EATING *in* MAINE

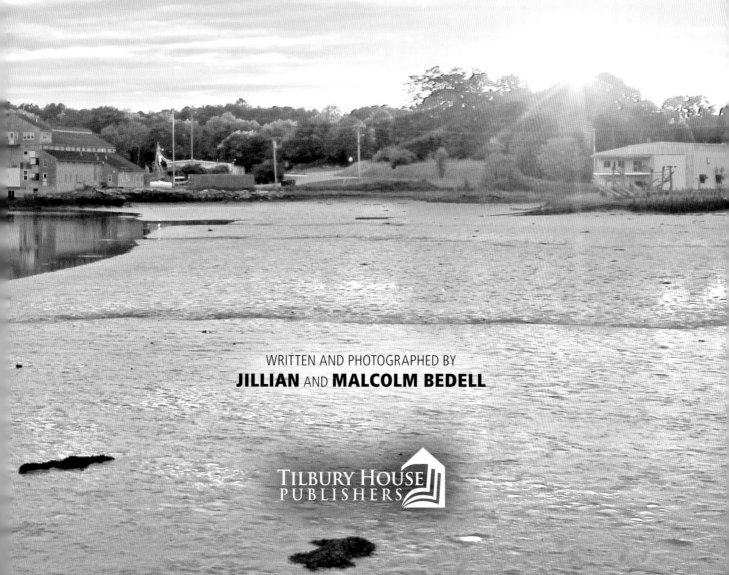

EATING in MAINE

AT HOME, ON THE TOWN and ON THE ROAD

WRITTEN AND PHOTOGRAPHED BY

JILLIAN AND **MALCOLM BEDELL**

TILBURY HOUSE
PUBLISHERS

Tilbury House, Publishers
12 Starr Street
Thomaston, Maine 04861
800-582-1899 • www.tilburyhouse.com

First edition: May 2014

ISBN 978-0-88448-355-7

Design by Lynda Chilton
www.booksdesigned.com

        Library of Congress Cataloging-in-Publication Data

Bedell, Jillian, author.
  Eating in Maine : at home, on the town, and on the road / written and
photographed by Jillian and Malcolm Bedell. -- First hardcover edition.
      pages cm
  Includes indexes.
  ISBN 978-0-88448-355-7
  1. Cooking, American--New England style. 2. Cooking--Maine. I. Bedell,
Malcolm, author. II. Title.
  TX715.2.N48B436 2014
  641.59741--dc23
                    2014007758

Printed by Versa Press, East Peoria, IL in the United States of America
14 15 16 17 18 19   VRP   10 9 8 7 6 5 4 3 2 1

TABLE *of* CONTENTS

INTRODUCTION   *9*

JANUARY   *15*

A New Year's Day Brunch Menu   15
Restaurant Review: Fore Street   21
Road Trip: The Best Breakfast Sandwich in Portland   23
A Snow-Day Menu   26

FEBRUARY   *32*

A Valentine's Day Dinner Menu   32
Road Trip: Pursuing the Maine Italian Sandwich   38
Restaurant Review: J's Oyster   41
A "Dear John" Letter   43
Dinners We Make Again and Again   44

MARCH   *51*

A Feast for St. Patrick's Day   51
Restaurant Review: Caiola's   63
Weekend Project: Scratch-Made Grownup Sloppy Joes   65
Restaurant Review: Trattoria Athena   68
Good Weekend Lunches   70

APRIL   *74*

A Menu for Easter Sunday   74
Restaurant Review: Suzuki's Sushi Bar   79
Restaurant Review: Micucci's   83
Weekend Project: Eggs Benedict   84
Restaurant Review: Long Grain   87
Food for the Great Spring Road Trip   90

Sweet Potato Soup, p. 17

American Chop Suey, p. 47

Scratch-Made Grownup Sloppy Joes, p. 65

Eggs Benedict, p. 84

MAY — 93

A Memorial Day Cookout Menu — 93
Restaurant Review: Local 188 — 98
Seasonal Ingredient: Rhubarb — 100
Restaurant Review: Po' Boys and Pickles — 104
Road Trip: Recommendations for a Food-Focused Three-Day Weekend in Portland — 106
Food for Upta Camp — 110

Asparagus Soup, p. 94

JUNE — 114

A Summer Solstice Celebration Menu — 114
Road Trip: The Curious Collection of Authentic Latin American Cooking in Maine — 120
Meals to Enjoy on Long Days and Cool Nights — 133

Hacienda Pancho Villa (Brunswick), p. 125

JULY — 137

A Menu for the Fourth of July — 137
Seasonal Ingredient: Lobster — 144
Restaurant Review: Hoss and Mary's — 151
Road Trip: Our Favorite Lobster Rolls — 155
Restaurant Review: Duckfat — 158
A Moxie Day Menu — 160

Lobster Dinner, p. 144

AUGUST — 163

Dog Days of Summer Menu — 163
Restaurant Review: Cook's Lobster House — 169
Weekend Project: Slow-Smoked Cooked Pork — 171
Restaurant Review: El Camino — 174
Restaurant Review: The Slipway — 178
Restaurant Review: Five Fifty-Five — 182
A Maine Lobster Festival Menu — 184

The Slipway (Thomaston), p. 178

SEPTEMBER — 186

Back-to-School Menu — 186
Maine Food Adventure: A Weekend on a Maine Windjammer — 191
Restaurant Review: Cod End Seafood — 196

Chocolate Moxie Whoopie Pies with Allen's Coffee Brandy Buttercream, p. 189

Weekend Project: **A Scratch-Made Ultimate Cheeseburger**   199

Road Trip: **Leaf Peeping in Northern Maine**   202

A Menu for Apple-Picking Season   206

OCTOBER   *211*

Halloween Nibbles Menu   211

Restaurant Review: **Big G's Deli**   220

Road Trip: **The Best Drive-In Cheeseburgers in Southern Maine**   223

Restaurant Review: **Wasses Hot Dogs**   229

Weekend Project: **Scratch-Made Lobster Roll**   230

Tricks and Treats Continued   232

Wasses Hot Dogs (Rockland), p. 229

NOVEMBER   *236*

A Thanksgiving Feast   236

Restaurant Review: **A1 Diner**   245

Weekend Project: **Porchetta**   248

Restaurant Review: **Clayton's Café**   251

Cake for Jillian's Birthday   252

Black Magic Grasshopper Cake, p. 256

DECEMBER   *258*

A Christmas Spirit Menu   258

Weekend Project: **The Ultimate Maine-Style Italian Sandwich**   266

Restaurant Review: **Moody's Diner**   268

Restaurant Review: **Hot Suppa**   272

More December Dishes: Everything in Moderation, Including Moderation   274

Yukon Gold Potatoes with Crème Fraîche and Lobster Roe, p. 274

INDEX TO RECIPES   *276*

INDEX TO RESTAURANTS   *284*

INDEX TO TOWNS   *285*

ACKNOWLEDGMENTS   *287*

ABOUT THE AUTHORS   *288*

INTRODUCTION

A Maine Food Journey • *Malcolm*

I grew up in Maine. In the 1980s of my memory, Maine's culinary landscape was populated with family-style fare. After enduring the seemingly endless car ride from Tenants Harbor to Portland to watch my mom spend hours marching through the mall, shopping for shoes that she insisted were better than any she could find in Rockland, we'd repair to DiMillo's Restaurant (which, to my seven-year-old eyes, represented the height of opulence) for baked haddock or to the Weathervane for piles upon piles of golden fried seafood.

Back home in the midcoast, the dining-out options were even fewer. You could get a perfectly good meal at Dave's Restaurant in Thomaston. I remember being fascinated in Dave's, watching the dim room full of flannel-clad grownups with thick accents who somehow managed to smoke cigarettes and stack empty steamer clam shells on their plates at the same time. For dessert you could enjoy Dave's pie or venture across Route One for an ice cream cone at Dorman's Dairy Dream, which is there to this day, having refused to sell out to the new Super Walmart that now looms behind them. If you wanted soft ice cream instead of hard, Rockland's Dairy Queen was a mile away. On the Thomaston waterfront, the Harbor View served hot fudge brownie sundaes in enormous brandy snifters.

In Rockland you could get steak and all the shrimp you could eat at Bonanza, whose North End location is long abandoned with grass poking through the asphalt parking lot, or at the Chuck Wagon in the South End. Mexican food was limited to whatever was being sold at El Taco Tico, across Main Street from the Chuck Wagon. In Tenants Harbor, Farmer's was busily transforming their village store into a full-fledged restaurant. For reasons never explained to me, my dad wasn't allowed to go to the Black Harpoon in Port Clyde. To this day I'm not sure if this was the restaurant's rule or my mother's.

The notion of "fast casual" dining hadn't yet taken root. There were no Applebee's, no Chili's, no cheeseball chains. During the summer you could buy a lobster roll at the gas station or a fried clam roll just about anywhere.

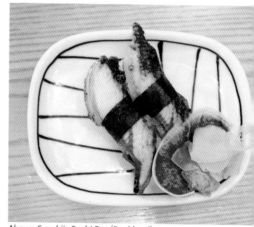

Above: Suzuki's Sushi Bar (Rockland), p. 79.
Opposite: Bourbon Cranberry Compote, p. 242.

Corned Beef Hash, p. 62

When the hammer of winter fell, your options for a quick meal dwindled to McDonald's or a convenience-store slice of pizza consisting of a big, slightly undercooked blob of dough topped with too-sweet tomato sauce, circling lazily in a warmer.

Mostly we ate at home. My mother was tremendously gifted in the kitchen, the kind of sprinkle-of-this, dash-of-that cook who never wrote down a recipe and rarely consulted a cookbook. She would put together elaborate meals for a ramshackle house full of kids, drawing inspiration from our travels overseas in the wake of my merchant seaman father. Her cooking always impressed me. While it may occasionally have wandered too far into the canned-artichoke-heart-and-crispy-Chinese-noodle pandemic of the 1980s, it was completely different from the cooking I saw out in the world, so different from the meals my friends' mothers made (which, though more traditional, were also delicious).

Life and career took me away from Maine for more than a decade, with stops in New Haven, where I met Jillian, New York City, and eventually to a run-down house in a tiny fishing village in Mexico, where we lived for four years. We moved a lot, learned a little about how many ways there are to live life, and had adventures, but we knew that when it came time to start a family of our own, we would end up back in Maine. It has always been home.

We returned to Maine in 2010, settling initially in Portland, and couldn't believe what we found. Maine's most cosmopolitan city was in the midst of an explosion of world-class restaurants and bars. The old eateries were still there, but now they were sitting shoulder to shoulder with new restaurants that were being opened at a dizzying pace by incredibly talented chefs. Food "from away," which had formerly existed only south of the bridge in Kittery, was suddenly everywhere. If you wanted sunchokes dolloped with porcini foam or French fries deep fried in duck fat, you could have them.

What's more, people were talking about it. National publications were tossing Portland's name into articles about the "foodiest" cities in the country, and a small group of independent publishers and bloggers had begun obsessively documenting their dinners, posting photos of meals and sprawling tales of recent debaucheries to the World Wide Web for all to read. We knew right away that joining their ranks would provide a structure for us to enjoy our new city and all the exciting new flavors it contained. We called our blog "From Away," bought a camera, and got to work.

We absorbed as much of Portland's food world as we could in that first year, reviewing and photographing meals at more than 100 restaurants in just a few short months. As our readership grew, our writing and research led us more and more frequently to towns outside Portland. Any time we needed a suggestion about where to get a sandwich, any time we planned a road trip north and east, a reader would point us to a small town I'd never been to before and a hole-in-the-wall restaurant famous only to the people who lived there. And almost every time, we would have an incredible meal.

In the years since, we've tried to absorb everything Maine's varied dining landscape has to offer, from the highest-end meals prepared by James Beard award-winning chefs to the boiled-ham Italian sandwiches the corner market has been dishing out for 50 years. They are all important. They all contribute to making Maine an exciting place to eat.

Meanwhile we've moved several times within Maine, inching our way up the coast before settling back in Rockland after our daughter was born, all the while cooking our brains out. We committed ourselves to publishing a new post on the site every day, which meant that several times a week we'd pick something from our travels and figure out how to cook and adapt it. Steamed pork dumplings from Chinatown? We could figure it out. Hand-rolled boiled water bagels? Thanks, Internet. The achiote-infused slow-cooked pork that I ate almost every Sunday from a street cart in the town square in Mexico? Surely we could figure out how to make it in Maine. We've worked hard to become better cooks and to bring home to Maine the flavors we've developed a taste for elsewhere.

These two simultaneous journeys have led to the book you are holding in your hands. In a place dominated by season, we've organized our recipes, reviews, and cooking projects into monthly themes and suggested menus for a crowd or a celebration. We want to honor this place that we love so much and to show you that anyone, regardless of culinary skill, background, or tools, can create amazing meals.

One final note: As you flip through these pages, you'll see that our emphasis is on great-tasting food to enjoy at home or in restaurants, food to enjoy with friends, family, and on special occasions, food with which to mark and highlight the passing seasons. Many of the foods we'll guide you to aren't things you should eat every day, but they are all delicious.

Top: Corned Beef Hash, p. 62. Above: Chorizo y Papas Grilled Cheese Sandwich, p. 70

Celebrating, Discovering, Exploring, Interpreting the New Maine Cuisine • *Jillian*

I'm not from Maine. I came to live here four years ago with my husband, Malcolm, who spent pieces of his childhood here. We met in college in Connecticut, where I grew up, then moved to New York— initially to a seedy neighborhood in Brooklyn and eventually to better, more brownstone-lined versions of the storied borough. In our late twenties we decided to defect from America and somehow buy a house on the beach in Mexico. Over the next four years we ventured to the Yucatan and

Top: Gluten-Free Two-Ingredient Banana Pancakes, p. 187. Above: Beef Wellington, p. 263

explored Mayan ruins deep in that green peninsula and the narrow, cobbled, Colonial streets of Merida, its capital city. We found ourselves a crumbling cement box smack on the Gulf of Mexico and lived in it while adding rooms, removing the roof and walls, putting in tiles great and small, and crafting smooth concrete features. We slept in hammocks, with doors and windows wide open to the breeze, though we did buy a proper bed and install air conditioning after we got married. When all that was completed, it was time to come home, to have a family and finally be more conventional. Maine was the safest, most comfortable place I could think of, and I began plotting what our lives would look like when we were just like everyone else.

I was lonely and hungry for layers after the simple, languid life in a fishing village. We chose Portland's West End because I wanted to walk on sidewalks to coffee shops and art exhibits. We immersed ourselves in the youthful culture, feeling lucky and free to explore the established restaurants and evolving food scene of a town becoming known for dazzling cuisine. We tasted much that was good and familiar and some that was thrilling, new, and sensational. It was good to be back in America, and our vision for a food blog slowly came together.

We started "From Away" in our first apartment, knowing from the beginning that we would have to dedicate ourselves to this project in a way we had never done before. We resolved to treat it seriously and with great diligence but not to take ourselves seriously, which is a funny line to walk. We wanted readers, because what is a blog without readers but a mere journal you leave open for someone to find? We wanted our readers to trust our sincerity and commitment, but we did not want to come off as feigning expertise in a field in which we had no formal training.

As the years passed, however, our readers (mostly friends and family, at first) came to think of us as "food people" even though we insisted otherwise. Eventually, having visited almost two hundred eating establishments around the state, we had to admit that we were on to something—or rather part of something—participating in and in some small way having an impact on Maine's burgeoning food scene. From Portland we migrated northeast to Topsham, a farming community lodged between pastoral Bowdoinham and collegiate Brunswick, moving into a sprawling farmhouse with a barn and goats and rhubarb. There were horses down the street and farm stands in both directions. We picked apples from our own front yard. This was a new lifestyle for us, an insight into yet another Maine. It was bucolic, yet ten minutes from a university town that is home to one of the best restaurants in the state. This is where we began our practice in earnest.

In Portland we had dabbled in the kitchen, experimenting with recipes and putting on a few elaborate party meals. But more often than not we had dined out, relishing the scene and devouring elegant dishes or massive quantities of mediocre Chinese-American take-out. At home in Topsham in a cozy, well-appointed kitchen, I made pies and cakes, stews and soups, breads, and some serious meat dishes. It didn't always work. There was a candy incident I don't care to recount. But I was learning what it was like to be in the kitchen, to follow a recipe and elaborate on or extrapolate from it, to explore the foods of my childhood, and to seek my mother and grandmother by making the foods of their girlhoods. I made pasta and cannoli and pizza dough in many iterations. I went often to the butcher shop up the hill that smelled of the sawdust and blood on the hands and coats of the clerks who worked the abbatoir next door. We got up early for donuts from Frosty's, a Maine Street icon recently reborn.

Apple Fritters, p. 218

We started following reader tips to insular, self-contained places that really made me feel from away. This interested us a great deal. We were inspired to devise our own versions of Maine's iconic dishes—elevated, stripped down, or in some cases pure homage. We went deeper into the interior, away from the coast; we saw the potato farms of wide-open Aroostook County and the hot dog and hamburger havens of a mid-century America that had been obsessed with youth and wealth and car culture. We ate lobster in rolls, stews, bisques, and chowders, and in take-out joints, fine restaurants, and the homes of friends who heaped upon us three and four steamed bugs and grinned as salty juice and butter ran down our chins.

We did our best to recreate the classics. We took everything we saw and learned and applied it to our blog. We wrote and revised and photographed everything we ate. All the while we saw the absurdity in it, but we couldn't stop. We were obsessed. There was so much good stuff going on at every level, in cities and beyond their icy outskirts. We tried never to dismiss a place because it was remote; we wanted to hold our cynicism in check, which has never been easy. I was becoming happily at home. I felt as if I had found the place where I could spend my future.

Somewhat nomadic, like herders following inconsistent sheep, we continued up the coast to Rockland, which was, for Malcolm, the you-can't-go-home-again homecoming he had been looking for. For me it was a soft landing in a sparkling, difficult, transforming town. I immediately loved it for its museum, theater, coffee shops, bookstores, antiques, ocean views, farmer's market overlooking the marina, a well-lighted Christmas parade in the freezing cold, and the way I felt embraced as I spent my days walking

Sun-Cooked Heirloom Tomato Pasta Sauce, p. 166

our new baby, Violet, around the town. Violet was born here in Maine, and I think maybe that counts for something. I'm the mother of a Mainer, and that roots me here as well. Maybe I chose to come here to have her so that we would always feel entitled to return, to buy a house, to be part of this community, this land; so that these woods and fields and harbors would always be for us, a place where we could rest, regroup, and recast ourselves.

Food has been a way for us to explore, to introduce ourselves and to forge new friendships. It is a lens through which we view a people and place, their history and our own. We all come together around a table, saying grace collectively or internally. We light the candles and dig in to the feast. We wanted to write about Maine and live Maine and love it because it is rich and bizarre and lovable. We have lived through the seasons, through suffocating winters and dazzling summers. Multiple springs and falls now soften our senses and remind us of years past. We try to convey all of that through what we share about cooking and eating, exploring, interpreting, and celebrating this place.

Call it discovery through appetite. We think this is the way food should be, not just in Maine but everywhere—simple and revelatory, making meaning through ritual and finding new things together. It's how we've always done it, Malcolm and I. No matter what comes next, we have this ingrained in our hearts, as a couple, as a family. We write about the world we live in now.

Toasted Almond Blondies, p. 73

JANUARY

O pen your eyes! It's the first day of a new year, the day to make resolutions, to dream and plan. It's the day to wake up early to meditate, to walk and contemplate the past, present, and future, or to sleep in after a night of revelry. What you do today sets the tone for January, maybe for the entire year. So of course you have to eat wonderfully and well and celebrate.

We suggest a festive, leisurely brunch for friends and the kids. This is something of a new tradition of ours now that we're parents and adults. Old and new friends toasting the New Year, enjoying warming and hearty food, sharing goals, both serious and silly. This makes us happy and grateful to be in these lives of ours.

A New Year's Day brunch like the one here, or any of its components, will thaw any cold January day and ring in the New Year spectacularly.

A New Year's Day Brunch
- Coffee Alexander Belle Orange
- Sweet Potato Soup
- Prime Rib Breakfast Hash
- Spinach and Gruyère Strata
- Sour Cream Coffee Cake

Coffee Alexander Belle Orange • *Jillian*

Makes 2 cocktails

INGREDIENTS

1 cup heavy cream

2 tablespoons confectioner's sugar

2 ounces La Belle Orange Cognac &

Orange Liqueur

Dash of vanilla extract

½ cup freshly brewed coffee

Dollop of sweetened whipped cream

Sprinkle of cinnamon

Sprinkle of grated orange peel

An elegant, gently intoxicating beverage is what separates brunch from breakfast. We love mimosas, all bubbly and citrusy, and we love a spicy, salty, acidic Bloody Mary, but for our New Year's Day brunch menu we created an elegant cocktail that is a nod to Maine's unofficial signature drink— Allen's Coffee Brandy and milk. We went through many happy iterations before coming up with this one. It is the ideal drink to proffer a party of New Year's Eve revelers who may require an eye-opener. We put out a large pot of coffee with cups and spoons and all the ingredients so guests can serve themselves, adding a lot or a little of the lovely orange liqueur, whipped cream, and other accoutrements. Fix a thermos or fill a flask with this warming drink and take the whole group out for a New Year's Day walk in the woods.

Method

1. Using a stand mixer, combine the heavy cream with the confectioner's sugar in a (chilled) bowl and whisk until stiff peaks are formed.

2. In each coffee glass, pour in 2 ounces cognac, vanilla extract, and the ½ cup of coffee. Add a dollop of sweetened cream. Finish with the cinnamon and grated orange peel.

Sweet Potato Soup • *Jillian*

Serves 4-6

Sweet and savory. Breakfast and lunch. Coffee and alcohol. Brunch is all about intersections of good things. When friends gather for brunch at home, we like to serve a little shot glass of some great soup. It's a somewhat unexpected but always welcome treat. This sweet potato soup is smoky, a little spicy, and super delicious, and it acquires a velvety texture without a heaping amount of cream. I like the idea of eating potatoes, a tuber, in the depth of winter; the symbolism of staying rooted while you grow toward the light is a nice thing to contemplate as you gather around the table or take a solitary morning walk.

Method

1. In a large soup pot, melt the butter over medium-high heat. Add the onions and sauté for 5 minutes. Add salt and pepper and stir. Add the potato, apple, ground ginger, and chipotle powder and stir to combine. Pour in 2 cups of water and bring to a simmer. Reduce the heat and cover, cooking on low for 45 minutes.

2. When the potatoes are very soft, transfer to a blender and blend until smooth. Stir in the chicken broth and heavy cream. Season with salt to taste. If desired, add a squeeze of lime.

INGREDIENTS

1 tablespoon unsalted butter

1 sweet white onion, diced

Kosher salt and freshly ground black pepper to taste

1 large sweet potato, peeled and chopped

1 tart apple, peeled and chopped

¼ teaspoon ground ginger

⅛ teaspoon chipotle powder

½ cup chicken broth

¼ cup heavy cream

Squeeze of lime, optional

Prime Rib Breakfast Hash • *Malcolm*

Serves 4

INGREDIENTS

¼ cup canola oil or any kind of beef drippings

2 cups boiled and cooled potatoes, cut into ¼-inch cubes

1 medium onion, finely chopped

2 cups cold roast beef, prime rib (trimmed), or pot roast, cut into ¼-inch cubes

2 cloves garlic, finely chopped

1 teaspoon fresh sage, finely chopped

⅛ teaspoon cayenne

⅛ teaspoon ground nutmeg

Kosher salt and freshly ground black pepper, to taste

½ cup heavy cream

2 tablespoons chopped parsley

Eggs, fried or poached

The best breakfast hash I've ever tasted can be found at Hot Suppa in Portland, Maine. They make their own corned beef, and it takes center stage. Their version of the dish is really more of an excuse to eat giant shredded hunks of beef, seared beautifully with a thick, crunchy crust. With two perfect poached eggs and a shot of Sriracha hot chili sauce, this hash leaves me hard-pressed to think of something I would rather have for breakfast.

My version uses leftover prime rib, potatoes, and onions, all sautéed in the drippings from a little bone marrow.

There are three keys to a successful homemade breakfast hash:

The ingredients must all be chopped to the same size. Aim for a ¼-inch dice. Refrigerate the boiled potatoes and meat before dicing. Do not skip the heavy cream. It's what brings the whole thing together with the consistency you expect. Use a cast-iron skillet, crusting, flattening, stirring, and recrusting the hash several times.

Method

1. In a cast-iron skillet over medium heat, brown the potatoes in oil or drippings, breaking them up as little as possible, about 10 minutes.

2. Add the onion and cook until soft and translucent, about 10 minutes. Add the beef, garlic, sage, cayenne, nutmeg, salt, and pepper, and continue cooking, stirring often, for 5 minutes.

3. Add the cream and reduce. When all the liquid is absorbed, flatten the hash in the skillet. Turn the heat to high and let cook, about 4 minutes. Flip the hash in sections, preserving the crust. Repeat until desired crispness is achieved, about 10 more minutes.

4. Garnish with the parsley and serve with fried or poached eggs.

Spinach and Gruyère Strata • *Jillian*
Serves 8

What's the best aspect of brunch? Is it eating at the dining table in your half-pajamas? The *Sunday Times* unpacked all over the floor, trailing after you for the rest of the day? Is it the interplay of sweet and savory, breakfast and lunch items getting incestuous together on the plate? No matter what kind of morning you're having, I assure you this strata is super easy to make and pleasing to all. Prep everything the day before, storing each component in separate containers, and put it all together before falling into bed. The next morning, just remove the strata from the fridge and bake.

Method

1. In a large skillet, sauté the leeks in the butter over medium heat until soft, about 5 to 8 minutes.

2. Whisk together the eggs, milk, and mustard, and season with salt and pepper.

3. In a buttered casserole dish, arrange the bread. Place the spinach on top of the bread, lay the leeks atop the spinach, and then sprinkle with the grated cheese. Pour in the egg mixture and grate the nutmeg over the entire dish. Cover and pop in the fridge for at least 8 hours before cooking.

4. Remove from the refrigerator while you preheat the oven to 350°F. Bake uncovered for 45 to 55 minutes, until golden-brown and puffy.

INGREDIENTS

1 leek, white and light green parts only, finely chopped

3 tablespoons unsalted butter

9 eggs

2 cups milk

2 tablespoons Dijon mustard

Salt and black pepper

8 cups hearty bread or bagels, cut into 1-inch cubes

10 ounces frozen spinach, thawed in cheesecloth and squeezed until dry

6 ounces Gruyère, grated

2 ounces Parmesan, grated

Whole nutmeg

Sour Cream Coffee Cake • *Jillian*

Serves 8

INGREDIENTS

For the cake:

¾ cup (1½ sticks) unsalted butter, softened

1½ cups granulated sugar

3 eggs at room temperature

1½ teaspoons vanilla extract

1¼ cups sour cream

2½ cups cake flour

2 teaspoons baking powder

½ teaspoon baking soda

½ teaspoon salt

For the streusel:

¼ cup packed brown sugar

½ cup all-purpose flour

1½ teaspoons cinnamon

¼ teaspoon salt

3 tablespoons cold unsalted butter, cut into pieces

I love waking up to a house full of friends. It reminds me of college—and just after—when we couldn't get enough of one another. We'd hang out for days on end watching *Comedy Central*, drinking a thousand beers, talking and laughing and making things, editing the literary magazine, writing papers due the next morning, ordering Irish nachos from our favorite neighborhood bar. We're so lucky to have these people in our lives still.

When we have weekend or holiday guests, staying up late playing board games and drinking wine, waking up for walks in the woods with dogs and the babies and toddlers who add depth and beauty to our evolving group, it's nice to have this coffee cake ready to go as we pad around the kitchen brewing the first big pot of coffee and cleaning up from the shenanigans of the night before.

Blow out the candles on this tasty cake and make a wish for the New Year.

Method

1. Preheat the oven to 350°F. Butter and flour a 10-inch Bundt pan.

2. In a stand mixer fitted with the paddle attachment, cream the butter and sugar. Add the eggs, vanilla, and sour cream.

3. In a large mixing bowl, combine the flour, baking powder, baking soda, and salt. With the stand mixer on low, slowly add the flour mixture until just combined.

4. In a separate bowl, using your fingers, crumble together the brown sugar, flour, cinnamon, salt, and butter.

5. Pour half the cake batter into the prepared Bundt pan and spread with a spatula. Top with half the streusel. Spread the remainder of the cake batter and top with the remaining streusel mixture.

6. Bake 50 to 60 minutes. A cake tester should come out clean. Cool the coffee cake completely before inverting on a plate.

RESTAURANT REVIEW

FORE STREET • *Jillian*
288 Fore Street, Portland, ME 04101; (207) 775-2717; forestreet.biz

When I stepped into Fore Street from the cold outdoors one winter evening, I was delighted to find a wood-burning oven glowing in the open kitchen and a vase of cherry blossom branches in the center of the woodsy restaurant. From our copper-topped table we enjoyed a dramatic view out the many-paned windows of the painted brick advertising for "W.L. Blake and Co. Mill and Industrial Supplies," advertising aged into art. Bathed in warm light, happy people were connecting over food and drink. This is the perfect place to dine on a wintry night in January.

Too often, really good restaurants present the idea of a meal, a delicious post-modernism that slightly alienates the diner even as she enjoys the scene. There is nothing clever or ironic about the food at Fore Street. It is poetry, the thing itself. The menu is impressive, extensive, and changes almost daily. I didn't know where to begin. Appetizers included roughly six choices for each of the following: Chilled and Raw Seafood; Wood Oven-Roasted and Wood-Grilled Seafood; Wood-Grilled and Pan-Fried Meats; Chilled Meats and Offal. Main course options offered four choices under Pan-Seared Seafood; Wood Oven-Roasted Seafood; Wood-Grilled Meats; Turnspit-Roasted Meats; and Vegetables.

Malcolm knew what he wanted immediately. His Exotic Mushroom and Bibb Lettuce Salad ($11) with pea tendrils, English peas, grilled ramps

JANUARY 21

(ramps ran rampant on the menu that night), and bacon and basil buttermilk dressing was languid yet nubile, like a Manet nude. Because the lettuce was so soft, the mushrooms seemed meatier and the peas popped. My Tagliatelle ($10) was totally badass, an elegant comfort bowl with a rather musky Comtè cheese as well as wild spring ramps, white wine dairy cream, and bread crumbs. I would have loved to have tried at least seven other starters, including a beet and rocket salad, razor clams, sweetbreads, and rabbit liver pate. So lovely and earthy and divine!

I vacillated among myriad amazing-sounding options for dinner, while Malcolm chose the chicken straight off. Not just any chicken, but Marinated Organic Chicken from Quebec (ooh la la!) ($23) with duck fat–fried sourdough and chard. In his own words, the duck fat–fried sourdough was what you hope to achieve when you sneak into the kitchen while the roast chicken is resting and use crusty bread to sop up the congealing fat and smack down the pope's nose when no one is watching. Rich. Satisfying. Melty. Melty food is my favorite.

I settled on the Summer Flounder Filet ($27) with braised greens, hon-shimeji, and ramp butter sauce. The edges were brown and crisp, and the meat was firm, white, and wholesome, with added greens and goodness all around. I loved the hon-shimeji mushrooms, sylvan little creatures that seemed like curative ancient friends. We shared the Butter-Roasted Sunroot Mash with Fresh Herbs ($6), which tasted like the woods. We both devoured our dinners, along with the Standard Baking Co. bread and sweet butter on the table and clean Ketel One drinks.

Our greatest regret: we left no room for dessert. There were sweets and ports and assorted ice creams. Next time! That's when I'll order wine and chocolate or cheese. And who knows what other mysteries await. Our server was knowledgeable and polite. I think we chose safely and well, and next time(!) I plan to be bolder. Here is a place to try things you've never had before or revel in the best version of a dish you've been eating all your life.

Fore Street is light and dark, masculine and feminine, elegant yet comfortable, and easy. It feels like unadulterated pleasure, the experience of adulthood I always longed to have. It provides respite from life's harsher realities, a most pleasing place to dine well, when you can.

The Best Breakfast Sandwich in Portland • *Malcolm*

Sometimes the only thing that can give me strength to start a new day is a perfectly greasy bacon, egg, and cheese sandwich from the corner deli. Over the years I've developed my platonic ideal for this sandwich: a New York–style hard roll with a half-dozen strips of crunchy, curled bacon and a thick layer of melted American cheese. The egg portion of my ideal sandwich is barely a factor; really it's just present as a gesture so that I can eat what is, essentially, a grilled bacon and cheese sandwich. A few shakes of hot sauce later, and you've got my favorite version of this quick, on-the-go sandwich. Add a nap, and you'll be (almost) ready to face the day.

But breakfast sandwiches don't always have to be cold-start fuels for especially tough mornings. We love them on just about any morning. Here are seven places in Portland to find our favorite versions of the classic breakfast sandwich:

PUNKY'S

186 Brighton Avenue, Portland, ME 04102; 207-773-8885

This is exactly the kind of small, independently run Maine sandwich shop that we really love. They make a mean fast food–style, cooked-to-order breakfast sandwich ($3) using a soft potato roll grilled in butter with a hard-cooked fried egg, a slice of white American cheese, and a few strips of crispy bacon. The steam from the tightly wrapped foil warms the bun through, turning the sandwich into a light, fluffy whisper of crunchy bacon, egg, and melty cheese. All of the ingredients are in balance, with no single element overpowering the others. It's inexpensive and profoundly filling.

158 PICKETT STREET

158 Benjamin W. Pickett Street, South Portland, ME 04106; 207-799-8998

On Saturday mornings in South Portland, this bagel shop and bakery is filled with young Mainers using smartphones and carb-loading after a strenuous jog. The atmosphere is somewhat edgy, and layers of stickers and flyers cover every surface, giving the place a decidedly punk-rock feel. Huge air pockets lend a lightness to the chewy, crisp boiled crust of the bagels, and they make for a hearty alternative to the wimpy English muffins or croissants served elsewhere. Try the Hogzilla ($7.50) on a toasted garlic bagel that's crisp-boiled, crunchy, and chewy. This portable sandwich loads absurd amounts of salty pork—thick-cut bacon, ham, and sausage that's cooked until it turns a sweet dark brown—atop a mountain of scrambled eggs and melted cheddar cheese.

MELLEN STREET MARKET
79 Mellen Street, Portland, ME 04101; 207-772-2206

Get to this nondescript neighborhood convenience store early enough and you'll find one of the best fast food–style breakfast sandwiches in the city. There's nothing fancy or overly creative about this sandwich, and some mornings, that's exactly what you're looking for. A budget-friendly $2.69 buys a tall stack of sausage, egg, and American cheese on an English muffin slightly steamed through from the heat of the glass warming case. The thin layer of fried egg here is barely a factor; the lightly spicy sausage patty and the warm melty American cheese do the heavy lifting, which suits me just fine. There's a $5 minimum on credit card transactions, so bring cash (or be prepared to eat two).

THE HOLY DONUT
194 Park Avenue, Portland, ME 04101; 207-874-7774; theholydonutmaine.com

There is no shortage of bright, friendly, tattooed twenty-somethings in Portland working hard to realize their particular culinary vision. The Holy Donut is no exception. Located diagonally across from Deering Oaks Park, the shop is building a reputation for excellent exotic donuts, including Dark Chocolate Sea Salt, Red Velvet, and Cheddar Bacon varieties. This same creativity is also present in their breakfast sandwich ($4), which combines pesto, bacon, egg, and cheddar cheese on a whole wheat English muffin. The pesto is flavorful, but the real star is the egg, which is neither fried nor scrambled but more like a slice of airy quiche. The whole wheat English muffin may even allow you to convince yourself that it's health food.

THE FRONT ROOM
73 Congress Street #A, Portland, ME 04101; 207-773-3366; hardingleesmith.com

When you wake up on a bleary Sunday morning craving a breakfast sandwich, the idea of a full sit-down meal may not sound like something you have the strength to manage. Stay in bed, though, and you'll miss the Front Room's take on this sandwich ($7): perfectly cooked fried eggs, blue cheese, bacon, and mayonnaise on grilled French bread. This may sound like too much, but somehow it manages to be light and crispy, and the blue cheese never overpowers the rest of the sandwich. Pair it with one of the restaurant's intensely spicy Bloody Marys and you may yet live to fight another day.

SCRATCH BAKING CO.

416 Preble Street Extension, South Portland, ME; 207-799-0668; scratchbakingco.com

This South Portland bakery only sells their breakfast sandwich ($4.75) on weekdays, and they sell out fast. Wait until 9 AM and you're likely to miss our favorite local twist on the traditional greasy, heavy breakfast sandwich. Served cold, it's a chewy Scratch bagel dusted with cornmeal and a spread of mustard stacked high with slices of boiled egg, prosciutto, and mixed greens.

HOT SUPPA

703 Congress Street, Portland, ME; 207-871-5005; hotsuppa.com

Though the restaurant may be more famous for its from-scratch corned beef hash, the same care and attention is given to their version of the humble breakfast sandwich. For $5.29 you get two strips of crispy bacon, a perfectly cooked over-medium fried egg, and a shellacking of white American cheese on an oversized English muffin, the real hero of this sandwich. It's crispy and charred on the outside, soft and chewy inside, with plenty of airy nooks and crannies to absorb the sandwich's liberal buttering.

A Snow-Day Menu

- "Japanese Big Mac" Pork Belly Buns
- Hungarian Mushroom Soup
- Short Rib Tagliatelle
- Snickerdoodle Cake with Brown Sugar Buttercream

I t's a new year and winter has only just begun. Now is the time to be creative, to learn a new language or cultivate a craft. It's time to take on challenging cooking projects and finally finish that David Foster Wallace novel you started months ago. We love to work on multistep recipes during these winter weekends. Make everything from scratch. Get to the bottom of breadmaking. Take your stomach on a tour of Thailand or Italy. Our recipes for this month are comforting, rich, hearty, and whimsical, because without a sense of humor and the occasional shot of Allen's Coffee Flavored Brandy, Mainers would never make it until spring.

The January thaw will come. Until then, let it snow, let it snow. Call some friends within walking distance to be at your house for dinner, and start cooking. You all need calories to combat the cold, and anyway, those New Year's resolutions are a distant memory now. Here's a menu guaranteed to melt snow.

"Japanese Big Mac" Pork Belly Buns • *Malcolm*
Makes 12 buns

The pork buns at **Pai Men Miyake** (188 State Street, Portland, ME 04101) get into your head. A thick slice of braised, fatty, salty pork belly nestled lovingly into a pillowy steamed bun, drizzled with gochujang mayonnaise, and finished perfectly with a bit of soft lettuce and a tart slice of pickle tends to leave an impression. What else leaves an impression? That these lovely buns cost nine dollars for an order of two. And if you're dining with a companion, I dare you—dare you!—to split an order and eat just one. Even for a light lunch, you're in for almost twenty bucks before you've even had a beer.

As nice as it is to dine in at Pai Men Miyake on a cold winter day, to wrap yourself in the smell of noodles in such a cozy little space with other similarly minded people, that price point means that we're not eating these buns nearly as often as we'd like. I thought I would take a stab at reverse engineering them at home.

I measured and weighed each ingredient carefully, and was surprised to find that I could get pretty close to these Momofuku-style buns right here at home for $1.92 per serving of two. As much as we enjoy the service and relaxation that one can expect from a hefty restaurant markup, learning to make these little munchkins at home, eating as many as we want, and watching *The Price Is Right* at the same time is nice, too.

Oh, sure, they're not made by a master chef. And I'm sure Sriracha and mayonnaise are poor substitutes for the sauce used at Pai Men. But I think if you give these a try, you might like 'em.

INGREDIENTS

For the dough:

½ package active dry yeast

2 tablespoons plus 2 teaspoons granulated sugar

1 tablespoon canola oil

½ teaspoon salt

1½ cups plus 2 tablespoons all-purpose flour

For the pork and toppings:

1½ pounds pork belly, boneless and skinless

½ cup kosher salt

½ cup granulated sugar

4½ cups water, divided

½ cup chicken broth

3 tablespoons mayonnaise

1½ teaspoons Sriracha

Boston lettuce, torn into small pieces

Sliced dill pickle chips

Method

For the dough:

1. Dissolve the yeast in a half cup of warm water. Add the sugar, the oil, and the salt. Let stand 15 minutes. Add the flour and knead until smooth, about 10 minutes. Place in a greased bowl, cover, and let rise in a warm place (about 80°F) until doubled in size, about two hours.

2. Punch the dough down and cut into 12 equal pieces. Roll each piece into a slightly oval round, and roll out until thin, about 3 inches long by 2 inches wide. Brush the top of each bun with the oil and fold in half. Place each bun on a 3-inch by 3-inch square piece of parchment or waxed paper, and let rise about 30 more minutes.

For the pork and toppings:

1. Brine the pork by combining the kosher salt, the sugar, and 4 cups of the water. Place in a sealed bag and refrigerate overnight or at least 12 hours.

2. Preheat the oven to 300°F. Discard the brining solution, and place the pork fat side up in a small baking pan. Add a half cup of water and a half cup of chicken broth. Cover tightly with foil and cook in the oven for 2½ hours. Remove the foil and cook an additional 30 minutes at 450°F or until the fat turns golden in color.

3. Let the pork rest for 30 minutes, and then slice against the grain into ¼-inch slices. Before assembly, the pork can be reheated in a 350°F oven for 10–15 minutes.

4. While the pork cooks, combine the mayonnaise and the Sriracha in a separate bowl, and shred the lettuce.

Assembly:

1. In batches, place the buns (including parchment or waxed paper) onto a steamer rack over boiling water, making sure the buns don't touch. Cover tightly, and cook until the buns puff up and are cooked through, about 3 minutes. Open each bun and add a healthy smear of the Sriracha mayo. Add a slice of pork, a dab of lettuce, and a slice of pickle. Serve immediately.

Hungarian Mushroom Soup • *Malcolm*

Serves 4–6

INGREDIENTS

2 cups onion, chopped

2 cups chicken stock

12 ounces mixed mushrooms (white button, portobello, shiitake, oyster), roughly chopped

1 tablespoon soy sauce

2 teaspoons dill weed

1 tablespoon paprika

1 teaspoon cayenne

2 tablespoons unsalted butter

3 tablespoons all-purpose flour

1 cup milk

2 teaspoons rice wine vinegar

½ cup sour cream

Kosher salt and black pepper

¼ cup parsley, chopped

We visit **Clayton's Café** in Yarmouth often for their terrific sandwiches and soups. I was inspired to recreate their Hungarian Mushroom Soup so that we always have it ready to serve at home or wherever we are, and on those days when the weather might keep us trapped indoors. Finishing this creamy, hearty, textured soup with sour cream, salt, and acid really makes it special. Serve it with an herb salad, crusty, buttered bread, and a crisp white wine.

Method

1. In a large skillet, sauté the onions in 2 tablespoons of the stock, seasoned with a little salt. Add the mushrooms, the soy sauce, the dill, the paprika, the cayenne, and a half cup of stock. Cover and simmer for 15 minutes.

2. In a soup pot, melt the butter and whisk in the flour, about 2 minutes. Slowly stir in the milk and stir until the roux becomes thick and has a smooth consistency. Add the cooked onion/mushroom mixture and the rest of the stock. Cover and simmer 15 minutes. Remove from the heat and stir in the vinegar, the sour cream, and the salt and pepper to taste. Stir in the parsley.

Short Ribs with Tagliatelle • *Malcolm*
Serves 4

There's something satisfying about starting with inexpensive, tough cuts of meat and slowly, over the course of a snow day, turning them into tender, fall-off-the-bone hunks of succulent flavor and fat. It's the kind of thing dads seem to know how to do automatically, and it's high time you learn it, too.

The secret ingredient in this dish? A finishing dust of shaved bitter-sweet chocolate. I'll admit that there's a moment of panic when you start shaving chocolate onto the finished pasta that you've slaved over all day, but you're just going to have to trust me on this one. As delicious as this sauce is on its own, the over-the-top beefiness of slow-cooked short ribs can border on being just a little bit funky and intense. A dab of bittersweet chocolate completely counteracts this and adds a mysterious depth to the dish that people won't quite be able to put their fingers on.

Method

1. Pour the olive oil into a heavy soup pot over medium heat. Add the pancetta and cook until crisp, about 4 minutes. Meanwhile, season the short ribs with salt and pepper, and coat with the flour. Using a slotted spoon, remove the pancetta from the pan and drain on paper towels. Add the short ribs to the rendered pancetta fat and brown on all sides, about 7 minutes total.

2. While the short ribs sear, add the onion, the carrot, the parsley, and the garlic to the bowl of a food processor and pulse until finely minced. Add the tomatoes and the tomato paste, and pulse again until combined.

3. Once the short ribs are browned, add the mixture from the food processor to the pot. Return the pancetta to the pot and stir. Add the rosemary, thyme, oregano, bay leaf, beef broth, and wine. Bring the mixture to a boil. Reduce the heat and simmer, covered, for 1 hour and 15 minutes. Remove the lid and simmer for another 90 minutes, stirring and turning the short ribs occasionally. Using tongs, remove the meat and bones from the pot. Discard the bones. Shred the meat, removing any large chunks of fat, and return the meat to the pot. Season with ½ teaspoon salt and ¾ teaspoon pepper, or to taste.

4. Bring a large pot of salted water to a boil. Add the pasta and cook until tender but still firm to the bite, stirring occasionally, about a minute less than the package instructs. Drain, reserving 1 cup of the cooking liquid. Add the pasta to the pot of sauce, and stir. Add the reserved pasta liquid ¼ cup at a time, as needed, to moisten the pasta. Transfer to serving bowls, and top with 1 teaspoon of chocolate shavings. Serve immediately.

INGREDIENTS

3 tablespoons olive oil

3 ounces chopped pancetta (about ½ cup)

2½ pounds short ribs

Salt and pepper

¼ cup all-purpose flour

1 medium onion, roughly chopped

1 carrot, peeled and roughly chopped

½ cup fresh parsley leaves

2 cloves garlic

1 can (14 ounces) tomatoes, whole or diced

1 tablespoon tomato paste

1 teaspoon fresh rosemary leaves, chopped

1 teaspoon dried thyme

½ teaspoon dried oregano

1 bay leaf

2½ cups beef broth

¾ cup red wine

8 ounces egg tagliatelle

4 to 6 teaspoons bittersweet chocolate, shaved

Snickerdoodle Cake with Brown Sugar Buttercream • *Jillian*

Serves 8

INGREDIENTS

For the cake:

1½ cups all-purpose flour

1½ cups cake flour

1 tablespoon baking powder

½ teaspoon salt

1 tablespoon cinnamon

1 cup (2 sticks) unsalted butter, softened

1¾ cups granulated sugar

4 eggs

2 teaspoons vanilla

1¼ cups whole milk

For the brown sugar buttercream:

¾ cup (1½ sticks) unsalted butter, softened

1 cup brown sugar

½ teaspoon cinnamon

3 cups powdered sugar

3 tablespoons half–and–half

It's pretty much the law that babies are allowed to devour an entire baby-sized cake with their bare hands on the occasion of their first birthday, and not a moment sooner. So I had to pray that no Internet-Parenting Big Brother eyes were on us when I caught our sweet, curious, eight-and-a-half-month-old Violet sucking brown sugar frosting from a paper towel I had dropped on the floor. Mostly, she eats bananas and squash and beets and quinoa and sweet potatoes and tofu and Greek yogurt, so it was probably a fairly momentous day for our little girl's taste buds. Of course, in addition to a dab of the sugar and butter frosting, today alone she ingested a feather from the throw pillows, a leaf, a bit of candle wax, my hair, dog hair, page 58 of the Restoration Hardware catalog, something white I couldn't identify, and playground mulch. Ingested isn't exactly accurate, since I catch her in the act absolutely every time and finger swipe that stuff right out. Then I vacuum, and we start all over again. To balance things out, I'm currently cramming her tiny fat fist with organic, gluten-free, green, superfood, quick-dissolve baby puffs. They're sort of a baby version of Veggie Booty. "Baby Booty," if you will. Stop the presses, I have to go patent that.

The point is, I am not a perfect parent. Or maybe the point is that despite your best intentions, your kid is going to get ahead of you and reach milestones before you're ready. Or maybe the point is that everybody likes brown sugar frosting. The important thing is that in addition to being a conscientious mother, I baked this cake with a pound of butter. A snickerdoodle is a cinnamon-butter-sugar cookie, the kind of cookie you make with your babysitter before eating the entire batch while she cries about her boyfriend. And you cry, too, because you get it, you totally sympathize—been there, done that—and you pour her another glass of milk because that's what your mom does for you when you're sad. Then you watch "The Little Mermaid" and pinky swear promise not to tell a soul that she knows all the words to all the songs. My mother-in-law brought some snickerdoodles over last week, and I remembered what a perfect cookie they are. And it occurred to me that I could bake a cake with the same ingredients.

Why is cinnamon so delicious and comforting? It really does make everything better. I suppose I'm supposed to say that of butter. Or is it bacon? This cake definitely has a lot of the former—almost four sticks, which is pretty ridiculous. Don't think about that, just bake. Go buy a big pack of butter; I'll wait here.

Method

For the cake:

1. Preheat the oven to 325°F and prepare two round cake pans with butter and flour, shaking out the excess flour.

2. In a large mixing bowl, whisk together the flour, the baking powder, the salt, and the cinnamon.

3. In the bowl of a stand mixer, cream the butter and the sugar until fluffy. Add the eggs, one at a time, beating after each addition, then add the vanilla.

4. Add the dry ingredients, alternating with the milk, and mix until just combined.

5. Pour the batter evenly into the two pans and bake for 35 minutes, until a toothpick comes out clean.

For the brown sugar buttercream:

1. Cream the butter, the brown sugar, and the cinnamon. Alternate between the powdered sugar and the half and half until everything is well combined. Do not frost until the cakes are completely cooled.

FEBRUARY

A Valentine's Day Dinner

- Steamed Artichokes with Roasted Garlic Aioli
- Maine Lobster Fondue with Oyster River Riesling and Bartlett Estate Wild Blueberry Wine
- Swordfish Puttanesca Rosemary Olive Oil Cake with Chocolate Ganache

Holidays like Valentine's Day are critical during a long Maine winter. Planning a night out—or better yet, a night in—keeps the spirits up. Spending February 14 at home, cooking together, opening a bottle of wine, and sitting down at the dining room table with candles lit and Van Morrison on the stereo is so much more our style these days. For an evening like this you want a menu that is simple, elegant, and romantic, and lobster fondue qualifies on all counts. Simple to prepare, this dish is so elegant it's decadent. Let's just agree that the Seventies got one or two things right, and fondue is one of them. It's sexy. There, we said it. Dipping perfectly cooked sweet lobster meat into rich, melty cheese redolent with blueberry wine is a quintessentially romantic endeavor that will warm you to the tips of your fingers and toes. Bundle up and take a winter walk, holding hands the way you did when you were young. Then come home and cook, alone together, cozy and sheltered from February in Maine. What else can winter be for?

Roasted Garlic Aioli • *Jillian*

Makes one cup of aioli

Recently in the From Away test kitchen, Malcolm was vivisecting a savory frozen toaster pastry while I was making aioli. I was feeling French and virtuous while my collaborator was coating his insides with Pillsbury goo. We've been conducting condiment experiments lately, and both of us have independently observed (that's how you know it's science) that childhood conditioning to Hellman's mayonnaise and Heinz ketchup makes the home-made versions appear strange at first, much like donning one of Aunt Gert's handmade sweaters after years of wearing the sweet Jordache ones from J.C. Penney. But the more accustomed we become to buying food from farms and making things from scratch, the less we expect visual perfection and the more we appreciate nonhomogeneous beauty. My aioli was neither gleaming white nor perfectly smooth, but the preparation was satisfying, whisking and all, and the result quite pleasing.

Everything should be dipped in aioli. Radishes, mushrooms, broccoli, tomatoes, cucumbers, endive, pretzels, Carr's rosemary crackers, grand-mas, sliced turkey, stuffed rabbits, Nestle Crunch bars, paper dolls, index fingers, sourdough bread, Big Macs, nectarines, submarine sandwiches, striped bass, lava lamps, tangrams, unicycles, and Chinese food. Every-thing. And certainly artichokes.

INGREDIENTS

1 room-temperature organic egg yolk

1 teaspoon white wine vinegar

1 teaspoon Dijon mustard

1 cup grapeseed oil

1 clove garlic

Salt, pepper, lemon juice

Method

1. Preheat the oven to 350°F. Wrap the garlic in foil and roast 1 hour. Let cool.

2. Separate the egg. In a bowl, incorporate the vinegar and mustard with the egg yolk. Very, very slowly, pour in the oil while whisking the mixture until it thickens. Mix in the cool, softened garlic. Season with salt, pepper, and lemon juice to taste. Covered and stored in the refrigerator, the aioli will keep for up to a week.

Maine Lobster Fondue with Oyster River Riesling and Bartlett Estate Wild Blueberry Wine • *Jillian*

Serves 8

Maine is the first place I've lived that I've really loved. It gets under your skin and you stay for years, without ever intending to or knowing where the time has gone. It's a haven for me after traveling abroad, a place to plant roots and let them grow. I haven't experienced this anywhere else. Whether I am landing at the Portland International Jetport or driving northbound across the Piscataqua River at Kittery, I sense a peace that has eluded me elsewhere. Slow and expansive, vibrating less furiously, with wild nature never more than a few blocks from your front door, Maine works on a wanderer. It makes me want things I've never wanted, and at the same time it makes me feel content and less anxious, as if I can rest for a while.

Fondue is a food I can't imagine hating. I suppose if you are lactose intolerant, a germaphobe, or detest the Swiss for their money laundering or their reluctance to choose sides in a war, fondue might not be for you. Otherwise, you have to love this dish. It's kitschy! And European! And melted cheese and wine are inarguably two of the best things on earth. I made my first fondue on a New Year's Eve in the Upper West Side apartment of my best friend's college boyfriend, a nerdy musician who played the lyre or lute or vibraphone or some strange thing. We felt so adult, staying in, cooking, and changing into party clothes to dance into the year 1998. We contemplated the universe over a chafing dish.

Making fondue forces you to slow down, adding the cheese a little at a time and making a meditation of constant stirring. Instead of the typical Kirsch, a cherry brandy, I like to substitute Bartlett Estate's wild blueberry dessert wine to intensify the Maine-ness of the dish. It adds at the end a pretty swirl and slight, sweet punch.

To develop this lobster fondue, I referred to a recipe from *The Fondue Cook Book* by Ed Callahan, published in 1968 by Nitty Gritty Productions in Concord, California, which I've been dragging around with me from city to city, country to country, and one dingy apartment to the next since college. The book is 104 yellowed pages of variations on the theme. Offering not just dipping fondues, but baked cheese specialties and rarebit recipes as well, this little book is a delight. Many of the recipes call for egg yolks, cream, crab, and sherry, but I didn't care to mess around with mid-century weirdness. I wanted to keep it classic, so I used the book's recipe for Fondue Sonoma as a guide for measurement and proportions, and tweaked it to suit my vision. I cooked mine on the stove in our big Le Creuset, then transferred the goods to a super Seventies fondue pot I found at Goodwill for three dollars. I got a little soft-shelled lobster at the market for five dollars and steamed him up in a flash. And while I have vacillated on the lobster/cheese issue for some time, I did find this a lovely addition to our Valentine's repast. The Maine wines worked perfectly, adding crisp depth and a fruity-spiked top note to the nutty meltness. This is a winner. Melt with it. Now, we sleep.

Method

1. In a pan over low heat, heat the wine.

2. Dredge the cheese in flour. Slowly add handfuls of the floured cheese to the pan and stir over medium-low heat. Stir in the seasonings. Keep stirring until the mixture is entirely incorporated, bubbling, and has thickened. Transfer to a fondue pot. Add the 2 teaspoons of the dessert wine.

3. Serve with cubed baguette bites, apple slices, and lobster pieces.

INGREDIENTS

2 cups Oyster River Riesling

½ pound grated Emmenthal

½ pound grated Gruyère

2 heaping tablespoons all-purpose flour

1 clove garlic

Pinch of salt, pepper, nutmeg

2 teaspoons Bartlett Estate Wild Blueberry dessert wine

Steamed lobster claw and tail meat, chopped into two-inch pieces, cubed baguette, and apple slices for dipping

Swordfish Puttanesca • *Malcolm*

Serves 3

INGREDIENTS

3 tablespoons olive oil

3 swordfish steaks (about 6 to 7 ounces each and ½ to ¾ inch thick), skin removed

Kosher salt and freshly ground black pepper, to taste

3 cloves garlic, finely chopped

1 anchovy in oil, finely chopped

1½ cups whole peeled canned tomatoes in juice, crushed by hand

½ cup large green olives, pitted and roughly chopped

2 tablespoons capers, rinsed and drained

¼ teaspoon crushed red pepper flakes

2 tablespoons roughly chopped parsley

2 teaspoons fresh lemon juice

Never having cared much for olives or capers, I was surprised by how much I have been enjoying the local supermarket's "Tuscan Gorgonzola" cheese spread, which tosses nearly every over-the-top strong flavor I can think of into a professional arm wrestling arena to compete for the custody of an estranged son who has been away at military school in the care of his domineering grandfather played by Robert Loggia. I'm not sure there's actually anything very Tuscan about it, unless the mere presence of olives and roasted red peppers makes something Tuscan. It has inspired me, though, to find other ways to introduce these unexpected elements—the briny zing of the green olives and the lip-smacking sharpness of the capers—into other, more familiar dishes.

This swordfish puttanesca works beautifully in this way. The strong, heavy flavors of the thick swordfish fillet perfectly balance the bright, vinegary, salty flavor of the olives and capers, along with the sweetness from the just-cooked crushed tomatoes. The finished product tastes like the sea. Ready in a snap, it's a somewhat lighter twist on a classic puttanesca. Using a big, meaty fish fillet in place of nutritionally void pasta adds tons of protein and flavor.

Method

1. Heat the oil in a large skillet over high heat. Working in batches, season the fish with salt and pepper and add it to the pan. Cook, flipping once, until golden-brown on the outside and medium rare inside, about 3 minutes total. Transfer the fish to a plate to rest.

2. Return the pan to the heat, and add the garlic and anchovy. Cook until soft, about 2 minutes. Add the tomatoes, olives, capers, and red pepper flakes. Cook until nearly all the liquid has evaporated, about 10 minutes.

3. Return the swordfish to the pan, add the parsley and lemon juice, and continue cooking until the fish has finished cooking through, about 2 minutes more. Divide the fish among the three plates and top with the sauce.

Rosemary Olive Oil Cake with
Chocolate Ganache • *Jillian*

Serves 8

I am in love with this unusual cake. It's light and rich, wintry and elegant, perfect for afternoon tea, or breakfast, or late at night with a small glass of port and an episode or two of *Downton Abbey* on DVR, or as a sweet treat to conclude a Valentine's Day dinner for two. Years ago, I discovered that a cake baked with olive oil is wonderful. It is a somewhat unexpected ingredient that adds a fragrant, fruity richness. Pouring a velvet layer of deep, thick chocolate ganache over an herb-flecked cake seems both decadent and sophisticated. It is just sweet enough for a February dessert and excellent with either port or champagne.

Method

For the cake:

1. Prepare an 8-inch cake pan with cooking spray. Preheat the oven to 325°F. In the bowl of a stand mixer thoroughly beat the eggs, add the sugar, and continue beating until light and fluffy. Slowly pour in the olive oil. Fold in the rosemary with a spatula.

2. In a large mixing bowl, combine the flour, baking powder, and salt. Stir the dry ingredients into the olive oil mixture until just combined.

3. Pour into the prepared cake pan and bake 25 to 30 minutes or until a toothpick comes out clean. Cool completely on a wire rack.

For the chocolate ganache:

1. In a double boiler, slowly melt the chocolate over medium heat. In a small saucepan, warm the cream over medium low. Stir the cream into the melted chocolate until the mixture is thick and shiny.

2. When the cake is completely cooled, spread the ganache over the cake and smooth with a spatula.

INGREDIENTS

For the cake:

4 eggs

¾ cup granulated sugar

⅔ cup olive oil

2 tablespoons fresh rosemary, very finely chopped

1½ cups all-purpose flour

1 tablespoon baking powder

½ teaspoon salt

For the chocolate ganache:

8 ounces semisweet chocolate, roughly chopped

½ cup heavy whipping cream

Pursuing the Maine Italian Sandwich • *Malcolm*

When February demands a cabin-fever reliever but you don't have cash to burn, maybe it's time for a Maine-style Italian. Head for town and walk the streets, scavenging that weak February sun, and when your stomach says it's time, head for Amato's or Anania's.

Any discussion of Italian sandwiches in Maine is fraught with peril. It's as sacred a cow as you're likely to find in Maine and incites at least as much passion as lobster-roll preparation and grange-supper etiquette.

The first thing to note is that in Maine any long sandwich with meat and vegetables is likely to be referred to by the generic term "Italian," much as people in other regions refer to hoagies, heroes, or grinders (though I personally have never heard anyone use the term "grinder").

To order a "Ham Italian" would be redundant; the ham is implied (the best ham always is) and included automatically unless you specifically request a "Turkey Italian." This can get confusing in some shops where ordering a combination sandwich using this naming convention would require you to (somewhat awkwardly) ask for an "Italian Cold Cut Combo Italian." But for the purposes of this road trip, we'll stick with the tried-and-true original Ham Italian.

AMATO'S
Locations Vary

At Amato's, and throughout Maine, there's not much about the Original Italian that I would associate with traditional Italian food. At first glance, the ingredients don't seem that special. Amato's bakes their own bread, a soft, chewy white loaf split lengthwise and flayed open to act as more of a tray for its fillings than an enclosure. A thin layer of nondescript white (American?) cheese is laid along the bottom, followed by a thin layer of rectangular ham. A sprinkling of raw, crunchy white onion and raw green bell pepper slices comes next. Then all hell breaks loose as tomatoes and slices of pickle are shaved in midair above your sandwich, falling where they may in irregular chunks and at great personal risk to the sandwich maker. A handful of black olives along with salt, pepper, oil, and vinegar finish the sandwich.

That's it. Nothing special or fancy about these ingredients. The recipe seems to follow a paint-by-numbers sandwich artistry in which individual sandwiches are indistinct from one another. A roast beef sandwich tastes like a turkey sandwich tastes like a salami sandwich, and instead of flavors,

your sandwich satisfaction is reduced to the pleasing contrasts in texture: soft layer, wet layer, crunchy layer, wet layer, soft layer.

But make no mistake, the Original Italian from Amato's is as addictive as the strongest street drugs. Quite literally, after having eaten my first one, I felt as if a giant omniscient being had grabbed me by the chest, pulled me through a tunnel of blurred, misconceived reality, and set me on my feet with new eyes, blinking back tears at the reborn world spread before me, clearly visible yet just beyond my grasp. I instantly began planning my next fix.

In short, the Original Italian is absolutely delicious, and I can only guess that there is something chemical at work to make me think so. There is a freshness to the assembled whole that other mass sandwich shops can't hope to reproduce. The overpowering flavors of the raw vegetables snap and burst in your mouth, the pickles have a wonderful tartness, and the juice of the tomatoes permeates everything. I am also completely smitten with the two other major features of this sandwich—the extreme saltiness and the black olives. These are two things I don't care about under most other circumstances.

There are few better purveyors of a Maine-style Italian sandwich than Amato's, who invented the sandwich on Portland's working waterfront 105 years ago. Sure, it's a little lowbrow and barely qualifies as Italian food, but it also happens to be stunningly, mysteriously delicious. Most days I buy a large, intending to eat half for lunch and the other half later on. I usually don't even make it to the table, instead inhaling the whole sandwich while leaning over my kitchen sink.

ANANIA'S
1227 Congress Street, Portland, ME 04102; (207) 774-8104

Anania's is my favorite sort of variety store, with a full sandwich menu, a fast-moving, friendly staff, and plenty of baked goods and snacks from independent manufacturers lining its shelves. Our Italian was made from scratch in just over a minute, and I was surprised by the compactness and weight of the finished sandwich.

The bread was marvelously soft and chewy and proved the perfect vehicle for what lay within. There was more ham than I expect in this type of sandwich and a layer of incredibly creamy American cheese, which helped protect the bread from the juiciness of the other ingredients. There were only a few slices of pepper and a few of the customary diced white onions. It was a nice change of pace; often, on this type of sandwich, the raw vegetables can be overpowering. I also liked that Anania's uses big, thick slices of tomato, which managed to be juicy and delicious despite the time of year. I can only imagine what this sandwich will be like in the summer when tomatoes are doing their thing locally. There were a few black olives (again, somewhat unusual for this type of sandwich; I am more accustomed to seeing Kalamatas used), which provided a mild, salty flavor. I was also happy to see big long spears of snappy, perfectly sour pickles as the top layer of the sandwich, with salt and pepper glistening on top.

I wasn't expecting anything beyond a standard-issue Maine-style Italian sandwich, but was pleasantly surprised by one of the best Italians I have yet tried. The careful balance of ingredients prevents that overwhelming "raw vegetable" flavor all too common in this type of sandwich, and the chewy bread and surprisingly creamy and flavorful cheese will stay in my mind a long time—or at least until I go back into the kitchen and eat the other half. Anania's has, for now, become one of my go-to stores for Italian sandwiches.

J'S OYSTER • *Jillian*
5 Portland Pier, Portland, ME 04101; (207) 772-4828; jsoyster.com

Alone, again. Valentine's Day is fast approaching, and you've destroyed another fledgling relationship with your neediness, your jealousy, your poor judgment during a night of drinking with his coworkers, or your unnerving penchant for dressing up your dog in period costumes.

In another scenario, that childish bastard has cheated on you, dumped you via text or Twitter, or gone out for milk and never returned. You've changed your Facebook status from "it's complicated" to "single."

In a third hackneyed scenario, you are alone by choice, mostly feeling like a badass single lady and reveling in not shaving your legs, watching every episode of *Game of Thrones* without interruption, and getting ever bolder venturing to the basement by yourself. You go, girl.

You know Valentine's Day is going to happen whether you like it or not. Mostly you've made your peace with the phony holiday. You consider its origins in sylvan Roman orgies and snicker at the teddy bears and paper hearts that oversaccharine what was once a most debauched occasion. In this spirit you decide to go out on the town alone in Portland. All your girlfriends are out with men who don't deserve them. Your guy friends have flown to Las Vegas for a four-day bender at the Spearmint Rhino. Even your dog has a date with the dachshund in 4A. What are you going to do and where are you going to go when every soul you know is coupled up, shooting stars into another's eyes, soppy love leaking through their sweaters like wet, red stains? You, my friend, are going to J's.

J's Oyster is seedy, salty, grimy, noisy, perfect. There is nothing romantic about it. It's not a place to hold hands, make plans, or declare boundless, heedless love. It's Romantic with a capital R, if you want to wear an oatmeal-colored Irish sweater and drink whiskey and look out to sea thinking of The Second Coming of Yeats. This is my prescription. Walk in and around the bar to the dark back corner. Order your liquor neat. Eat a dozen oysters without ceremony or decorum, 'cause let's face it, oysters aren't sexy. Order a cup of haddock chowder. It is always soul-satisfying. Then have the decades-deep waitress bring you a lobster. The reddest they've got. The one that was angry going into the pot. Twist off its claws and tail with abandon, because you don't care who sees you, because really, no one is looking. Slosh some of the liquid around. Get it on your sweater. Get up to your elbows in butter and the green goo from within. Demand mussels with lots of doughy rolls for dunking up the garlic broth. And finally, just to really grind down your solitude and fill your belly, ask for a big bucket of gritty steamers.

All of this will likely cost you half what it would anywhere else in the city. The preparation is basic, but seafood this fresh requires little more. You won't be the drunkest person there. You won't be the only one who is lonely, raw, and bitterly sad, whose heart aches and who has lost it all and expects to lose it all again. You go to J's not because you have no hope, but because you have too much. Love hurts. Life hurts. J's is there to help. It heals all with its elixers from the cask and the sea. They do not take reservations. This Valentine's Day, stay home if you are superficially bitter. If you are childish and annoyed, if you are going to heckle the happy lovers and invoke the phrase "Hallmark Holiday," stay home and read your Nicholas Sparks novel. Stay home and eat your fro-yo. Stay home and stalk ex-boyfriends online, write vitriolic blog posts about how their loss is your gain and how they will never find another girl like you. But if you want to be a bit cooler than that and have a hell of a meal in the process, put on your boots and walk the plank to J's. Tell them love sent you.

A "DEAR JOHN" LETTER

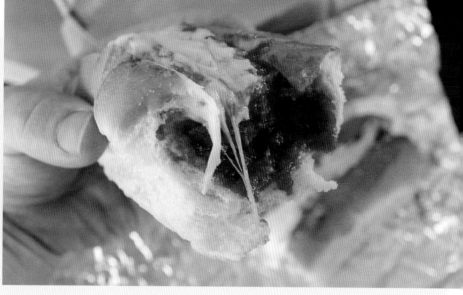

Dear Meatball Parmigiana Sandwich from Amato's,

Can you believe that it's been almost three years since we met? I have to confess that it wasn't exactly love at first sight, if I can even find it within myself to believe in such a thing anymore. When we first met, I was going through a weird time in my life, and there you were, ready to fill the emptiness inside me. I was living in Mexico, returning to the States only for a week each winter. And what whirlwind trips those were, filled with every manner of processed food and frozen wonders that I could cram into the tiny freezer in our rented condominium. I was dubious the first night we met, but to be fair, I hadn't really explored the width and breadth of the menu you came from. Oh sure, I'd had my dalliances with the Amato's Original Italian and gone round and round with some of your bohemian cousins, like the amazing weekend I spent in the Catskills with your second cousin, the Spaghetti Calzone. But it was you, Meatball Parmigiana Sandwich from Amato's, it was you who ultimately won my heart.

At first I just didn't understand what you were about. I'll never forget how I felt the first time I held you in my hands, your weight and heat bleeding through your tinfoil wrapper. A few minutes on a conveyor-style oven will do that to a sandwich, won't it? Even today, writing this letter, I remember the rush I felt as I peeled the waxy, translucent paper off the layer of provolone and mozzarella cheese melted onto your surface, a cheesy barrier that served to protect both of us from the oddly sweet molten tomato sauce beneath, a sauce only too eager to leap forth from your bun and soil my favorite sweatshirt.

But oh, you weren't without your faults, were you? Meatball Parmigiana Sandwich from Amato's, you've never been shy about pointing out my shortcomings, and for once, I am going to respond in kind. I'm sorry it has to be in a letter, but you know what it's like when we get together in person. I'm just worried that all those old feelings are going to come rushing back, and I want for once to be honest. Honest with you and maybe even honest with myself.

For one thing, you only contain two meatballs. Did you think that if you had them cut in half I wouldn't notice? Where I come from, they call that "false advertising,"

Meatball Parmigiana Sandwich from Amato's. And that shellacking of cheese you have up top? You can't tell me that's anything more than a salt layer, which may be melted the moment you come hot out of the oven but—and it pains me to say this—quickly solidifies into a rubbery crust. And I know I said I would never mention your soft bun again (a genetic gift from your mother, no doubt), but it just doesn't work for you. It turns you from pleasantly plump to squishy and disintegrated before I can even finish ravaging your first half.

How is it, then, that despite all your faults my attraction only grew stronger as the years went by? Before long we were meeting for six-minute-long trysts over the sink in my kitchen or, if we just couldn't control ourselves, in the front seat of my car. It didn't take long for that initial spark to blossom into a full-blown romance, and soon I was hungrily gobbling your gray, school lunch–style meatballs as many as two times a month. You were like a drug, and I was a hungry, helpless addict.

In our hearts, though, we both had to know it wouldn't last. We have to do the adult thing and admit to ourselves that sometimes in this crazy, mixed-up world, love just isn't enough. I've had to go up a T-shirt size, and when I bend over to tie my shoes too quickly, I start breathing heavily and nearly pass out from the exertion. Things are even worse for you, what with being ground into a mash by my teeth and then utterly destroyed by the acid in my stomach. In spite of our best intentions, I can't help but feel that this relationship always had an expiration date. I'll always have a special place for you in my heart, Meatball Parmigiana Sandwich from Amato's. We had some good times, but I think we must finally move on.

Fondly yours, Malcolm

Dinners We Make Again and Again

- Spicy Lamb Meatballs with Roasted Golden Beets and Moroccan Couscous
- Yankee Pot Roast
- American Chop Suey
- Cranberry Cardamom Monkey Bread with Clementine Glaze

As food bloggers for the past several years, we've created a lot of new recipes. We cook a lot and we test a lot. Some dishes work, and occasionally, some don't. But we are always looking for new recipes, filling the fridge with our mostly tasty experiments. Not every one of them goes into the regular rotation. When we're not cooking new recipes or heading out to dinner, we like to keep it fairly simple: a cheeseboard or homemade pizza or classic comfort foods such as meatloaf or spaghetti.

On Groundhog Day, Presidents' Day, Will-February-Never-End Day, or any other day of the year that drags its sorry carcass into evening begging to be graced by a can't-miss repast, these are the recipes we go back to again and again. They're comforting and cozy dishes that we just can't quit making.

Spicy Lamb Meatballs with Roasted Golden Beets and Moroccan Couscous • *Jillian*
Serves 4

INGREDIENTS

1 pound ground lamb

1 cup grated feta cheese

1 cup olive oil

Kosher salt and freshly ground black pepper

½ cup onion, chopped

1 garlic clove, minced

½ cup dry vermouth

½ cup beef broth

1 cup canned diced tomatoes

4 small dried chiles japoneses, reconstituted in boiling water

2 tablespoons basil leaves, ripped

6 beets

1 cup couscous

Good lamb is so fantastic, it really needs nothing else—just a little feta to hold it together. But it's the sauce that will become your new favorite thing ever. You will be spooning it out of the pan and dunking anything you can find into it. It's spicy, but nicely balanced by the sweetness of the roasted beets.

Method

1. In a large mixing bowl, combine the lamb and the feta. Form the mixture into 1-inch meatballs. Heat the olive oil in a large skillet over medium-high heat. Season with salt and pepper, brown the meatballs for 4 minutes, then remove them to a plate.

2. Turn the heat down to medium-low and add the onions and the garlic to the pan, cooking until soft, about 5 minutes. Pour in the vermouth and cook another 5 minutes.

3. In a food processor/blender, blend the onion mixture with the beef broth, the diced tomatoes, the chiles, and the basil. Return the sauce and the meatballs to the pan and simmer over low heat for 10 minutes.

For the beets:

1. Preheat the oven to 350°F. Scrub and dice the beets and toss with the olive oil, salt, and pepper. Roast 35–40 minutes, stirring/shaking once or twice.

For the couscous:

1. Cook one cup of couscous in two cups of chicken stock, simmering 10–15 minutes. Toss the beets with the couscous. Plate the meatballs on a bed of couscous, and spoon the sauce over everything.

INGREDIENTS

½ pound thick-cut bacon, diced

3–4 pounds beef chuck roast

Coarse salt and freshly ground pepper, to taste

2 tablespoons (¼ stick) unsalted butter

1 large yellow onion, diced

4 cloves garlic, minced

3 tablespoons (about 3 branches) fresh rosemary leaves, chopped

1 cup dry red wine

½ cup water

1 can (14 ounces) diced tomatoes

1 pound small white potatoes, halved

1 bunch of small carrots, cut into 2-inch pieces

3 stalks of celery, cut into 2-inch pieces

2 cups pearl onions, trimmed and peeled

Yankee Pot Roast • *Malcolm*

Serves 6–8

Learning how to make pot roast is one of the more satisfying culinary endeavors you can undertake. There's something immensely reassuring about taking big, cheap, tough cuts of meat and whether through slowly smoking or in this case through braising, turning them into the moistest, most flavorful, most tender roasts ever that fall apart under the lightest pressure from a dinner fork.

This is the kind of meal you will need to keep you warm until the next summer begins—sometime in mid-July, I suspect.

Method

1. Preheat the oven to 325°F. In a large Dutch oven, brown the bacon over medium heat, stirring occasionally, until the bacon begins to crisp. Using a slotted spoon, transfer the bacon to drain on paper towels.

2. Pat the beef dry, season liberally with salt and pepper, and add the beef to the Dutch oven. Using tongs, turn the meat on all sides to brown in the bacon fat. Transfer the beef to a plate.

3. Reduce the heat to medium, add the 2 tablespoons butter to the pan, and add the yellow onions. Cook, stirring occasionally, until the onions begin to turn translucent, about 6 minutes.

4. Add the garlic and the rosemary and cook until fragrant, about 3 minutes. Add the wine and the water and cook, scraping the brown bits off the bottom of the pan with a wooden spoon, about 1 minute.

5. Add the tomatoes (and juice) and check the seasoning, adding more salt and pepper, if needed. Return the beef to the pot and bring to a simmer over high heat. Cover, transfer to the preheated oven, and cook until the beef is almost tender, about 3 hours.

6. Remove the pot from the oven. Scatter the potatoes, the carrots, the celery, the pearl onions, and the cooked bacon around the roast. Cover, return to the oven, and cook until the vegetables are tender, about 1 hour. Remove the beef from the pot and let rest 15 minutes, then slice against the grain. Arrange on a platter with the cooked vegetables, and drizzle with the braising liquid.

American Chop Suey • *Malcolm*
Serves 4–6

Everyone who lives west of Massachusetts thinks they know what this dish is when I describe it. "Oh," someone from Wisconsin will say, "We eat that, too. It's called Goulash." Or someone from Arizona will say, "That's easy to make; that's Cheeseburger Macaroni."

No. No, it's not.

American Chop Suey is a uniquely New England dish comprised, in its most basic (and economical) iteration, of ground beef, elbow macaroni, and some sort of tomato slurry, whether tomato sauce, tomato soup, or V-8 juice. To me, it's quintessential Maine comfort food, served in healthy economic times and in bad, in grammar school cafeterias, VA hospitals, at bean suppers, and, to this day, in many homes throughout the state.

I was first exposed to this dish in 1983 at my best friend Joel's house. His mother, Lee, a pharmacy technician at Laverdiere's in Rockland, introduced me to what I really came to think of as "Maine food." My first bright-red hot dog swimming in a plateful of baked beans? Hers. My first baked hamsteak topped with pineapple ring and accompanied by scalloped potatoes? Hers. A blue, scratched translucent plastic Tupperware container full of sticky coffee bars (which never tasted as good when my mom made them), or powdered sugar–dusted lemon squares? They also were hers, and were stored in the cupboard to the left of the sink, high above the ancient, huge, wood-paneled microwave. As a little kid, I ate as many meals at their house as I did at my own. Sometimes I took it upon myself to stop by and help myself to a snack from their fridge even when Joel wasn't home.

INGREDIENTS

3 tablespoons olive oil

1 medium yellow onion, finely chopped

1 green pepper, seeded and finely chopped

1 pound 80/20 ground beef

½ pound hot Italian sausage, ground

2 teaspoons garlic powder

2 teaspoons onion powder

1 teaspoon paprika

2 teaspoons crushed red pepper flakes

Salt and pepper, to taste

1 can (28 ounces) whole peeled tomatoes

2 cans tomato sauce, 15 ounces each

2 tablespoons tomato paste

1½ teaspoons granulated sugar

¼ teaspoon ground cinnamon

1 pound box "Large Elbow" macaroni

Grated Parmesan cheese, to garnish

Sourdough bread

And it was for good reason: Joel's mom's cooking was different from my mom's, who was always trying to muck up my five-year-old taste buds with hearts of palm and water chestnuts. Joel's mom's food was delicious. After a particularly rough day at school, a day in which I didn't make the basketball team (again) or that little bastard Jamie Robbins smashed my Huffy "Dirt Dog" for the fourth time (that week), I didn't run home for my mom's kielbasa and artichoke heart stir-fry that she had slaved over all day. I went to Joel's for a two-liter bottle of cold Pepsi, a loaf of white bread, a tub of Country Crock, and a big, endless bowl of American Chop Suey.

Jillian and I have worked hard to create a recipe for the best possible version of the dish without changing what it essentially is. Our version of American Chop Suey knows its roots and would probably pass muster with the most die-hard, grange-hall ACS eaters—even with Joel and his parents. And no, that doesn't mean I'm putting canned condensed tomato soup in it.

Our version uses both a dab of ground hot Italian sausage and a generous amount of red pepper flakes. If you like things a little less spicy, or if you are using particularly spicy sausage, start with just one teaspoon of red pepper flakes and adjust from there. Make a big pot of our American Chop Suey, change into your footie pajamas, light a fire, and get a good game of Rush'n Attack going. It's comfort time, baby.

Method

1. Heat the olive oil in a large pot over medium-high heat. Add the onion and the green pepper, and cook until just softened, about 8 minutes. Add the ground beef, the ground sausage, the garlic powder, the onion powder, the paprika, the red pepper flakes, and the salt and pepper. Cook, stirring occasionally, until lightly browned, about 5 minutes. Add the whole tomatoes (and juice), crushing the tomatoes with your hands as you add them. Wear an apron. Add the tomato sauce, the tomato paste, the sugar, and the cinnamon, and stir well. Bring to a boil, reduce the heat, and simmer, uncovered, stirring occasionally, until the sauce thickens, about an hour.

2. While the sauce cooks, cook the pasta according to the package directions, reducing the cooking time by 2 minutes. Drain the pasta and rinse with cold water. Transfer the macaroni to the pot of sauce and stir until combined. Add more salt and pepper if needed, and cook until the flavors combine, about 10 more minutes. Serve with the grated Parmesan cheese and hot, buttered Sourdough toast.

Cranberry Cardamom Monkey Bread with Clementine Glaze • *Jillian*

Serves 6–8

Monkey bread is the perfect wintertime treat. Make it for an open house, brunch, or dinner party, and you will have every guest standing around the kitchen pulling apart and munching on this warm, sweet bread. I have happily made the easy version—open a can of Pillsbury biscuits, roll them out, soak them in butter and cinnamon sugar, and bake. The following, somewhat more refined recipe is not that much harder to make, and the result is cozy and pretty. I always have a big bowl of clementines in the house during the winter, and the cardamom adds such a lovely aromatic richness. Look for it sold in bulk at the natural foods store so you can buy only the amount you need.

Method

For the dough:

1. In the bowl of a stand mixer, combine 2 cups of the flour, the yeast, the sugar, the salt, and the cardamom. Mix using the dough hook attachment.

2. Heat the milk until lukewarm, 120–130°F. Add the warm milk, the butter, and the egg to the dry ingredients. Mix and scrape down the sides. Add the remaining flour, a half cup at a time, until the dough leaves the sides of the bowl.

INGREDIENTS

For the dough:

3½ to 4 cups all-purpose flour

2¼ teaspoons active dry yeast

¼ cup granulated sugar

1 teaspoon salt

1 teaspoon ground cardamom

1 cup milk

¼ cup (½ stick) unsalted butter, room temperature

1 egg, room temperature

For the coating:

¼ cup (½ stick) unsalted butter, melted

Zest of 2 clementines

1 cup granulated sugar

1¼ teaspoons cinnamon

1 teaspoon ground cardamom

½ cup dried cranberries

For the glaze:

Juice of 2 clementines

½ cup confectioner's sugar

3. Turn the dough onto a lightly floured surface and knead until smooth and elastic. Coat a large mixing bowl with baking spray. Place the dough in the bowl, turning it once, so that it is completely oiled. Cover and let it rise in a warm spot for about an hour.

4. Punch down the dough, cover, and let it rise again, about 30 minutes. After the second rising, form the dough into approximately 30 balls the size of walnuts.

For the coating:

1. In a small saucepan, melt the butter over medium heat. In a medium-sized mixing bowl, combine the clementine zest, the sugar, the cinnamon, and the cardamom. Dunk the dough balls in the melted butter, then roll them in the sugar mixture. Arrange them loosely in a Bundt or tube pan and sprinkle with the dried cranberries. Cover with plastic and refrigerate overnight.

2. Remove from the refrigerator while preheating the oven to 350°F. Bake 35–40 minutes.

For the glaze:

1. Stir the fresh-squeezed clementine juice into the confectioner's sugar until it dissolves. Spoon or pour the glaze over the hot bread just after it's out of the oven.

MARCH

How do you make the most of March, a month that is tedious and barren? Even in beautiful Maine, with its picturesque summers and (mostly) white winters, this month is a bit of a bummer. It's definitely not spring, not even yet "mud season," that peculiar in-between time when everything melts and looks, well, muddy. It can be bitterly cold, and you will definitely want warming soups and hearty fare. We are still deep in our cozy hibernation.

One way to make the most of this month is with St. Patrick's Day, which has evolved into—what else—an eating and drinking holiday, which we are always game to celebrate. Theming meals for a special occasion or event, even if the meaning is not quite clear, is a good excuse to celebrate with friends and narrow the focus of meal planning. We love all things Celtic—a crackling fire, a pint of Guinness, and a warm, woolly sweater. A boiled dinner might seem plain, but toting the last root vegetables up from the cellar and enjoying a satisfying meal of cured meat is one way to eat locally in New England in March.

A Feast for St. Patrick's Day

- Welsh Rarebit Bites
- Brown Ale and Cheddar Soup
- Scratch-Made Corned Beef and Cabbage (New England Boiled Dinner)
- Chocolate Guinness Cupcakes with Jameson Ganache and Bailey's Buttercream

BONUS!
Leftover Corned Beef Hash

Welsh Rarebit Bites ● *Malcolm*

Serves 12 as an appetizer

INGREDIENTS

1 pound super thick-cut bacon (about 8 slices)

2 tablespoons (¼ stick) butter

2 tablespoons all-purpose flour

8 ounces good cheddar, grated or chopped

¾ cup Guinness beer

1 tablespoon Worcestershire sauce

2 teaspoons dry mustard

1 teaspoon paprika

1 teaspoon pepper

1 French baguette, cut into slices

Olive oil

2 fresh tomatoes, seeded and chopped

2 green onions, sliced

No one is 100% sure where the moniker "Welsh Rarebit" for a dish consisting of toast covered in cheese sauce came from. One thing's for certain, though: The Welsh were probably being made fun of. The phrase used in the eighteenth century was "Welsh Rabbit," and the consensus seems to be that there was sarcasm at play. All but the most poverty-stricken English families could at least afford rabbit in the 1700s, whereas the Welsh were notoriously poor—so poor, the name suggests, that they would have to eat cheese sauce in place of meat.

Where, then, did the "rarebit" come from? No one's sure of that either. It has been suggested that "Rabbit" had to be modified to Rarebit when too many pub customers started wondering why the rabbit they had ordered wasn't on the plate set before them. I've also read that "rarebit" was coined long after the dish's creation in an attempt to make a peasant dish seem more sophisticated.

These are issues for linguists and grammarians to parse at boring dinner parties. My concerns about this dish are much more direct: With spring right around the corner, how can I possibly justify eating hot cheese sauce for lunch?

When I was growing up, this was a perfect dish for March. My mom would make piles of sourdough toast, layer the toast with bacon and big fat slices of tomato, and ladle cups and cups of hot, bubbling cheese on top. It was hearty, satisfying fare—food that should really only be eaten by someone who has just been shoveling snow for two hours. I wanted to lighten it up, miniaturize it, and make it suitable for any season or even as a party hors d'oeuvre. Some experimenting led me to this recipe. It uses much, much less cheese sauce, which makes it a much lighter dish—or as light as anything that includes cheese poured over bacon can possibly be. The taste of mustard, beer, and cheddar cheese is still very much present and combines wonderfully with salty, super thick-cut bacon and the freshness of chopped tomatoes and green onions.

Method

1. In a medium skillet, cook the bacon until crisp, turning often, about 12 to 14 minutes. Drain the crisp bacon on paper towels.

2. Melt the butter in a medium-sized saucepan. Slowly add the flour, stirring constantly, and cook over medium heat until toasted, about 3 minutes. Add the cheese, beer, Worcestershire, mustard, paprika, and pepper. Cook, stirring constantly, until the cheese is melted and smooth, about 3 minutes. Remove from the heat.

3. Brush each baguette round with olive oil and arrange on a baking sheet. Broil until the bread just begins to toast and turn brown.

4. To assemble, place a half strip of bacon on each slice of bread and drizzle with 1½ teaspoons of the hot cheese sauce until it begins to flow over the edges of the toast. Top with the chopped tomato and sliced green onions, and serve immediately.

Brown Ale and Cheddar Soup • *Malcolm*

Serves 8

Okay, so this may not be the kind of meal you want to eat before doing anything strenuous, such as running headlong into a burning schoolhouse to save dozens of screaming orphans. It's probably not what you want the night before you run the New York City Marathon or before your first day of basic training for the Marines. It may not be ideal for anyone looking to tackle a predawn jog or even make it into work on time. Full disclosure: It's not even for anyone who has a pressing need to put on pants the next day. Let's just say this and then not speak another word about it: Save this supper for a night when your only major obligation is to continue the basic intake of oxygen and expulsion of carbon dioxide and maybe, just maybe, make sure the latest rerun of *Teen Mom 2* is set to be DVRd. Anything more involved may be too ambitious.

Why is that? Because this is a soup made of cheese and beer and bacon, for goodness' sake. Any soup that uses bacon pan scrapings as one of its major flavoring agents just isn't going to be that good for you. Even calling it "soup" may be putting lipstick on a pig. This is a bowl of rich, hot cheese. It's liquefied Welsh Rarebit. It's a lightly spiced, soul-warming coppa d'oro. It's excessive and gross and hedonistic and awful, and it's also wonderful and delicious and heavenly and I'm eating another bowl even as I type this.

Use the best cheddar you can buy, since it's such a major player in this soup, and a decent brown ale, such as Newcastle, or a pale ale such as Bass. If you don't like a lot of heat, scrape as much of the inside of the jalapeño as you can with the edge of a spoon before dicing. Top each bowl of soup with more bacon, jalapeño, thyme, or diced fresh tomato, and serve with plenty of crusty bread. Call me when spring gets here.

INGREDIENTS

A 12-ounce package of thick-cut bacon, diced

3 large garlic cloves, minced

1 celery rib, finely chopped

1 small onion, finely chopped

1 tablespoon chopped thyme

1 large jalapeño, ribbed, seeded, and chopped

A 12-ounce bottle brown or pale ale

About 2¼ cups low-sodium chicken broth

4 tablespoons (½ stick) unsalted butter

¼ cup all-purpose flour

1 cup heavy cream

¾ pound sharp cheddar cheese, coarsely shredded

Salt and freshly ground pepper

Additional sliced jalapeño, bacon, thyme, and/or diced tomato to garnish

Crusty bread

Method

1. In a large saucepan or Dutch oven, cook the bacon, stirring occasionally, until the fat renders and the bacon is crisp, about 8 minutes.

2. Using a slotted spoon, transfer the bacon to drain on a paper towel. Crumble any overly large pieces between your fingers or chop quickly with a knife.

3. Add the garlic, celery, onion, thyme, and jalapeño to the rendered fat in the saucepan. Cook over moderate heat, scraping up any brown bits from the bottom of the pan, stirring often, until the vegetables soften, about 8 minutes.

4. Add half of the beer and cook until reduced by half, about 5 minutes.

5. Add 2¼ cups chicken broth and return to a simmer.

6. In a small skillet, melt the butter.

7. Whisk in the flour, making a roux, and cook over moderate heat, stirring until lightly browned, about 2 minutes.

8. Whisk the roux into the soup until combined and bring to a simmer. Cook until thickened, about 8 minutes.

9. Add the heavy cream, cheddar cheese, and the remaining beer and simmer, stirring occasionally, until thick and creamy, about 5 minutes.

10. Stir in the cooked bacon and season with salt and pepper. Top with additional jalapeño, bacon, thyme, and/or diced tomato. Serve immediately with plenty of crusty bread.

Scratch-Made Corned Beef and Cabbage (New England Boiled Dinner) • *Malcolm*

Serves 6–8

Once you come to understand that your days of drinking pale green-tinted beer until you lose vision in your right eye and wake up with a bloody nose are probably behind you, the biggest remaining component of a St. Patrick's Day celebration is the food. Last year we tackled a traditional corned beef and cabbage, or "boiled dinner" as it is called in New England. To me, a boiled dinner is really just a necessary prelude to eating leftover corned beef hash with runny eggs—and I'm willing to consume a few pieces of boiled cabbage in order to get there. To make it more interesting, I decided to corn my own beef, which means pickling a flat cut of beef brisket in a salted-water-and-brown-sugar brine before cooking. It's a great way to annoy your significant other, since the wet curing process takes 7 or 8 days and requires replacing much of the refrigerator's ordinary contents—vegetables, fruits, eggs, etc.—with a 5- or 6-pound slab of slowly graying beef.

INGREDIENTS

For the brine:

6 cups water

1½ cups coarse kosher salt

1 cup brown sugar

A 5- to 6-pound flat-cut beef brisket

1½ tablespoons Insta-Cure #1 (optional; see sidebar on page 59)

A 1.5-ounce jar pickling spice

One cinnamon stick, broken into pieces

One bottle Yuengling or other lager beer

Additional water as needed (see below)

For the corned beef and vegetables:

4 bay leaves

1 tablespoon coriander seeds

1 tablespoon whole mustard seeds

1 tablespoon whole black peppercorns

A 12-ounce bottle Guinness stout beer

Water

6 to 8 unpeeled, red-skinned potatoes

6 medium carrots, peeled

3 medium onions, peeled and halved

2 medium parsnips, peeled, cut into 2-inch lengths

1 head of cabbage, quartered

Mustard and/or horseradish cream sauce

Our method calls for cooking the corned beef and vegetables separately and combining them at the end. Boiled dinner purists may scoff at this; my editor's wife, who traces her lineage to County Cork, argues vociferously (sound Irish?) that the whole point of the exercise is to have the otherwise bland cabbage partake of the corned beef's salt and fat. What can I say? While it is certainly possible to coordinate your timing and cook everything together in one pot, I prefer to cook the meat and vegetables separately for greater control over doneness.

Method

For the brine:

1. In a medium saucepan, warm the water over medium heat just until air bubbles form. Remove from the heat, add the salt and sugar, and stir until dissolved. Let cool completely, adding ice if you are in a hurry.

2. Add the uncooked brisket to a large roasting pan. Pierce the meat all over with a paring knife to allow the brine to penetrate deep into the meat. Poor the cooled salt and sugar water solution over the meat and add Insta-Cure (optional), the pickling spice, cinnamon stick, and lager beer. If needed, add more water until the meat is completely covered. Cover the pan with foil or plastic wrap and place in the refrigerator to cure for 7 or 8 days, flipping the meat over each day and stirring the brine.

To prepare the corned beef and vegetables:

1. Remove the brisket from the brining liquid and rinse with cold water to remove excess salt and spices. Set aside.

2. Using cheesecloth, tie up the bay leaves, coriander seeds, mustard seeds, and peppercorns. In a large stockpot over high heat, add the brisket, the Guinness, enough water to cover the meat, and the cheese cloth pouch. Bring to a boil, then cover, reduce the heat to low, and simmer for 2½ hours.

3. Using tongs, remove the meat to a baking sheet and set aside. Add all the vegetables to the stockpot with its remaining simmering liquid and cook until the vegetables are cooked through, about 25 minutes. Transfer the meat back to the pot to heat through, about 5 minutes. Using tongs or a slotted spoon, remove the meat and all the vegetables to a large wooden board. Slice the meat against the grain and serve with mustard and/or horseradish cream sauce.

THE COLOR OF CORNED BEEF

There is a choice to be made when you are making your own corned beef. As part of the process, the beef will take on a harmless grayish-brown color. If you want your corned beef to turn out bright pink and vibrant, you need to add a few spoonfuls of Insta-Cure to your brining liquid. This is a controversial choice, since Insta-Cure is mainly sodium nitrate, used mostly by sausage makers to inhibit bacteria growth and prevent botulism. The word "nitrate" scares a lot of people because of concern a few years ago that nitrates were linked to cancer. This study has since been largely debunked by the American Cancer Society and the National Research Council, who agree that consuming low levels of sodium nitrate (which incidentally is also present naturally in foods, including spinach, carrots, celery, and, for that matter, anything grown in the ground) poses no increased risk of cancer.

This doesn't make Insta-Cure any easier to get your hands on: I couldn't find any at Hannaford (though I've since heard it can be purchased there) or at Whole Foods, where one employee acted as though I were asking for anthrax. If deep-pink corned beef is important to you, Amazon carries it, as do some specialty sausage shops. I skipped it, and although my corned beef was not quite as photogenic as it otherwise would have been, it tasted fantastic.

Chocolate Guinness Cupcakes with Jameson Ganache and Baileys Buttercream • *Malcolm*

Makes 12 cupcakes

I've never been much of a novelty drinker. I will choose a glass of whiskey with a cube of ice over some mixologist's overwrought ginger-infused absinthe concoction any day. Because I went to college, though, where $40,000 in student loans taught me mostly how to open a beer bottle with a cigarette lighter, I make an exception for the Irish Car Bomb. It's a staple among crowds of rookie drinkers: Drop a shot glass filled with equal parts Irish whiskey and Baileys Irish Cream into a pint glass filled three quarters of the way with Guinness draught beer. When the liquor hits the beer, all hell breaks loose—the drink immediately overflows, curdles, and explodes. Tilt the whole mess back in a few big gulps, the foamy mixture of beer and booze sliding easily (and quickly!) down your throat and directly onto your liver.

My last experience with Irish Car Bombs was three years ago at a restaurant called The Whale's Tail in Oxnard, California. It was the kind of place with Bloody Mary–soaked wall-to-wall carpeting and tipsy septuagenarians tilting back gin and tonics at noon on

INGREDIENTS

For the cupcakes:

½ cup Guinness stout

½ cup (1 stick) unsalted butter, room temperature

6 tablespoons Dutch-process cocoa powder

1 cup all-purpose flour

1 cup granulated sugar

¾ teaspoon baking soda

1¼ teaspoons salt

1 egg

1 cup sour cream

For the Jameson dark chocolate ganache filling:

4 ounces bittersweet chocolate

1 cup heavy cream

1 tablespoon butter, room temperature

1½ teaspoons Jameson Irish whiskey

For the Baileys buttercream frosting:

1 cup (2 sticks) unsalted butter, room temperature

2½ cups powdered sugar

3 tablespoons Baileys Irish Cream

a weekday. What should have been a breezy family lunch changed course rapidly when my sister, herself no stranger to a barstool, casually mentioned that she had never tried an Irish Car Bomb. Ever the loving little brother—and with my mother looking on—I insisted she try one immediately. We received our drinks, and on a count of three dropped our shot glasses into our beers, where they immediately overflowed their glasses, sending my sister into a fit of giggles so severe that she was unable to finish her drink. The very patient waitress and I explained that she shouldn't worry and should try again with another one. Fresh drinks, 1-2-3, clink, foam, giggle fit, curdled beer, sighing waitress. Try again. Fresh drinks, 1-2-3, clink, foam, giggle fit, curdled beer, sighing waitress. On the fourth attempt, she was finally able to compose herself and down her Irish Car Bomb without spilling a drop. Meanwhile, in my capacity as coach, I had finished the four I'd been served in about twenty minutes, which made walking across the room surprisingly difficult and has kept me from having another since.

This year there won't be any Irish Car Bombs, any public intoxication, or any fistfights with someone in a "Kiss Me, I'm Irish" T-shirt. Jillian and I have a new daughter, and my sister is married with a son of her own. This St. Patrick's Day, the closest we will come to that kind of debauchery is consuming our Guinness, whiskey, and Baileys in cupcake form.

All of the elements of this cupcake work beautifully together. The Guinness adds a subtle richness to the chocolate cake, which develops just the slightest crispy crackle on its exterior. The cupcakes are filled with a Jameson-spiked dark chocolate ganache, and the whole shebiggle is topped with a surprisingly light, definitely boozy Baileys-soaked buttercream frosting. With just one bite, that combination of sugar, fat, and booze is enough to quicken your pulse and make the world seem like it's spinning off its axis. In other words, they're perfect for your St. Patrick's Day celebration.

Method

For the cupcakes:

1. Preheat the oven to 350°F. Line a cupcake or muffin pan with 12 cupcake liners. In a medium saucepan over medium heat, bring the Guinness and butter to a simmer. Add the cocoa powder and whisk until smooth. Remove from the heat and allow to cool slightly.

2. In a large bowl, combine the flour, sugar, baking soda, and salt. Using a stand mixer, beat the egg and sour cream until combined. Slowly add the Guinness and chocolate mixture, and stir until combined. Add the flour mixture, and continue stirring until completely combined.

3. Fill each cupcake liner to two-thirds full. Bake until a toothpick inserted into the center of a cupcake comes out completely clean, about 17 to 20 minutes. Remove the cupcakes from the pan, and allow to cool completely on a wire rack.

For the Jameson dark chocolate ganache filling:

1. Finely chop the chocolate and place in a heat-safe bowl. In a small saucepan, heat the cream until simmering and pour over the chocolate. Let stand for 1 to 2 minutes, and then stir with a rubber spatula until smooth. Add the butter and whiskey, and continue stirring until combined. Let cool while you prepare the buttercream frosting.

For the Baileys buttercream frosting:

1. Using the whisk attachment in your stand mixer, whip the butter on high speed for 5 minutes. Reduce the speed to low (unless you want to cover your kitchen and, ahem, camera, in a fine mist of powdered sugar) and gradually add the powdered sugar until incorporated. Add the Baileys and increase the speed to whip for another 2 to 3 minutes.

To assemble the cupcakes:

1. Using a paring knife, carefully cut a cone-shaped hole about two-thirds of the way down into the cooled cupcakes, eating the removed cupcake centers as you work. Transfer the ganache to a piping bag with a wide tip and fill the cupcakes with the ganache.

2. Fill another pastry bag with the buttercream frosting, and pipe onto the tops of the cupcakes. Finish with sprinkles if desired.

BONUS! Corned Beef Hash • *Malcolm*

Serves 4

INGREDIENTS

4 tablespoons (½ stick) unsalted butter

1 poblano chile pepper, cut into medium dice (about ½ cup)

2 to 3 cups potatoes, cooked, cut into a ½-inch dice

2 to 3 cups fully cooked corned beef, shredded into ½-inch pieces

2 to 3 carrots, peeled, cooked, cut into a ½-inch dice

1 large onion, cooked, cut into a ½-inch dice

¼ head of cabbage, cooked, cut into a ½-inch dice

2 tablespoons chile sauce

1 teaspoon Sriracha hot chili sauce

1 to 2 tablespoons whole grain mustard (optional)

¼ cup heavy cream

4 large eggs

Kosher salt

Freshly ground black pepper

2 tablespoons fresh parsley, chopped

For me, a traditional New England boiled dinner, complete with potatoes, carrots, parsnips, and cabbage, is only a necessary stop along the path from "not eating corned beef hash" to "eating corned beef hash." There's nothing really wrong with a boiled dinner (especially if you have lots of whole-grain mustard and horseradish cream on the side), but it's not a dish I crave. Corned beef hash, on the other hand—and more specifically, corned beef hash with lots of Sriracha, ketchup, and a few soft-boiled or poached runny eggs—is a dish that occupies my brain and gives me something to look forward to with the leftovers from my corned beef and cabbage dinner.

If you have a great corned beef hash just once in your life, you'll find yourself forever chasing the experience, a journey that ultimately ends when you find yourself eating the canned stuff at three in the morning in a diner somewhere in New Jersey. Our version has little in common with the mushy pink canned stuff; ours has big chunks of shredded corned beef and recognizable vegetables. It makes a great light supper for late winter and early spring.

Try to cut all the meat and vegetables to roughly the same size, and when cooking your hash, use a spatula to keep forming a new crust by mixing the hash, pressing the mixture down in the pan, flipping the mixture, and repeating the process several times. Use our recipe as a guideline for getting the proportions right. Really, though, part of the fun of making corned beef hash is in adapting it to the leftover ingredients you have on hand, so you should feel free to add or subtract ingredients as needed. It's like jazz, man. This recipe assumes you are working with cooked leftovers; you can start with raw vegetables as well, simply increasing your cooking time accordingly.

Method

1. In a large nonstick skillet over medium heat, melt the butter. Add the diced poblanos and sauté until just softened, about 3 to 4 minutes. Add the potatoes, corned beef, carrots, onion, cabbage, chili sauce, Sriracha sauce, mustard (optional), and heavy cream. Stir until thoroughly mixed.

2. Using the back of a spatula, press the mixture into the bottom of the pan and let cook undisturbed 3 to 4 minutes. Scrape the pan with a spatula, folding brown bits back into the mixture. Flatten into the pan and cook undisturbed for 3 to 4 minutes. Scrape and mix. Repeat 3 to 4 more times until the hash is browned with lots of crusty bits, 15 to 20 minutes total.

3. Using a spoon, make 4 shallow indentations in the top of the hash, and break an egg into each one. Season with salt and pepper to taste, cover, and cook until egg whites have set but yolks are still soft, about 5 minutes. Sprinkle the hash with chopped parsley. Serve immediately.

CAIOLA'S • *Jillian*

58 Pine Street, Portland, ME 04102; (207) 772-1110; caiolas.com

Finally, a gorgeous meal in a charming restaurant. Supper at Caiola's was everything I wanted it to be: an intimate dinner for two at a good—really good!—neighborhood place just around the corner from our apartment. I called for reservations and was told 7:15; we were seated immediately upon arrival in the front section of the small dining room. It was cozy, rustic, amber-hued, and warm. Every table seemed to have at least one bottle of wine, and laughter floated from all corners of the room. The single-page menu (which changes daily) proffered numerous options for each of us. But first we had a martini. It was perfect. Clean and cold like a colonial bath in the midst of heathen country. I felt better and lighter already.

We agreed that, to start, we should order warm dates stuffed with manchego and served with pancetta and seasonal vegetables. Every component of this appetizer was excellent. Sweet and savory, gooey and crisp, and as pleasing to the eye as to the palate. After devouring the rich fruit, meat, and cheese, I dove into bitter endive, red cabbage, apple matches, and pomegranate seeds. Eating pomegranate makes me feel ancient, wicked, beautiful, and desperate. It is one of my favorite things. I dipped my index finger into the swath of jam on the plate, licking every sticky swipe. I only wish there had been an even number of dates. Shouldn't they come in pairs?

Based on the recommendations of our server, Malcolm ordered scallops and I the chicken marsala, which, like veal piccata or communism, is not something I would ordinarily consider. It seems Cold War boring, better in theory than practice. I was so very mistaken. Chicken marsala à la Caiola's is wonderful—sweet, light, and lovely. I was expecting a pounded-down breaded chicken cutlet smothered in a weird sauce. The most appropriate adjective to describe what I was served escapes me: I just know I didn't want to stop tasting it. And this delectable protein was served with a mound of penne in red sauce with greens and Parmesan that was so pure and elegant in its simplicity, it was almost mathematical.

Though Malcolm's scallops were smaller and less seared than he had imagined them, the nicely sweetened sauce complemented their richness perfectly. The purple roasted potatoes were tasty and even more delicious when he realized they weren't beets. The mashed sweet potatoes were sweet and cinnamony, the French beans stringy and perfectly cooked. Our only small complaint was the service, which was slow. The staff was super helpful and personable, but I was ready to leave about 20 minutes before we were able, when we ran across the street to Cumberland Farms for a bottle of wine and a pack of Rolos to finish our night in style back on the couch at home. I am so delighted we finally went to Caiola's, a neighborhood place that's ideal for a delicious dinner with a husband, wife, or group of friends on a chilly March evening.

WEEKEND PROJECT:
Scratch-Made Grownup Sloppy Joes • *Malcolm*

Makes 4 big sandwiches

Is there a more quintessentially American food than the Sloppy Joe? Okay, so the sandwich, a slurry of beef, onion, and sweet tomato sauce, isn't exactly the darling of the gourmet food world. Maybe it's because of a 1980s-era association with Manwich, the canned Sloppy Joe sauce that removed most of the "cooking" from "cooking dinner." Those old Manwich commercials had a weirdly aggressive air about them, convincing you that feeding your family any kind of lesser, inferior sandwich meant that you didn't love them, and that no matter how tired and child addled you might be at the end of the day, surely you could find the strength to brown some ground beef, dump a tin of Manwich sauce on top, and spoon the mixture over a few hamburger buns.

I don't think I'd had a Sloppy Joe since the forgettable ones I must certainly have gulped down in high school hot lunches 20 years ago. But this sandwich has been on my mind lately because I see no reason why it shouldn't be great. It's a quick, easy, inexpensive, kid-friendly convenience food that you can cook by the bucketload and serve all week. It's like a chili with no beans, served on top of bread and sweetened for that inner child weaned on S'mores and Pop Tarts. It's comfort food for the ten-year-old that lives inside your adult body.

Our version of this classic keeps the elements that make a Sloppy Joe a Sloppy Joe—ground beef, onion, tomato sauce, and some sugar. But we also wanted to make it a little more interesting for the adult palate, so we added a touch of heat and spice. We serve it on buns specially made for Sloppy Joes, full of cheddar cheese and more onion, with a slightly crispy, chewy outside that stands up to the sauce while staying soft and warm on the inside. As a final statement, we melt a slice of homemade American cheese and sprinkle a few sliced jalapeños on top of the Sloppy Joe mixture. The result? A satisfying, interesting spin on a childhood favorite.

INGREDIENTS

1 tablespoon vegetable oil

½ red bell pepper, chopped

1 yellow onion, chopped

2 celery ribs, chopped

3 cloves garlic, minced

4 ounces fresh Mexican chorizo

1 pound 80/20 ground beef

Salt and pepper to taste

A 15-ounce can of whole tomatoes

¼ cup ketchup

¼ cup chili sauce

1 tablespoon Worcestershire sauce

1 tablespoon white wine vinegar

2 tablespoons brown sugar

Pinch ground cloves

½ teaspoon dried thyme

Pinch cayenne pepper

4 Sloppy Joe buns (recipe follows)

4 tablespoons (½ stick) unsalted butter

4 slices American cheese, sliced pickles, or sliced jalapeño, to garnish

Method

1. In a large, deep skillet over medium heat, add the vegetable oil, bell pepper, onion, and celery. Cook, stirring occasionally, until the onions turn translucent, about 5 minutes. Stir in the garlic and cook about 1 minute. Transfer the vegetables to a bowl and set aside.

2. In the same pan, add the Mexican chorizo and the ground beef, crumbling the meat as you add it to the pan. Add salt and pepper and cook, stirring occasionally, until the ground beef is well browned, about 7–10 minutes.

3. In the bowl of a food processor, pulse the tomatoes until nearly puréed, making sure to leave some chunks of tomato.

4. Add the tomato mixture to the pan with the meat, along with the reserved vegetables, ketchup, chili sauce, Worcestershire sauce, vinegar, brown sugar, cloves, thyme, and cayenne.

5. Let simmer over low-medium heat 10 minutes, adjusting the seasoning and the consistency with a bit of water if needed.

6. While the filling simmers, split 4 buns in half and butter the cut sides. Arrange cut side down on a hot skillet, allowing the buns to brown slightly.

7. Arrange the buns on plates, top with the meat mixture and, optionally, the cheese, pickles, and jalapeño.

Sloppy Joe Buns

Makes about 2 dozen

Method

1. In the bowl of a stand mixer, combine the yeast, water, and sugar. Let the yeast bloom for about 5 minutes, then add the milk, salt, egg, garlic powder, cheddar cheese, onion, butter, and flour.

2. Using the mixer's dough hook attachment, knead the mixture on low-medium speed until smooth and elastic, about 10 minutes. Remove from the mixer and form into a ball. Transfer the dough to a greased medium-sized bowl and flip the dough over so that the top is also lightly greased.

3. Cover with a clean kitchen towel and let rise in a warm, draft-free place for 1 hour until the dough has doubled in size.

4. Punch down the dough and return it to the mixer. Knead on low speed for 10 minutes. Remove from the mixer and roll the dough to ½-inch

INGREDIENTS

1 tablespoon active dry yeast

1 cup warm water

2 tablespoons sugar

¾ cup milk, room temperature

2 teaspoons salt

1 large egg, lightly beaten

1½ tablespoons garlic powder

1 cup shredded mild cheddar cheese

1 small yellow onion, finely chopped

¼ cup (½ stick) unsalted butter, soft

6 cups bread flour

1 egg white

Poppy seeds

thickness on a smooth floured surface. Cut the dough into 3- to 4-inch rounds. Place the rounds 2 inches apart on a greased cookie or baking sheet. Cover with a clean kitchen towel in a warm, draft-free place and let rise for 45 minutes or until doubled in size. Preheat the oven to 375°F.

5. In a small bowl, use a fork to lightly beat the egg white. Brush each bun with the egg white. Sprinkle the buns with poppy seeds. Bake for 20 minutes or until the buns are golden-brown. Let cool on a wire rack.

TRATTORIA ATHENA · *Jillian*
25 Mill Street, Brunswick, ME 04011; (207) 721-0700; trattoriaathena.com

At Trattoria Athena, you sit by the kitchen, or near the windows, or at the bar. Despite the cozy space, each table feels private and insular while remaining a part of the whole. And you want to be part of this tiny dining establishment. It transports. And at the same time, you are exactly here, where you should be, on a one-way street in Brunswick, within the chalk-board-, map-, and wine-lined walls where friends meet unexpectedly and on purpose. We were invited out with a group recently and found ourselves tucking into a reclaimed wood table for six at seven o'clock on a Saturday night. The place was full of happy, hushed voices, and it was rosy-warm inside as the temperature dipped outside.

The menu is Greek-Italian, local, and seasonal. It struck me as an authentic choice rather than a zeitgeist thing. It's how this food is meant to be. Red wine was poured into stemless glasses before I had a chance to question it. All I know is that it was spicy and delicious. We started with a trio of spreads ($10): tara-masalata—fish roe, bread puree; tzatziki—Greek yogurt, cucumber, and dill; and htipiti—feta and grilled hot peppers served with crusty bread. I had never had htipiti before and was pleasantly surprised by the bite that was balanced by tangy cheese. The bright, creamy tzatziki and lovely taramasalata were the best I've had since I used to haunt Sahadi's on Atlantic Avenue in Brooklyn. Enhanced joy from sharing good food and wine soon became evident at our table.

The blackboard behind me was covered with copious notes concerning the specials, but having prepared by browsing the menu online, I was already settled on the short ribs ($24). Rich and meaty, more akin to a slow-cooked Sunday pot roast than any other preparation of beef, this dish was soul warming. In a fit of spontaneity, Malcolm ordered a pasta dish from the daily board. It was a work of beauty composed of duck egg and white truffle oil, corzetti pasta with butter-poached lobster, white wine, shallots, sungolds, and corn ($24). I had three or four bites and still could not begin to discern the multiplicity of flavor combinations. Each taste was a new world of sensual delight. Marvelous! This was the dish of the night; their pasta is not to be missed.

Others in our party ordered meatballs aromatic with cumin, a salad covered in figs, a bowl of fresh ribbon pasta ready to be turned unctuous with an orange egg yolk balanced at its center, and ravioli filled with goat cheese. The ensemble was a feast for the senses, selflessly shared in forkfuls drifting perilously over others' plates. We sensibly ordered a smattering of desserts: Tiramisu, baklava, ekmek—such musical and evocative names for sweet bites—as well as a deep chocolate hazelnut torte and a special that evening, deep-fried ricotta spheres with orange zest and dripping with honey. These provided a coda and closure to a rustically elegant meal; all of them were outstanding, but the gooey baklava and complex ricotta were, in my opinion, extraordinary.

I love how each dish was carefully prepared, not at all fussy but not accidental, and complex and perfected. The service was unobtrusive but knowledgeable, and even though it is a small restaurant, it was not loud or claustrophobic. We both felt that this was one of the single best meals we've had in Maine and agreed we would be returning as soon as possible. Trattoria Athena seems settled and unassuming; it doesn't make a show-offy performance of the business of making food, which is why it's the kind of place we like most.

Good Weekend Lunches

- Chorizo y Papas Grilled Cheese Sandwiches
- Eggs Florentine Burgers
- Toasted Almond Blondies

Most families spend weekdays away from each other, at school, at work, working at home. That makes weekend lunches special. While I love going out for lunch at our local pub for no reason at all, or picking up road food while we're traveling or running errands, we have a particular fondness for the homemade weekend lunch. And though a good weekend lunch is welcome any time of year, I crave it most during the transitional seasons. When it's a little chilly outside but you're busy spring cleaning or doing a fall yard cleanup, what better time to make a pot of soup and a good grilled cheese? Call a temporary halt to the around-the-house busyness and watch a movie with commercials on cable. It's the little things in life that are so sweet.

Chorizo y Papas Grilled Cheese Sandwich • *Malcolm*
Makes two sandwiches

Poke your head through the kitchen window of nearly any household in Mexico around breakfast time, and you're likely to find a family with a skillet full of bright red, ground, fresh chorizo sizzling away with diced potatoes and sometimes a few scrambled eggs. Folded into fresh corn tortillas and served with a side of beans, this is as common a breakfast staple in that country as, say, bacon and hash browns are in the United States.

It's a filling, comforting breakfast that I haven't gotten to enjoy in a while due to the mysterious dearth of fresh Mexican chorizo in midcoast Maine. Because I can't find chorizo in the big local supermarkets, I'll go to great measures to score the good stuff. That means I'll make it myself. I'll drive all the way to a big box store in South Portland, which often seems to inexplicably carry big plastic tubes of finely ground, brightly spiced fresh Mexican chorizo. I'll even order it on the Internet. Whenever I do find a place to buy it, I get as much as I can reasonably fit into the freezer.

I cracked a fresh package one morning at that weird in-between hour when you've skipped breakfast but it still feels too early to dive into lunch. I was leaning toward a sandwich, so rather than prepare my chorizo y papas the traditional way, I adapted the concept into grilled cheese form, adding crisped Tater Tots for extra texture.

The resulting sandwich delivers acres of spicy ground chorizo directly into your stomach on a wave of melted cheese. I used a combination of habanero cheddar for spice as well as processed American for texture and melt. If habaneros bring too much spice to the sandwich for your taste, feel free to substitute pepper Jack. You can use sliced leftover baked potatoes if mass-produced frozen tater smithereens aren't your thing, but I strongly

INGREDIENTS

4 slices good white bread

4 tablespoons (½ stick) unsalted butter

½ cup ground Mexican chorizo

½ yellow onion, thinly sliced

6 slices habanero cheddar or pepper Jack cheese

6 slices American cheese

Handful of Tater Tots (about 12), cooked according to package directions

Sliced pickled jalapeños (optional)

Sour cream (to serve)

suggest trying the Tots and offering no apologies. And if you like things really spicy, you can even throw in a few pickled sliced jalapeños. Go ahead. This sandwich is already ridiculous, and it will shorten your life by at least a few hours. You might as well enjoy yourself.

Method

1. Combine the Mexican chorizo and the sliced onion in a medium-sized skillet, and cook over medium-high heat until the chorizo is cooked through and the onions are soft, stirring often, about 10 minutes. Transfer the mixture to a plate lined with paper towels, and allow to drain.

2. For each sandwich: Butter a slice of bread with a tablespoon of butter, place it butter side down in a nonstick skillet, and layer it with half of the habanero cheddar or pepper Jack. Top with half of the chorizo and onion mixture, then half of the cooked Tater Tots, then half of the American cheese and optional pickled jalapeños. Finish with half of the American cheese. Butter the other slice of bread, and use it to top the sandwich, butter side showing.

3. Cook covered over low heat, flipping as needed, until the cheese is melted and the bread is brown and crispy. Serve with a side of sour cream.

Eggs Florentine Burgers • *Malcolm*
Makes three burgers

Immediately after our daughter Violet was born, I purchased a life insurance policy with the idea that, in the case of my untimely demise, my wife and daughter would at least be able to console themselves in their time of grief by buying a new house or a car with a leather interior. As part of this process, the insurance company sent an elderly doctor to my house to collect blood for a series of tests, in order to determine my monthly premium.

I was a little nervous. Having lived for years outside the United States and away from routine medical care, and having practiced a somewhat laissez-faire approach to physical wellness while indulging a penchant for Scotch and cheese sauce, I wondered what kind of numbers I would see. What kind of havoc had I been wreaking on my internal organs all these years?

As it turned out, the numbers weren't bad. My cholesterol is a little high, but certainly not redlined, compared with other 34-year-olds. "It's the kind of number you can probably reduce just by having a bowl of Cheerios every day," my new doctor said.

INGREDIENTS

For the burgers:

1 pound ground beef

Kosher salt and pepper to taste

3 cups fresh spinach

3 eggs

Splash of white vinegar

3 hamburger buns, split

For the hollandaise sauce:

3 egg yolks

1 tablespoon Dijon mustard

2 tablespoons freshly squeezed lemon juice

¾ cup (1½ sticks) unsalted butter, melted

Salt, pepper, and cayenne pepper to taste

"So," I replied, "do you mean like eating rare hamburgers topped with a poached egg and hollandaise sauce?"

"No," he said, "I don't mean anything like that at all."

This burger will try to kill you. I suggest defending yourself with a knife and fork.

Method

For the burgers:

1. Divide the beef into three equal balls, and flatten into hamburger patties. Work the beef with your hands as little as possible, just enough to shape the hamburger patties. Season both sides with salt and pepper, and cook in a skillet over high heat until medium rare, about 2 to 3 minutes per side.

2. Add a tablespoon of butter to the burger drippings. Add the raw spinach and cook over medium heat until the spinach begins to wilt.

3. Crack an egg into a small dish, and set aside. Fill a small saucepan halfway with water, and add a splash of white vinegar. Heat the water over medium heat until millions of bubbles appear, the point just before the water starts to simmer. Reduce the heat to low and, holding the edge of the small bowl with the egg as close as possible to the nearly simmering water, slip the egg into the water. Adjust the heat as needed to keep the water from boiling or simmering vigorously. Cook until the yolks are just set, about 4 minutes, and remove with a slotted spoon. Repeat with the remaining eggs.

For the hollandaise sauce:

1. Fill a small saucepan with 2 inches of water, and place over medium heat. When the water simmers, reduce the heat to maintain a gentle simmer, and place a small metal or heat-safe glass on top of the pan as a double boiler. Add the egg yolks, the mustard, and the lemon juice, and whisk until combined.

2. In a slow, steady stream, pour the melted butter into the egg yolks, whisking constantly. Using a candy thermometer, make sure the egg yolks reach 140°F and remove from the heat. Keep whisking until the sauce thickens, about 3 minutes more. Season to taste with salt, pepper, and cayenne. The finished sauce can be kept warm in a thermos, insulated coffee cup, or over very low heat until ready to assemble.

Put it together:

Place a cooked hamburger patty on the bottom of each bun. Top with some cooked spinach, a poached egg, and finish with a few spoonfuls of hollandaise (and a side of Lipitor).

Toasted Almond Blondies • *Jillian*

Serves 8–10

I never got to buy hot lunch in elementary school. I considered this a great injustice in the third grade, when everyone who was cool got to stand in line and pass two dollars to the lunch lady for a piece of pizza cut with scissors, fruit cocktail, and a carton of milk on a plastic tray. It seemed so grown-up to be part of the world of commerce and eating food your mother hadn't made. I longed for an imagined freedom I simply wasn't experiencing with my once-a-week allowance for dessert. Instead my lunches were always well-balanced and made with love, a highly embarrassing and far too babyish state of affairs for someone as worldly as I felt at age eight.

To mitigate my humiliation at being so well cared for, I went for what I considered the most sophisticated ice cream novelty sold in the Joel School cafeteria—the toasted almond bar. It sold for thirty-five cents, which I kept in a red rubber change purse you had to squeeze closed to open. God, that almond bar was heaven. Crunchy bits, sweet white "vanilla" ice cream. I even liked the wooden stick, which I would hold onto as long as I could, letting the last of it linger in my mouth while our tables were called and we spilled our refuse and freezer packs into garbage cans, then queued up to file back to class.

I remember the din of a hundred kids kicking their feet on metal benches, teasing and trading secrets for sandwiches. Life was simpler then. I make these blondies as a way to reminisce, since the only way to truly time travel is with food.

INGREDIENTS

¼ cup chopped almonds

¼ cup chopped walnuts

1 cup (2 sticks) unsalted butter, melted

1 cup packed dark brown sugar

1 egg

1 scant teaspoon vanilla extract

¼ teaspoon almond extract

1 cup all-purpose flour

½ teaspoon baking powder

⅛ teaspoon baking soda

Pinch of salt

Method

1. Preheat the oven to 350°F. Grease and flour an 8-inch by 8-inch pan. In a dry skillet, toast the almonds and the walnuts over medium-high heat until fragrant; be careful not to burn them. Set aside.

2. In the bowl of a stand mixer, cream the butter and the sugar. Add the egg, the vanilla, and the almond extract.

3. In a large mixing bowl, whisk together the flour, the baking powder, the baking soda, and the salt. Incorporate the dry ingredients until just combined, and fold in the nuts. Spread the mixture in the prepared pan, and bake 20 minutes or until a toothpick comes out clean. Allow them to cool in the pan before cutting into squares.

APRIL

Easter Sunday Menu
- Deviled Ham
- Kale and Artichoke Soup
- Leek and Goat Cheese Pie
- Braised Leg of Lamb

Even if it isn't 75 degrees and sunny, even if the weather is still damp and chill, in April we celebrate new life—regeneration, rebirth, renewal. And it feels so good. Signs of spring pop up all around us. Birds chirp cheerily, or so it seems. Crocuses and early daffodils bloom against south-facing foundations. The air at midday is softer, and in the evening, spring peepers send forth waves of song from every wetland. It is the season of lambs, buds, and all those symbols of life that tell us the earth is restoring itself once again and will keep on doing so every year without end. We celebrate with pastel dresses and white straw hats, peeking under rocks in search of the jelly beans and painted eggs left there by a man-sized bunny. Spring is definitely on the rise. For us, Easter is a holiday for visiting and for welcoming visitors. We look forward to a fairly informal meal with one great, braised leg of lamb as the centerpiece and lots of fun snacks and sides for friends and family to partake of while sipping mimosas and sneaking candy from the kids' brightly colored baskets. Balance out all the chocolate and marshmallow goo with leeks, artichokes, and kale.

Deviled Ham • *Malcolm*

Serves 6-8, as an appetizer

I realize that I've taken a big chance with the name of this recipe. Some of you—maybe even most of you—will read that name and move right along to another section of the book or abandon it altogether, perhaps for a dessert cookbook filled with 100 percent more Thin-Mint-and-Nutella-filled cupcakes and at least 50 percent less ground up, spicily seasoned pork paste.

Some of you may be unable to dissociate your images of deviled ham from those tiny tins of Underwood-brand Deviled Ham with its pitchfork-wielding red devil leering ominously from the white paper package. Others may have a visceral negative reaction to the notion of blending cooked ham with mayonnaise. But if you've run out of things to do with five pounds of leftover Easter ham, and if you've found yourself standing in your bathrobe in front of the open refrigerator at three in the morning while eating what you swear is your last slice, deviled ham is the solution you need. Trust me.

With origins in the mid-1800s, the process of "deviling" can be applied to almost any food, including hard-boiled eggs, organ meats, or in this case, cooked leftover ham. The remains of our honey-glazed, spiral-cut ham are ground up and mixed with mustard and other spices and used as a flavorful, unique spread for crunchy crackers or for (not so) fancy tea sandwiches with the crusts cut off and eaten with pinky extended. Still not on board with the idea? Then close your eyes and pretend that you are being treated to "Downeast country pâté" on a fancy charcuterie board at a sidewalk cafe, along with a few toast points, a handful of cornichons, and an ice cold beer, all of which cost more than a used iPad.

Method

1. Combine all ingredients in the bowl of a food processor. Pulse in one-second bursts, scraping down the sides of the bowl with a rubber spatula as needed. Pulse until very well combined but not quite a smooth paste (some texture here is good).

2. Cover and chill in the refrigerator for at least 1 hour to allow the flavors to meld. Serve on crispy crackers or on white bread.

INGREDIENTS

1½ cups cooked ham (about half a pound), chopped

1 cup mayonnaise

2 teaspoons whole grain mustard

3 tablespoons onion, chopped

1 teaspoon whole capers, drained

3 to 4 tablespoons curly parsley

1 teaspoon Worcestershire sauce

1 teaspoon Sriracha hot chili sauce (or your favorite hot sauce, to taste)

1 teaspoon sweet pickle relish

INGREDIENTS

2 tablespoons olive oil

1 yellow onion, diced

3 large garlic cloves, minced

Kosher salt and freshly ground black pepper

1 parsnip, peeled and diced

2 cups kale, stems removed, roughly chopped

A 15-ounce can of artichoke hearts, drained and rinsed

1 tablespoon unsalted butter

32 ounces chicken broth

2 dashes cayenne

1 dash nutmeg

1 cup cream

Parmesan cheese

Baguette or crusty bread

Kale and Artichoke Soup • *Jillian*

Serves 6-8

After waiting all winter, the first edible plants we get from the farmers' market are leafy, vitamin-packed greens. In Maine we are especially grateful for food that is nutrient dense and satisfying, foods such as kale, beet greens, and chard. I can feel myself growing stronger, healthier, and renewed as I sip this purée of earth's goodness. We still require warming meals at this time of year, so this vegetable soup is just what the Easter Bunny ordered as part of an Easter holiday feast or for a simple and satisfying dinner any chilly night in transformative April.

Method

1. In a Dutch oven, heat the olive oil over medium heat. Add the onions and garlic, season with salt and pepper, and cook until softened.

2. Add the parsnips, kale, artichoke hearts, and butter. Stir and cook down, about 5 minutes.

3. Add the chicken broth, cayenne, and nutmeg and bring to a boil.

4. On low heat, add the cream and simmer 10 minutes.

5. Blend in the pot using an immersion blender, or in batches in a food processor, until soup is smooth. Garnish with Parmesan cheese and serve with a slice of toasted baguette and a drizzle of olive oil.

Leek and Goat Cheese Pie • *Jillian*

Serves 4-6

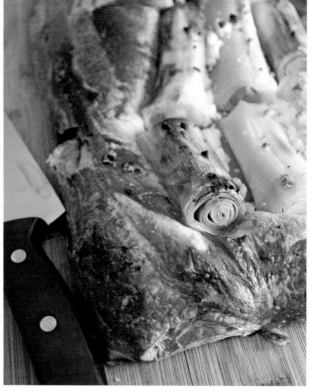

On Easter we keep things casual. We have an open house—an all-day, bring-your-new-girlfriend-and-her-dog-and-her-cousin's-hairdresser-and-we'll-open-another-bottle-of-wine affair. We like to make lots of little plates of edibles, both high-brow and low-brow, haute and country. Pimiento cheese certainly falls in the latter category, and this leek and goat cheese pie is its easy and elegant complement, which is what I am always going for in every aspect of my life. Leeks are so early spring, so young and green, with just enough onion bite. If you don't care for goat cheese, try ricotta salata or a simple crumbly farmer's cheese instead.

Method

1. Preheat the oven to 400°F. Thaw the puff pastry on the counter while you prepare the leeks. Remove the dark green stalks and layer of outer leaves. Halve the leeks lengthwise and cut each into 3 pieces. Simmer the leeks in the wine and butter seasoned with salt and pepper, about 20 minutes. Remove the leeks from the liquid and pat dry.

2. Fold each piece of puff pastry in half, layer one atop the other, and roll the dough into a rectangle. Use the back of a knife to score the pastry like a picture frame, making a one-inch border. Nestle the leeks into the dough. Sprinke with the goat cheese and brush the edges with the egg white. Bake for approximately 25 minutes. Let stand for five minutes before slicing and serving.

INGREDIENTS

1 package (2 sheets) puff pastry

2 medium-sized leeks, thoroughly washed

½ cup white wine

1 tablespoon unsalted butter

Salt and freshly ground pepper to taste

½ cup crumbled goat cheese

1 egg white, lightly beaten

INGREDIENTS

A 3-pound leg of lamb

Salt and freshly ground pepper, to taste

3 tablespoons extra-virgin olive oil

A bottle of white wine

10 sprigs each fresh rosemary, oregano, and mint

14 cloves garlic, peeled, or a whole head of garlic

Iraqi-style flatbread or Indian-style naan

Packaged tzatziki dip

Braised Leg of Lamb • *Jillian*

Serves 6

Little lamb, who made thee? I did, thanks, and you were delicious. My dad was a mint jelly guy. There was always a jar of the neon-green stuff on the door of our fridge, and once I made the mistake of slathering it on my peanut butter sandwich. Don't try that at home—or anywhere else. To this day I cannot tolerate its taste and texture, but fresh mint in this Mediterranean-inspired lamb is lovely. What I love about this entrée is that you wake up early, pop the lamb in the oven, and it mostly takes care of itself. Then, whenever friends arrive, they can serve themselves. This lamb works nicely hot, cold, or at room temperature. And be sure to reserve a bit just for yourself. There is nothing sweeter than the last hours of a holiday—the guests have gone home and the children have been tucked into bed. You and your significant other can now go over the happy details of the day, have a cocktail and a "leftovers" sandwich, and watch silly reruns on the couch.

Method

1. Preheat the oven to 250°F. Salt and pepper the leg of lamb on all sides. In a large Dutch oven, cover the bottom in olive oil and brown the lamb on all sides. Remove to a cutting board.

2. Add the wine, the stalks of herbs, and the garlic to the Dutch oven. With a wooden spoon, scrape up the bits of lamb in the bottom of the pot and return the leg of lamb to the pot.

3. Cover the pot and place in the oven. Baste the lamb every hour for 4 hours. Remove the lamb from the pot and place it on the cutting board.

4. Pour the cooking liquid through a strainer, removing the herbs, garlic, and bone. Reduce over low heat until slightly thickened. Use a fork to break the lamb into chunks, then drizzle with pan sauce.

5. Serve with buttered, Iraqi-style flatbread or naan (found at any large supermarket) and a dollop of tzatziki.

Cooking like this after time spent away feels cozy, grounding, and life affirming. We welcome spring in Maine.

SUZUKI'S SUSHI BAR • *Malcolm*

419 Main Street, Rockland, ME 04841; (207) 596-7447; suzukisushi.com

Suzuki's Sushi Bar sits directly on Rockland's Main Street. The small front half of the elegant dining room stands in sharp contrast to the wings-and-beer specials advertised on the sidewalk chalkboard at the bar across the street. Walking through the front door and into the intimate dining room feels a little conspiratorial, like being let in on a secret by an old friend. The decorations are spare in the quiet room; an antique eel spear takes up one whole wall in a room with just a few tables and a sushi bar with a few stools. Behind the counter, Chef Keiko Suzuki Steinberger is a quiet whirlwind of knifework and bright smiles, offering a sincere greeting to each entering party and a sincere farewell to each departure.

Jillian: A confession: I don't hanker much for sushi. I find it pleasant, like a summer rain, when it's good, but it isn't food I crave or miss when it's not around. I don't think I'd ever tasted sushi that could be considered outstanding before I visited Suzuki's. Of all the surprises Rockland has up her strange sleeve, a tiny Japanese spot where a female chef/owner is creating beautiful dishes all year round was one of the more unexpected. I love how quiet and spare the space is; I love how the windows of the small shop begin to steam up and your face gets warm as you sip cold sake and savor the raw fish. It is a garden of earthly delights in a way I find foreign yet familiar and unforgettable.

Keiko is an anomaly in the world of sushi chefs, a field that has traditionally been dominated entirely by men. The historical explanations for this gender bias are varied. Some traditionalists insist, irrationally, that women's hands are too warm to handle raw fish and that their fiery sensibilities cook the flesh of the fish even as it is being prepared. Others maintain that the mechanics of handling seafood are too physically demanding to concern women. Fortunately, traditional Japanese gender politics aren't a hot-button issue in a town like Rockland, and Keiko seems determined to put an end to these old wives' tales once and for all by staffing her sushi counter exclusively with female chefs.

Of much more interest, however, is the seafood itself. The ingredients used at Suzuki's are hyperlocal and are constantly rotated based on availability. The oysters are grown in nearby Cushing. The mackerel is caught on lines cast from the Rockland Harbor breakwater. An advertisement that runs in the local free weekly not only gives the restaurant's location and hours but invites local fishermen, growers, and foragers to peddle their products to Suzuki's for incorporation into the nightly specials. The resulting dishes feature seafood that, in many cases, was pulled from the water just hours before service, artfully arranged with a precision that we have been hard put to find elsewhere, and served by a staff whose knowledge of the subject borders on the obsessive.

Jillian: Each time we visit, we are amazed once more by the consistency, quality, elegance, and composition of each piece and each plate. It's almost mathematical, like the mystical math of the music of the universe and nature and symphonies. Recently we returned with out-of-town friends who insisted on a second visit after an earth-shattering experience the previous fall. Each time we go, we throw ourselves willingly and gleefully into the hands of the chef.

"Let me tell you a little bit about some of the specials Keiko is preparing this evening," our server explains. And that's how it feels at Suzuki's—not like ordering tired staples from a standardized menu that a burned-out chef has prepared thousands of times before, but rather as though the beautifully designed plates arriving at your table are delivered straight from Keiko's imagination. The server always asks if there is anything we dislike or are allergic to; the answer to the first part of this question is no, and it should be for you, too.

On our most recent visit, we began with two appetizer specials, the first being a monkfish liver paté sliced with scallion, onion, cucumber, and soy sauce and served in a small dish. I had no previous experience with this dish but ordered it without compunction, knowing that anything on special at Suzuki's would be exquisite. It was buttery and rich, and the strong flavors of the sea were offset by the bright saltiness of the soy.

Jillian: The monkfish liver was fattytoothsome, which is an adjective I made up just this second while trying to recall how it felt in my mouth. So many textures and tastes here are unexpected and without precedent in my world of cooking and eating.

The second special, a raw diver scallop carpaccio, was similarly divine, with thin slices of sweet diver scallop topped with mixed microgreens, slices of starfruit, and a few flecks of gold leaf for good measure. The dish is staggeringly beautiful, and the delicate flavor of the scallop perfectly represents the sweet flavor of the ocean. It's a dish that would be equally appropriate at the beginning or end of a meal.

Jillian: It was so demure, so wild, so thoughtful, as if the result of decades of living on a deserted beach when the castaway has finally discovered how to create sublime food from the grass and slime of the shore and shoals.

After choosing a few of the appetizer specials, we often order the chef's-choice omakase for two ($58). What appears a few minutes later makes our jaws drop every time. The enormous white platter that serves as a base for the omakase is dotted with preparations that change each day but follow a few basic themes. There is always a maki roll of some sort, a few pieces of nigiri and sashimi, and a few hand rolls. Some days, tiny, sweet Maine shrimp are the star ingredient. Other days, diver scallops, eel, mackerel, or clams are the focus. One night we were served sweet Maine crabmeat overflowing from two gigantic hand rolls, along with tuna and two rolls overflowing with uni. Each bite of the sea urchin caused my eyes to close, the nutty flavors of the uni filling me with joy and with a weird, inexplicable sadness that is difficult to articulate but that I find completely and utterly addictive.

Jillian: I love the halibut that slips like silver over your tongue, and the sweet local shrimp are creamy in the way they melt in your mouth. Tragically, Gulf of Maine stocks of the Northern shrimp, *Pandalus borealis,* have collapsed due to ocean warming, and the 2013–14 shrimp-fishing season was cancelled. We can only hope—for the sake of Maine's hardworking fishermen and the health of its coastal towns—that the shrimp

return next year. Meantime, Suzuki's eel dishes also melt in your mouth. The cooked eel, sitting zazen on a mound of rice and tied up simply with seaweed, is like a party you think you don't want to attend, but when you do, you can only think "whoa," like Keanu Reeves's character in *The Matrix*. Every detail is exquisite: the thinly sliced ginger to cleanse the palate; the dab of wasabi that makes a sharp pain in the base of your skull; the warm washcloth before the meal that begins to cleanse and prepare you for truth and beauty. This is not hyperbolic.

By this point in the meal, we have usually given ourselves completely to the experience. We order a few more plates, nigiri sold by the piece, featuring either our favorites from the omakase we have just eaten or the roundup of dishes that we have been dreaming about since our last visit. Keiko, who has been watching our approach to each piece she sends to our table, suggests other items for us to try, often including complimentary extra bites on the plate after plate of food that keep appearing from behind the counter: a hamachi and scallion roll; another order of diver scallop sashimi. After two more orders of broiled eel, the smoky, oily flesh barely held in place by a thin strip of nori, the windows of the restaurant begin to fog up from the collective, excited breath of everyone in the room, obscuring our vision of the street outside.

Another pint of beer and the room starts to spin, not from the alcohol but from the buzz brought on by eating such delicate, impeccably prepared food. It is only the surviving bits of self-control, some last remaining shreds of propriety, that stop us from ordering more and force us to ask for the check, which is always shockingly more manageable than we expect.

Jillian: When you visit Rockland, you may want lobster and fried shrimp and clam rolls—who doesn't?—but have one meal at Suzuki's too. Once you try it, you'll be back. This is a place that gets in your head—mindful, joyful dining.

Suzuki's Sushi Bar offers a rare opportunity to surrender your judgment to a chef who begins to feel like a trusted friend, guiding you through a culinary landscape that may seem unfamiliar but that ultimately rewards all your senses with a precise clarity of flavor that has been, quite simply, unmatched by almost any other restaurant we have tried. Our close proximity to Suzuki's is one of the perks of living in midcoast Maine. It may be reason enough to put your house on the market, take your kids out of school, and uproot your entire life to move to this small town. This is so much more than fish. This is master-level, life-changing cooking.

MICUCCI'S • Jillian

45 India Street, Portland, ME 04101; (207) 200-9669; micuccigrocery.com

I was unabashedly charmed by the India Street Italian market and pizzeria called Micucci Grocery. Maybe it was the weather, or perhaps I was hallucinating and high on premature spring temperatures, but I felt as if I had been there before—even though I hadn't—as I added chickpeas and Pellegrino to my basket. Up the stairs and to the left, I found bakers' shelves stacked with freshly made imperfect squares. Without further ado, I boxed one up, paid, and high-tailed it home.

And then, on my next visit, I discovered the pizza, and everything changed. If you haven't had Micucci's pizza, we are living in parallel realities. I am different than I was before I tried this sublime pizza, unlike any I have known. How can something called The Sicilian Slab taste so sweet? Thick as the name implies, but not at all heavy, the dough of the crust is soft and airy. The sauce is fruity but not cloying. And the cheese layer inspires the best of us to employ a lighter hand when slinging mozarella. Each component has integrity and complements the whole. Each bite invites the one that follows until the inevitable end. Also, in case you had not gleaned from the name, it is enormous. Our ruffian technique was to rip the giant slice in two and consume it while standing in the kitchen.

My favorite pizza in the world resides, not on New Haven's storied Wooster Street, but at Modern Apizza on State Street in New Haven, a dirty stretch of road below I-91. My favorite pie in this good old town is white with spinach, garlic, and lemon wedges served on a gleaming dais above a red-checked plastic cloth. It is nothing like The Slab. But now that The Slab exists, my heart has been opened just a little wider.

INGREDIENTS

English Muffins:

½ cup (1 stick) unsalted butter

1½ teaspoons sugar

8 ounces milk

½ package active dry yeast
(¾ teaspoon)

1 large egg, beaten

8 ounces all-purpose flour (about two
fluffed cups)

¾ teaspoon kosher salt

1 teaspoon baking powder dissolved in
1½ teaspoons water

Cornmeal, for dusting

Hollandaise Sauce:

3 egg yolks

1 tablespoon dijon mustard

2 tablespoons freshly squeezed
lemon juice

¾ cup (1½ sticks) unsalted
butter, melted

Salt, pepper, and cayenne pepper,
to taste

Putting It Together:

4 slices thick-sliced uncured ham

4 large eggs

Splash of white vinegar

Freshly ground pepper

2 tablespoons chopped chives

WEEKEND PROJECT:
Eggs Benedict • *Malcolm*
Serves 4

I'm not sure what your approach to a brunch buffet is, but I never, ever go with eggs Benedict. Give me the omelet bar. Or the carving station. Or the fruit plate. Bulk-prepared eggs Benedict is usually one of the worst: hard little pucks of under-toasted English muffin made soggy from the hard-yolked poached egg on top, a slice of Canadian bacon whose only defining characteristic is its thick casing, and blobs of congealing, gummy, made-from-a-powder Hollandaise sauce. It can be a depressing display of a classic dish gone bad when what you really want from a satisfying brunch is mimosas and zing and zip and shazaam and "YAY, it's Sunday." For our signature version of this society staple, we wanted to start from the ground up.

The English Muffin The foundation of any great Benedict is its muffin, and we knew that store-bought Thomas' muffins weren't going to do the trick. The Internet offers dozens of recipes for making them, but most produce results that are more like crumpets or some kind of skillet cake. We finally settled on a recipe by Michael Ruhlman. It uses a wet batter that is almost like a pancake batter but with tons of yeast. Just prior to cooking, a swirl of baking powder dissolved in water is added to create even more nooks and crannies. Perfectionists can buy special ring forms for making English muffins, or you can use any can from the pantry with the ends cut out. I even like the results that come from not using a mold at all; the muffins may not be perfectly round, but they are easier to flip and control on the hot griddle. Whether you use a mold or not, you may find that your muffins are lopsided after flipping; don't be afraid to correct this by pressing down lightly with a spatula. Don't forget to sprinkle some cornmeal on the cooking surface—this extra texture is important for proper English muffins. Finally, be careful about burning. If the surface of the muffin starts to get too brown, you can always finish baking them in

the oven. Split them with a fork (for even more increased cranny action) and use them warm from the griddle or toast them before use to coax out a little more flavor and texture.

The Interstitial Layer This is really the only element of a Benedict that offers any room for creativity, and we wanted to do something special. Canadian bacon is usually pretty soulless stuff, adding salt and texture and little else. We considered using spinach as in eggs Florentine. We considered corned beef hash as in a so-called "Irish" Benedict. Being Maine-centric, we considered lobster. Because we love Mexican cuisine, we considered fresh chorizo and refried beans. We considered braised pork belly, but that's been done to death, hasn't it? Pancetta? Nah. A duckfat-fried breaded portobello mushroom cap? Nope. Anything too exotic would take away from the flavor of the perfectly poached eggs and the Hollandaise, which we believe should really be the stars of the dish. Besides, this should be a classic Benedict. We settled on some nice, thickly cut uncured ham, which we flashed in a hot pan for a few minutes to add some color.

The Poached Egg We've tested nearly every method for poaching eggs that you can imagine. It's not as hard as people tend to make it. You don't need special equipment, a microwave, or, for goodness' sake, one of those $80 egg-poaching pans from Williams-Sonoma. We'll go into more detail in the recipe, but all you need is this: A pan of water that's just about to simmer, a splash of white vinegar, a small dish, a slotted spoon, and four minutes of your morning. That's it. No fancy technique needed, and perfect eggs every time.

The Hollandaise Sauce Hollandaise seems difficult on the surface, what with the whole "cooking (but not scrambling) egg yolks, while not poisoning yourself with the result" thing. It doesn't have to be if you take your time and can come to terms with the idea that, if all goes according to plan, you will be pouring melted butter and more eggs on top of eggs. A double boiler is key, as well as adding the melted butter in a slow, steady stream. Made correctly, it won't show any separation, and once you've successfully achieved your emulsion, the sauce will stand up to a fair amount of abuse, including refrigeration and freezing, or being kept warm over low heat, or even temporary storage in a thermos or insulated coffee cup.

Method

English Muffins:

1. In a small saucepan over medium heat, combine the butter and sugar, stirring to dissolve. Add the milk and stir until just barely warm, about 20 to 30 seconds. Remove from the heat, and stir in the yeast and egg.

2. In a mixing bowl, combine the flour and salt. Add the milk mixture and stir until well combined. Cover with a dishtowel and set aside for 1½ hours.

3. Preheat the oven to 375°F. On the stove, heat a griddle over low heat. Butter the muffin rings if you are using them. Stir the dissolved baking powder into the batter, and sprinkle the skillet with cornmeal. Scoop quarter-cup portions onto the griddle, either free form or in the rings. Cook for about 7 minutes, being careful not to burn them. Flip the muffins and press lightly to flatten them. Continue cooking until done, about 7 to 10 more minutes. If the muffins begin to burn without cooking through, finish in a single layer on a baking sheet in the pre-heated oven.

4. Allow muffins to rest for at least 10 minutes.

Hollandaise Sauce:

1. Fill a small saucepan with 2 inches of water and place over medium heat. When the water simmers, reduce the heat to maintain a gentle simmer and place a small metal or heat-safe glass container on top of the pan as a double boiler.

2. Add the egg yolks, mustard, and lemon juice, and whisk until combined. In a slow, steady stream, pour the melted butter into the egg yolk mixture, whisking constantly. Using a candy thermometer, make sure the sauce reaches 140°F, then remove from the heat. Keep whisking until the sauce thickens, about 3 minutes more. Season to taste with salt, pepper, and cayenne pepper. The finished sauce can be kept warm in a thermos, insulated coffee cup, or over very low heat until ready to assemble.

Putting It Together:

1. For each plate, split an English muffin with a fork and toast until lightly browned. Place both muffin halves on the plate.

2. Add the ham to a skillet over medium-high heat and cook until slightly browned. Remove each slice and place on an English muffin half.

3. Crack an egg into a small dish and set aside. Fill a small saucepan half-way with water and add a splash of white vinegar. Heat the water over medium heat until millions of bubbles appear, the point just before the water starts to simmer. Reduce the heat to low and, holding the edge of the small bowl with the egg as closely as possible to the water, slip the egg into the water. Adjust the heat as needed to keep the water from boiling or simmering vigorously. Cook until the yolk is just set, about 4 minutes. Remove with a slotted spoon. Place an egg on top of the ham.

4. For each plate, ladle 1 to 2 tablespoons of the Hollandaise sauce over the assembled Benedict. Top with freshly ground pepper, and a sprinkle of chives, and serve with the other half of the English muffin.

LONG GRAIN · *Jillian*
31 Elm Street, Camden, Maine 04843; (207) 236-9001

The first time I had Thai food, I was a college freshman in Boston. My dad came up to check on me and ask if I was already behind in science (I was) and how I'd managed to spend $300 in two months at the Campus Convenience store (Marlboro Reds and milk for White Russians, obviously). As we sat alone at lunchtime in an otherwise empty dining room slurping spicy and sweet and savory noodles, discussing my uncertain future, I really had no idea how any of it would turn out. Sixteen years later I'm sitting in a different Thai restaurant with another man I love and trust, and we're sampling some of the best food I've had in a very long while, still with no idea how any of this happened.

Long Grain is nothing like that place on Commonwealth Avenue. In fact, I can't compare it with any other Asian restaurant, and I'm not fully qualified to write about the complexities of each of the dishes I tried. I can only recount the experience and describe it with my limited vocabulary. The flavors are concentrated, layered, vivid. But it's more than taste; the chef-owners are creating food that engages every sense.

About the mussels: Get them, I beg you. They are plump, fresh, and sweet, but what's even more important is the sauce that they are swimming in. It's one of those broths you can't stop slurping up. Use the mussel shells

as rustic spoons, and use every last grain of rice they serve on the side to deliver this coconut-based elixir to your taste buds. We really could have stopped there. Sharing that appetizer and a bottle of the Snow Beauty unfiltered sake would make for a simply gorgeous meal.

Malcolm: Never one to let the limitations of my vocabulary or lack of knowledge of a particular cuisine sway me from blurting out 3,000 words on the subject, I find these mussels a perfect place to begin. I texted a message to a friend detailing my dinner plans, and his three-word reply read, "Get the mussels." He was right. A perfect meal could be made from this appetizer alone, eaten at the bar while drinking entirely too much hot rice wine. The mussels themselves are divine and call to memory just how many shriveled, dried versions of the shellfish I have been served in other establishments. Here, they are as juicy and fat as they should be. It hardly matters, though. It's the sauce they are swimming in that will bring you back for another serving, a thin coconut curry spiked with heady punches of lemongrass. I would eat it poured over anything, or, as we did this night, slurped straight from a spoon.

In my dinner, the Pad Kee Mao ($12.50), there were mushrooms that looked like noodles and noodles that resembled onions. And, I think, actual onions. But I forgot to ask, because by the time we left, I was so intoxicated on delicious food, Prosecco, and sake that I could hardly walk or reason and had to be rolled home in a wheelbarrow.

Pad Kee Mao is the Thai menu staple more commonly known as Drunken Noodle, a dish I've ordered 8,700 times before. But this was unlike any that I have had. The Long Grain version is brimming with pork belly (or not, your choice), and our favorite fatty protein lent even more depth and dimension to an already multifaceted meal. My plate also included leafy, toothsome kale, three kinds of locally foraged mushrooms—including hen-of-the-woods—and pieces of hand-cut broad rice noodles, plus, I believe, bits of egg and basil. All of these more or less humble ingredients created endless combinations with every taste. I ate well past the point of hunger or decorum. I kept saying, "This is my last bite," only to let my fork fall back in the bowl for another half-drunken go-round.

Malcolm: I had an enormous steaming bowl of the Spicy Night Market Noodle Soup ($10), a rice noodle soup flavored with chunks of pork, ground sausage, and chopped peanuts. The first flavor to register in your brain is a bright sweetness, followed by a spicy jump-punch to the back of the head that builds cumulatively with each mouthful. It may be my new perfect food. The garnish of pork rinds become bloated and fat with the pungent broth as I worked my way through the bowl.

Everything about the place is sensational. It's small, but not so small that you're sitting on the laps of strangers. The service is laid back but enthusiastic, and all are happy to steer you in the right direction. The decor is minimal but not stark. Long Grain is a comfortable neighborhood place serving food that is astonishingly good. I'd read before we went that the flavors were "strong," which conveyed a negative connotation to me. But I understand what the reviewer meant. Words like "bright" and "bold" and "concentrated" almost begin to describe this food, but they somehow fail.

Malcolm: I went ahead and used them anyway.

I've seen Long Grain described as "fusion," which is too vague and cheesy for this place. I have read that it is authentic Bangkok street food with influences from many parts of Asia. Okay, I'm sure it is. I know that they are using local ingredients in traditional forms, which is super-glorious-hip-fantastic.

Malcolm: We can't call the food being presented at Long Grain "fusion cuisine," because this isn't 1994 and I'm not standing in a strip mall. We also can't call it New Thai, because, well, eww. Instead, we'll concentrate, as they do at Long Grain, on the ingredients. There's not a dish of tepid yellow curry with crinkle-cut carrots anywhere in sight. Instead, a focus on what's available locally combined with a creative flair for Thai-influenced dishes delivers inexpensive, innovative twists on a cuisine I only thought I knew, all for less money than the generic Chinese takeout from the place sandwiched between the Shaw's and the Gamestop. It's a place we'll return to often.

The conclusion? Long Grain is eight tables, plus a few bar stools, of communal space. This is a place where I want to go every chance I can to eat everything I can as I try to plan what is essentially the unknown path of my destiny.

Food for the Great Spring Road Trip

Hibernating, holing up, and waiting for the spring thaw. As Mainers, we know this condition all too well. Winter starts off cozy and joyful as we bask in home and art projects, books and movies, but it winds up like *The Shining*. By April, no matter the temperature, we need to get out, stretch our muscles, breathe the outside air, and discover something new in the world. We drive, find a pretty place, put on three sweaters, and go exploring before getting back in the car forty-five minutes later, freezing. We listen to a comedy podcast or *Car Talk*, sing, talk, seek out new scenes such as Fort Knox or a great state park. And while we are fans—big fans—of roadside snack stands, nut houses, drive-throughs, and all the weird food ephemera to be found at a gas station convenience store, it's much nicer, healthier, and more cost effective to pack a lunch. Fill a thermos with coffee and retrieve your picnic basket from the attic—it's almost time for spring! Hallelujah!

Boiled Egg, Sautéed Asparagus, and Pickled Red Onion Sandwich • *Malcolm*

Makes two sandwiches

Without a foot of snow on the ground, it's difficult to be inspired by chowder and comfort food recipes. Who can eat a big bowl of chili when the birds are chirping, the daffodils are shooting out leaves, and the rhubarb is cracking through the surface of the soil?

This lunch is like springtime in sandwich form. The crunch of the bright green asparagus pairs perfectly with the creamy boiled eggs, and the pickled onions add a touch of acidity. A sprinkle of dill and a squeeze of lemon, with a dab of Dijon, bring everything together and make you feel fancy and French. Enjoy this taste of spring before tomorrow's cold front moves in.

Method

1. Cut the baguette into two lengths, roughly matching the length of your asparagus spears. Split lengthwise, and remove some of the inside of the bread to make room for the sandwich ingredients.

2. In a medium-sized sauté pan over medium heat, drizzle a little olive oil. Add the garlic and the asparagus. Cook until tender, tossing often, 4–6 minutes. Remove the asparagus from the pan and set aside.

3. Place the bread cut side down in the pan drippings, and toast lightly. Remove from the pan and set aside.

INGREDIENTS

1 French baguette

Olive oil

1 clove garlic, peeled and smashed

10–12 asparagus spears, peeled with woody ends removed

2 tablespoons mayonnaise

1 tablespoon Dijon mustard

⅛ teaspoon dried dill

2 eggs, hard boiled, peeled, and sliced

2–4 tablespoons pickled onions

Lemon

4. In a small bowl, combine the mayonnaise, the mustard, and the dill. Stir until combined.

5. To assemble each sandwich, spread one side of the toasted bread with about a tablespoon of the mustard mixture. Top with 5 or 6 asparagus spears, one sliced boiled egg, and 1–2 tablespoons pickled onion. Top with a squeeze of lemon and an extra shake of dried dill.

Brown Butter and Bacon Chocolate Chip Cookies • *Malcolm*

Makes about three dozen cookies

I love these cookies, probably because of the insane combination of bacon and chocolate. BACON. And CHOCOLATE. Fat and happiness. It's really like a drug. They have a sort of yin and yang, male and female, sweet and salty thing going on, which is absolutely divine. I'm telling you, anywhere you take these bad boys, you will be loved and adored. Obscure countries will make you their monarch, and you will die a revered and honored saint.

Food for the Great Spring Road Trip
- Boiled Egg, Sautéed Asparagus, and Pickled Red Onion Sandwich
- Brown Butter and Bacon Chocolate Chip Cookies

INGREDIENTS

10 strips bacon, chopped

14 tablespoons (1¾ sticks) unsalted butter

½ cup granulated sugar

¾ cup packed brown sugar

1 teaspoon salt

2 teaspoons vanilla

1 large egg

1 large egg yolk

1¾ cups all purpose flour

½ teaspoon baking soda

1 cup dark chocolate chips

3 tablespoons milk chocolate, grated

Method

1. Place an oven rack in the middle of the oven, and preheat the oven to 375°F.

2. In a large skillet over low heat, cook the bacon until crisp but not burned, turning often. Drain on paper towels and roughly chop the bacon to approximately ¼-inch pieces. Set aside.

3. In a medium-sized saucepan, heat 10 tablespoons of the butter over low heat, swirling and stirring often, until the butter is a warm golden-brown, about 8–10 minutes. Remove from the heat, add the remaining butter, and allow to melt.

4. In a large mixing bowl or in the bowl of a stand mixer, combine the granulated sugar, the brown sugar, the salt, the vanilla, the egg, and the egg yolk. Slowly incorporate the melted butter, and stir until all the sugar crystals have melted. The batter should be smooth and shiny.

5. Add the flour and the baking soda, and stir until no pockets of flour remain. Add the chocolate chips, the grated chocolate, and the chopped bacon. Stir until combined, but don't overwork the batter.

6. Line a large baking sheet with parchment paper and, working in batches, place heaping teaspoon-sized dollops of batter onto the prepared baking sheet.

7. Bake until the edges are golden but the middle is not quite set, about 11–14 minutes.

8. Transfer the cookies to a cooling rack, and cool completely.

MAY

May is our recompense for the past winter's chill, freezing rain, nor'easters, massive icicles, blizzards, numb fingers and toes, gusting winds, shoveling, and digging out of cars before first light. We are good friends with winter. We have a thing for seasons, most especially autumn, and we honestly believe that warm weather is not as sweet if it isn't well deserved. How can we appreciate hot without cold, or floral profusion without the stark landscape of winter? In Maine we do not take late spring and summer for granted. We enjoy every moment from May until September—walking, hiking, kayaking, peering in tidepools, flying kites, riding bikes, grilling, swinging in hammocks, dipping our toes in the bracing Atlantic. It all starts here and now. Kick off the season right with a cookout of epic proportions.

Memorial Day Cookout Menu

- Strawberry Rhubarb Sangria
- Asparagus Soup
- Watermelon Salad Bites
- Beer & Bison Burgers with Garlic Pub Cheese and Bacon & Egg Potato Salad
- Macaroon Whoopie Pies

INGREDIENTS

1 bottle crisp white wine

1 cup white rum

2 cups lemonade

6 strawberries, hulled and sliced

2 rhubarb stalks, chopped

1 lemon, sliced into rounds

1 teaspoon grated fresh ginger

1 cup sparkling water

Strawberry Rhubarb Sangria • *Jillian*
Serves 6

A boozy wine punch is an excellent way to entertain casually in the spring and summer. Sangria makes any small gathering of friends feel like a party. This one is the perfect combination of sweet and tart. I am in love with lemons right now—they are so refreshing and clean. The rhubarb tints the sangria a pretty pink, and the ginger adds a little something earthy and extra. Your guests will never know what hit them!

Method

1. Combine all the ingredients except the sparkling water in a large pitcher or jar and let the mixture marinate for a day or overnight in the refrigerator.

2. To serve, splash the seltzer into each glass and include some of the fruit in every serving.

Asparagus Soup • *Jillian*
Serves 8-10

INGREDIENTS

5 tablespoons unsalted butter

3 pounds asparagus, woody ends removed

2 leeks, white and light-green parts only, chopped

2 tablespoons all-purpose flour

4 cups chicken stock

½ cup heavy cream

Salt and pepper to taste

1 tablespoon lemon juice

Spring finally arrives in Maine with golden-yellow dandelions carpeting fields of green, delicate pink blossoms decorating dogwood trees, and fat bumblebees buzzing lazily about the daffodils. After many months of looking stark, gray, and bare, limbs are painted with color, saturated and brilliant. Spring always takes me by surprise. I catch it in the corners and hope that it's real and lasting. Asparagus heralds the promise of the bright and sunny season, making new life not only manifest but edible. If you've been waiting patiently, now you are rewarded.

A spring brunch menu should be neither light nor heavy. You never know when the weather will turn sour, and you will want a comforting cup of soup or warming beverage while it rains.

Asparagus soup is nutty, creamy, fresh, and exceedingly green after so many months of gray. It is rich with butter and cream; you only need a taste. Roasting half the asparagus makes it extra wonderful. When we have guests for Memorial Day, the holiday tends to become a weekend-long affair. With this soup in the fridge, we can present a beautiful lunch without much extra effort.

Method

1. Preheat the broiler and move an oven rack to the top third of the oven. In a medium-sized soup pot, melt one tablespoon of the butter. Arrange half the bunch of asparagus on a baking sheet, toss with the melted butter, and broil for 5 minutes, until they just begin to wilt.

2. Dice the rest of the asparagus spears into pea-sized pieces. Melt the remaining butter in the pot, add the leeks, and sauté until translucent, about 5 to 8 minutes. Stir in the flour until well combined with the buttery leeks. Continue stirring and pour in the chicken stock.

3. Increase the heat to high and bring to a boil. Reduce the heat and simmer 3 to 5 minutes. Add all of the asparagus to the simmering broth. Turn the heat down to medium-low and cook uncovered, about 5 minutes.

4. To blend, either purée the soup in a blender in batches or use an immersion blender right in the pot (removed from the heat source). When the soup is smooth, pour in the cream and slowly heat on low. Season with salt, black pepper, and the lemon juice. Serve immediately.

Watermelon Salad Bites • *Malcolm*

Serves 8-10 as an appetizer

I'm always tickled by foods that don't arrange themselves into a cohesive whole until you take that first bite, when disparate ingredients come together to make a whole new surprise flavor.

During my bachelor party years ago in Mexico, I learned that I could make a perfectly acceptable margarita by taking a healthy swig of tequila followed by a pull from a bottle of margarita mix, completely forgoing the use of a glass.

Okay, so that may not have ended so well. In this case, though, the combination of sweet watermelon, acidic lime juice, spicy slices of serrano chile, and crumbled salty feta cheese don't strike your guests as a "salad" until they take a bite. Then the flavors rearrange and combine into something all new—startling, cooling, and satisfying. They're inexpensive, perfect for a crowd, and easy to prepare (especially if you start with a seedless watermelon). The presentation may be a little more modern than most of the things we cook, but these self-contained, bite-sized watermelon salads are always a hit.

Method

1. In a large bowl, combine the lime juice and olive oil. Stir well to combine. Add the watermelon and toss to coat evenly.

2. Arrange the watermelon cubes on a serving plate, and top each piece with a little bit of feta and a slice of serrano chile. Sprinkle with salt to make the flavors really pop.

3. Serve immediately or within a few hours; if prepared too far in advance, the watermelon will release too much of its juice.

INGREDIENTS

2 limes, juiced

2 tablespoons olive oil

1 small ripe seedless watermelon, peeled and cubed

8 ounces feta cheese, crumbled

½ to 1 serrano chile, sliced thinly

½ to 1 tablespoon kosher salt, to taste

Beer & Bison Burgers with Garlic Pub Cheese and Bacon & Egg Potato Salad • *Malcolm*

Serves 4

INGREDIENTS

Beer & Bison Burgers:

1 pound ground bison

¼ cup rolled oats

¼ cup amber ale such as Gritty's Vacationland, divided

2 teaspoons olive oil

Salt and pepper, to taste

Garlic Pub Cheese:

1½ large garlic cloves

4 ounces cream cheese

1 cup grated sharp white cheddar cheese

Putting It Together:

4 hamburger buns or soft Kaiser rolls

2 tablespoons unsalted butter

2 cups alfalfa or broccoli sprouts

Ground bison can be shaped into burgers and grilled just like ground beef, but the result is a substantially looser, leaner burger, much lower in fat than its ground-beef cousin. On a hot grill, bison burgers have a tendency to fall apart; we use rolled oats to bind the patties slightly with the beer. Because they are so lean, they tend to get a little dry, which is where our homemade pub cheese enters the picture.

Eating a lower-fat burger justifies spooning what is essentially cream cheese on top, and as soon as the pub cheese hits the hot burger, it runs and drips in rivulets throughout the grassy, earthy, protein-rich meat. It's a delicious alternative to a basic burger, perfect for days with nothing to do but sit around the grill, drinking beer and thinking about America.

Method

1. In a large bowl, mix the ground bison, oats, and 2 tablespoons of the ale. Form into four ½-inch patties, brush with the olive oil, and sprinkle with salt and pepper.

2. For the pub cheese, pulse the garlic in a food processor until diced. Add the cheeses and continue pulsing until smooth.

3. Grill the burgers, turning once, about 6 minutes total for medium. While the burgers grill, brush the buns with butter and grill until lightly browned. To serve, arrange the burgers on the bottom half of the buns and top with the sprouts. Spread the tops of the buns with the cheese mixture and serve immediately.

Bacon & Egg Potato Salad • *Jillian*
Serves 4

I like my potato salad jammed with vegetables and condiments. Feel free to add more potatoes if copious quantities of starchy tubers are more your thing.

Method

1. Cube and cook the potatoes in salted, boiling water until fork tender. Toss with the lemon juice, Worcestershire, and salt and pepper. Combine gently with the other ingredients and refrigerate until ready to serve.

Macaroon Whoopie Pies • *Jillian*
Makes about a dozen sandwich cookies

It is impossible to talk about Maine food without mentioning, in no particular order, lobster, blueberries, and whoopie pies. And now that the Maine food scene has gone national, I'm sure everyone knows that a whoopie pie is, essentially, two cakes hugging a half cup of frosting. Upscaled or reduced to their lowest common denominator, whoopie pies can be found just about anywhere, even at church sales and gas stations, where they're made with lard, or worse, margarine. What in the world is margarine and how did the government ever convince us it was food? This is one of my interpretations of a classic Maine treat—every New England kid's favorite sweet.

Method

For the cookie:

1. Preheat the oven to 325°F. Grease and flour a cookie sheet. In a large bowl, whisk together the coconut, flour, sugar, and salt. Stir in the egg whites and almond extract until well blended.

2. Make thin, palm-sized flats and drop them onto a cookie sheet. Bake 20 minutes or until the edges are brown.

For the filling:

1. In the bowl of a stand mixer with the whisk attachment, combine all the ingredients. Process approximately 10 minutes, until white and fluffy. Spoon a heaping tablespoon dollop of the filling between two of the macaroons for a super sweet treat.

INGREDIENTS

16 ounces fingerling potatoes

1 teaspoon lemon juice

Splash of Worcestershire sauce

Dash of paprika, dill, and garlic powder

Salt and pepper

4 hard-boiled eggs, chopped

2 scallions, thinly sliced

2 celery stalks, diced

½ cup yellow bell pepper, diced

4 strips of bacon, cooked and crumbled

¼ cup sour cream

¼ cup mayonnaise

INGREDIENTS
For the macaroon cookie:

A 14-ounce package shredded coconut

6 tablespoons all-purpose flour

⅔ cup granulated sugar

¼ teaspoon salt

4 egg whites

1 teaspoon almond extract

For the filling:

½ cup (1 stick) unsalted butter, room temperature

½ cup Crisco shortening

1 cup granulated sugar

1 tablespoon flour

1 teaspoon vanilla

½ cup warm whole milk

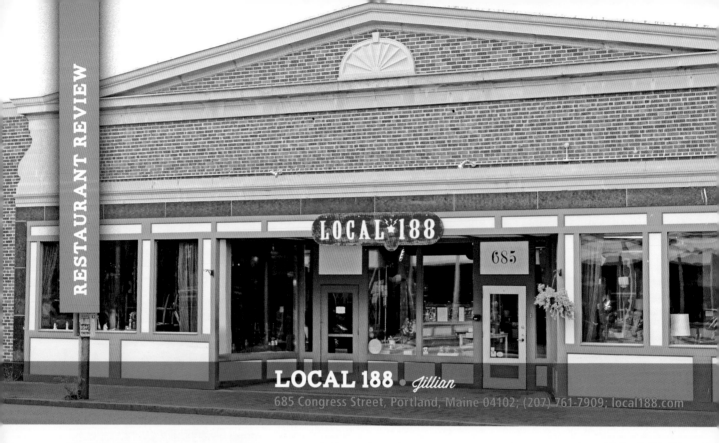

LOCAL 188 • Jillian

685 Congress Street, Portland, Maine 04102; (207) 761-7909; local188.com

We have known for some time that Local 188 is an excellent place to drink. Every cocktail served there is wonderful. It feels like your grandmother's house, the one she lived in when you were little, before she moved into a condo, before she became truly old, though you didn't know she wasn't then. The Formica tables are perfectly homey; there should be a deck of cards and a dish of hard candy on every one. You sit around a table with your friends—so much better than sitting abreast at a bar—and talk, imbibing many sidecars. Why we waited so long to eat there, I don't know. Was it that we didn't want to be disappointed? If so, our fears proved misguided once again. We had a great evening in their dining room and walked back to our apartment sated.

If you are going to be a grown-up and have only one drink, we certainly recommend the Dropkick Murphy: Jameson and root beer with a Murphy's stout float. Thank goodness, food arrived almost as soon as we had ordered it, or we would have quickly been in our cups. Spread before us was an assortment of olives, lamb keftedes over lightly seared cucumber strips and mint crème fraîche from the tapas list, braised short ribs and house-made gnocchi, and a three-radish salad, a special that night. Our tiny table was covered by giant white plates as we dug in and began exclaiming over almost everything. Even the bread plate, including a doughy, herby, caramelized oniony square, was delicious. Beware of overindulging in the bread—my weakness.

The dish of olives could have fed every wedding guest in Cana. I ate every one of the bright green Castelvetrano olives, my new favorite, and not a few Kalamatas, and we still had plenty to take home. Keftedes are, at least here, oblong meatballs made from ground lamb, and they were juicy with a beautiful, thick, seared crust, not too rich, and complemented by the warm cucumber ribbons in a light, creamy sauce. We each had one and wished for another; a foolish idea, as we had more than enough extremely satisfying food. The radish salad was good, with bitter microgreens and a buttermilk dressing sparingly used, but the sugary walnut pieces were the best part, nicely played against the rooty bites of radish. I want to like radishes more than I do; I am not, after all, a Fraggle.

My dining companion won the entrée competition this time around. My gnocchi were well made, but the busy happening of condiments made this dish a bit of a muddle, though one I couldn't quit popping into my mouth. Let me see if I can elaborate. As potato dumplings go, they were small and light and I would have loved them simply done with sage butter or fresh marinara. I couldn't quite place the sauce, which was reminiscent of a British beef–flavored potato crisp—better than it sounds, weird but good. Then there were barely cooked chopped red onions, dabs of goat cheese, halved grape tomatoes, and a drizzle of balsamic across the whole diverse ensemble, which added up to too many textures and tastes that didn't quite blend for me.

Getting back to Malcolm and the short ribs (band name alert!): They. Were. Awesome. Four compact bales of meat, stacked and glazed like an offering to a god I haven't yet met. Though it may be clichéd to say this, still it must be said: The ribs were fall-off-the-bone, melt-in-your-mouth buttery, with a kick. Our waitress (who was great) was able to tell us that the sauce contained "everything but the kitchen sink," including beer and smoked paprika, almost like a riff on the lowbrow A-1 and cola, but more elegant and completely amazing. I really get a kick out of vegetables, and even dabbled in the sort of adolescent vegetarianism that persists among a certain type of girl, but a life without short ribs would be so much less wondrous.

As is our habit, we skipped dessert, though cookies and milk are such a fantastic idea, coming back around to home, family, and coziness. Everything should be shared, passed around, and eaten until you are so full that all you want to do is recline and watch TV. The dining room at Local 188 has a din like a cafeteria, as if every table is the kids' table and all the kids are having fun. There's art on the brick walls. It's bright, like the gin mill I used to frequent with my grandfather when I was small. He was a plumber, union man, and steamfitter who drank boilermakers, so I can't help but think of him here, too. Local 188 is the neighborhood place I wish we had discovered sooner. Everyone needs a local.

INGREDIENTS

For the tacos:

2 large white onions, sliced into 1-inch-thick rounds

6 cloves garlic

¼ teaspoon cumin

Juice from one lime

½ teaspoon salt

A 1-pound flank steak

12 flour or corn tortillas

Lime wedges, for serving

For the salsa:

1 tablespoon olive oil

½ medium onion

4 cups diced rhubarb

½ cup brown sugar

¼ cup raisins

3 tablespoons canned chipotle sauce or two habanero peppers, stemmed, seeded, and chopped

½ teaspoon smoked paprika

¼ teaspoon cinnamon

¼ teaspoon allspice

¼ teaspoon ground ginger

½ teaspoon sea salt

¼ cup apple cider vinegar

SEASONAL INGREDIENT: RHUBARB
Featuring recipes for Grilled Flank Steak Tacos with Chipotle Rhubarb Salsa / Sparkling Rhubarb Water / Vanilla Roasted Rhubarb and Strawberries

You know what's a reasonable thing to have in your garden? A rhubarb plant. You know what's less reasonable? Having ten enormous rhubarb plants. A bumper crop of rhubarb, each plant producing dozens of thick, crimson red rhubarb stalks, has left us scrambling for new ways to use the tart flesh of this vegetable. While it freezes beautifully, we thought we would explore some new recipes that go beyond the usual jams and pies to help inspire you with new ideas for using rhubarb.

Grilled Flank Steak Tacos with Chipotle Rhubarb Salsa • *Malcolm*
Makes 12 tacos

This amazing chipotle rhubarb salsa uses chipotle chiles and a little sugar to perfectly balance the tart rhubarb. The canned chipotle sauce lends a smokiness and a mild spice that works beautifully with the rhubarb. For a

ABOUT RHUBARB

Before growing it ourselves, we didn't know rhubarb would grow so tall. We didn't know about its fluttering flowers, fleeting stalks, or the shameless pink of its overground roots, or how satisfying it is to pull from the ground. Rhubarb is amazingly prolific, maximizing its all-too-brief season. Raw, tart, and green tasting, it pairs well with strawberries. In fact, a strawberry-rhubarb pie is a little bit of heaven. May and June mark rhubarb's time in the sun, so let's make the most of it! A few notes to remember:

Rhubarb is usually harvested in late May or early June. Choose stalks that are about an inch in diameter. Stalks can be red or green; pay more attention to size than color. Before using, remove the inedible leaves from the tops of the rhubarb stalks; they contain oxalic acid, which is toxic to humans. We also trim the white part at the opposite end of the stalk.

Rhubarb should be refrigerated until ready to use, but it also freezes beautifully for up to eight months.

little more heat, you can substitute two habanero peppers for the chipotle; the result is a completely different salsa in which an initial sour sweetness is followed immediately by a bright, burning heat. I can't decide which I like better, but one thing's for certain: Both variations are amazing when spooned liberally over thinly sliced flank steak and folded with grilled onions into tacos.

Method

For the tacos:

1. Add about a fourth of the onion rounds, the garlic, the cumin, the lime juice, and the salt to the bowl of a food processor. Whirl in the food processor until puréed. Place the flank steak in a baking dish and rub the marinade over all sides of the meat. Cover, refrigerate, and let marinate for at least 1 hour.

2. Heat a grill to medium high. Lay the remaining onion rounds on the grill and let cook, turning occasionally, until blackened in spots and softened, about 10 minutes. Transfer to a serving platter and break the rings apart (if they haven't broken apart already).

3. Remove the meat from the marinade and grill until browned on the hottest part of the grill, turning once, about 2 minutes per side for medium rare. Let the flank steak rest for 5 minutes, then slice thinly across the grain.

For the salsa:

1. In a large saucepan, heat the olive oil over medium heat. Add the onion and rhubarb and sauté until the rhubarb softens and the onions begin to turn translucent, about 10 minutes. Add the remaining ingredients and bring the salsa to a boil. Reduce the heat to simmer, and cook for 20 minutes. Use an immersion blender (or let cool slightly and transfer to a regular blender) and blend until smooth.

Assembling the tacos:

1. Warm the tortillas on the hot grill. Evenly divide the sliced flank steak, the grilled onions, and the rhubarb salsa among the 12 tortillas. Top each with a squeeze of fresh lime.

Sparkling Rhubarb Water • *Jillian*
Serves 4

INGREDIENTS

4 cups boiling water

2 pounds rhubarb, cut into pieces

¾ cup granulated sugar

juice of 1 lemon

Recently, I drove to a little farm in Topsham. Alongside the burdock growing for the goats were rows of luminescent pink rhubarb stems hidden under overgrowing green leaves. I came home with an armful of the tart fregetable (vruit?)***** but didn't feel like making a pie or crumble. Instead, I brewed this recipe for a marvelous and refreshing pink drink. Thanks to my SodaStream, my only embellishment was making it fizzy. Serve it over crushed ice with a strawberry garnish and possibly an artful splash of gin for a summer-in-the-tropical-colonies cocktail. I'm calling it "The Kipling." Take my advice and distill this delightful beverage before rhubarb season ends—it's fleeting!

*Rhubarb is usually considered a vegetable; however, a New York court decided in 1947 that since it is used as a fruit in the United States, it should be treated as one for purposes of regulations and duties.

Method

1. Pour the boiling water over the cut-up rhubarb, cover with plastic, and leave to steep on the kitchen counter overnight. The next day, strain and discard the rhubarb. Boil the liquid with the sugar and lemon juice for 5 minutes. Chill and enjoy in the sunshine.

Vanilla-Roasted Rhubarb and Strawberries • *Jillian*

Serves 4

This dessert requires very little cooking. Stir up the components, spoon them into a parchment-paper pouch, bake, and then serve over yogurt or ice cream with honey and nuts. The interplay of temperatures and textures is a delicious treat at any backyard barbeque or sophisticated summer dinner party under the stars. String up lanterns between trees and light votive candles in mismatched teacups. Make simple and delicious food from what is local and lovely. What a wonderful way to spend these glorious months. It's why we love living in Maine all spring and summer long.

INGREDIENTS

4 rhubarb stalks, cut into 2-inch pieces

12 strawberries, hulled and halved

¼ cup bourbon

¼ cup granulated sugar

1 vanilla bean, split lengthwise, seeds removed, cut into 4 pieces

Greek yogurt

Honey

Chopped pistachios

Method

1. Preheat the oven to 425°F. Combine the rhubarb, strawberries, bourbon, sugar, and vanilla bean in a medium bowl. Spoon the mixture into four 16-inch by 12-inch pieces of parchment paper and fold or crimp the edges to close into a purse. Bake on a baking sheet, about 10 to 15 minutes.

2. Carefully open the packets and transfer the contents into individual bowls. Serve with a dollop of Greek yogurt, a generous drizzle of honey, and chopped pistachios. You can also make packets with heavy-duty aluminum foil and cook them on the grill over a medium flame. Peach or blueberry ice cream would be a delightful and sweeter alternative to the tart yogurt.

PO' BOYS AND PICKLES • *Malcolm*
1124 Forest Avenue, Portland, ME, 04103; (207) 518-9735; poboysandpickles.com

Any review of Po' Boys and Pickles should start with something along the lines of "I never expected a little sandwich shop on Forest Avenue to be making anything even remotely similar to what I think of as an authentic New Orleans po' boy, but my goodness, wasn't I pleasantly surprised." Unfortunately, I can't begin our review this way for two reasons. First, anyone who has spent any time reading Portland-area food writing knows that Po' Boys and Pickles is no slouch when it comes to frying up seafood and laying it on a roll. And second, I don't have any idea what "authentic" New Orleans po' boys are like. Sure, I spent the weekend in New Orleans once, hanging from balconies and soaking myself in sickly sweet, syrupy hurricanes that were served in comically oversized novelty cups. But I don't know my remoulade from my tartar sauce. When I think of the sandwiches I've eaten down South that fit the po' boy description, my memory calls up ridiculously oversized sandwiches flooded with white sauce and three or four gigantic fried oysters that either explode burning ocean into your mouth on first bite or are chewy to the point of making the whole sandwich eating experience frustrating and confusing. In spite of what I thought I knew about Po' Boys and Pickles from coverage in the local food blogs, I was pleasantly surprised by the atmosphere of the restaurant. There are a few outside tables for pleasant-weather dining. Inside, instead of the cold, gray cafeteria-style interior I was for some reason expecting, we were greeted by a friendly, outgoing staff working in an open kitchen beneath several giant black chalkboards with the menu scrawled in an appropriately New Orleans–style wacky handwriting.

We ordered two "regular"-sized po' boys, one oyster and one shrimp. (Okay, to be clear, I ordered "poor boys," which always makes me feel silly, but not as silly as I would feel saying "po' boys" out loud. I don't say, "Nawlins," either.) A side of fried pickles, a Brooklyn lager, and a Capt'n Eli's Root Beer later, we were in for $23.54.

After about 10 minutes, one of the staff brought our lunches to the table. Jillian's oyster po' boy wasn't like anything I had ever seen. Instead of big, wet oysters with soggy breading clinging limply to a bun, Jillian's sandwich was piled high with little round balls of fried perfection. The oysters were small enough to make the fried-batter-outside-to-soft-salty-inside ratio exactly perfect. Similarly, my shrimp were the ideal size: not big enough to need two bites, but not those sad little 70-count flavorless "cocktail" shrimp either. Like the oysters, the shrimp were seasoned nicely, battered in cornmeal, and fried precisely the right amount, with good color and crunch.

Both sandwiches were topped with cool, crunchy iceberg lettuce and slices of ripe tomato, which was a bit of a surprise for this time of year. The bread hit a nice middle ground between the soft hero rolls I am used to seeing in these parts and the kind of baguette that would be too crusty and chewy for this kind of sandwich. These rolls had a nice resistance on the outside that gave way to just enough chew in the middle.

Each sandwich was topped with a satisfying smear of sauce: red pepper mayo on Jillian's oyster sandwich and tartar sauce on my shrimp. I would be hard-pressed to describe the difference between the two sauces; however, there isn't enough of either to overwhelm, and neither sauce is the star of the sandwich. The main event here is the fried seafood, and it's nice to see a sauce that doesn't compete with that or turn your sandwich into a big, gloppy mess. Po' Boys and Pickles also makes sure each table has a bottle of Crystal hot sauce in case you want to dial up the spiciness of your sandwich.

So the big question: Is Po' Boys and Pickles serving authentic New Orleans–style fried seafood po' boys? How should I know? I can say with certainty, though, that Po' Boys and Pickles is serving unbelievably delicious, crunchy oyster and shrimp sandwiches, and a lot of thought and care are given to the menu, the food, and your experience. We were asked no fewer than three times by the staff if we were enjoying everything, not because they're pushy, but because the staff at Po' Boys and Pickles seems to genuinely care what kind of food they're producing and how they're serving it. A "how was everything, folks" isn't a mere gesture of restaurateur politeness at Po' Boys and Pickles; it is a genuine expression of curiosity about your experience, and that investment in the restaurant's customers and the quality of its food will beckon us to return again and again.

Recommendations for a Food-Focused Three-Day Weekend in Portland • *Malcolm*

A reader of our blog once mentioned that he and his wife were planning to spend a three-day weekend in Maine and were interested in visiting as many off-the-beaten-path eateries as possible while maintaining a focus (naturally) on seafood and lobster rolls and avoiding high tourist prices. It got us thinking about what we would do if we were limited to eating every meal out during a long weekend in Portland. We're going to assume four things: You have access to a car (because, frankly, we're not sure how you would get from the Kittery bridge to Portland without one); you've got plenty of time to get from one restaurant to the next; you want to stick close to Portland (though this limits your lobster roll options somewhat); and you have a healthy appetite.

SATURDAY BREAKFAST

Maybe you're hitching a ride on the mailboat for an impromptu tour of the islands of Casco Bay. Maybe you're taking a free tour of the Shipyard Brewing Company. No matter your plans, you've got a big day ahead of you, and it's critical to start properly. And nothing spells "boundless energy" like a warm belly full of corned beef hash and eggs. We're head over heels in love with the corned beef hash being slung at **Hot Suppa** (703 Congress Street, Portland; 207-871-5005). It's a perfectly crusted combination of hand-cut potatoes, carrots, and onions, piles of house-made shredded corned beef, and a side of hash browns—with a healthy shot of Sriracha sauce squeezed on top. Bon Appetit named it "Portland's Best Breakfast Dish" in 2009, and we can't think of a better way to start your visit to Portland. (See also our recipe for homemade corned beef hash in the "March" chapter.)

SATURDAY LUNCH

If you've come to Portland in late spring or summer, you've probably got lobster rolls on the brain—that classic combination of chilled, freshly picked lobster meat tossed with a touch of mayo and served in a warm, grilled split-top New England hot dog bun. Though this may be a controversial choice, we don't see any reason why you'd go anywhere but the **Lobster Shack at Two Lights** (225 Two Lights Road, Cape Elizabeth; 207-799-1677) for your first lobster roll of the trip. It's not a favorite among all locals; with only four to five ounces of lobster meat per roll and a price of about $14, it's not the biggest or the least expensive lobster roll in town. You'll be amazed, though, at just how much better a lobster roll tastes when you're sitting smack on the coast on a huge slab of granite looking at a lighthouse while Atlantic Ocean spray moistens your face. This lobster shack has one of the most scenic "dining rooms" on the East Coast, and it's what you imagine when you picture eating a lobster roll on a perfect summer day in Maine.

SATURDAY DINNER

After a day spent on or near the water, it's nice to have a shower, rinse the salt off your skin, and get a tiny bit gussied up for dinner. For times like this, **Fore Street** (288 Fore Street, Portland; 207-775-2717) strikes the perfect balance: a casual restaurant offering James Beard award-winning food in a warm, rustic atmosphere with thoughtful service that never feels pretentious. This is the kind of restaurant in which you order the roast chicken because you know their version of such a simple preparation will be one of the best you've ever tasted. Fore Street serves whatever is in season or available locally, and thus, the menu is always changing. You can almost always sit at the bar and enjoy an enormous bowl of mussels and a glass of wine. Reservations are recommended; thanks to plenty of attention from the likes of *Frommer's* and *Gourmet* magazine, tables can sometimes be tough to get. (See the "January" chapter for a full review.)

SATURDAY LATE NIGHT

Finding a kitchen that stays open late enough to serve the post-bar crowd used to be tricky in Portland and well-nigh impossible in much of the rest of Maine, but fortunately, this is changing. In addition to the food carts that seem to pop up around Portland's Old Port late at night, **Otto Pizza** (576 Congress Street, Portland; 207-773-7099) has established itself as a staple of late-night noshing, serving rotating varieties of specialty slices, including a mashed potato, bacon, and scallion pie that just might have the power to prevent hangovers.

SUNDAY BREAKFAST

Portland offers several good options for brunch, but our favorite is still **Caiola's** (58 Pine Street, Portland; 207-772-1110). This small, cozy restaurant in Portland's West End is fantastic for dinner, but they really put on a show at brunch, where you'll find not just a perfectly respectable eggs Benedict, but also a spicy spin on huevos rancheros (theirs is called an Egg Tostada and features plenty of Mexican chorizo), a bastard child of French toast and bread pudding called Warm Lost Bread that is served with Maine maple syrup, and a homemade cinnamon-and-sugar-filled Pop Tart. This is cozy, homey food served in a small dining room that is just like yours but better. You'll feel like you should be in your jammies. For a full review of Caiola's, see the "March" chapter.

SUNDAY LUNCH

Sure, it's touristy, particularly during the summer. Okay, so it's a tad on the spendy side for a lobster shack. And fine, the branding and logos all seem a little too spot-on and on purpose. But the **Portland Lobster Company** (180 Commercial Street, Portland; 207-775-2112) also happens to be smack on the water in the heart of the Old Port where you can watch the

boats come in and out of Portland's rapidly disappearing working water-front. After placing your order for a lobster roll, full lobster dinner, or bucket of steamers, you can elbow your way in at the counter or make your way out to the seating area on the dock. When the weather cools and the patio heaters come out, I can think of few better places to tilt a pitcher of Geary's, listen to some live music, and eat a pile of fried shrimp as big as my head.

SUNDAY DINNER

Tonight we want you to give your palate a break and go a little ethnic with some of Maine's best Mexican-influenced cuisine. What's that? Did reading "Maine" and "Mexican" in the same sentence make your eyes go googly? It did ours, but every time we return to **Zapoteca** (505 Fore Street, Portland; 207-772-8242), our belief is reaffirmed that this purveyor of authentic New Mexican cuisine is one of Portland's finest restaurants. Forget the sour cream–drenched nachos and buffalo chicken enchiladas famous in Portland's other Mexican restaurants. Instead, try the carnitas de puerco served with a spicy tomato purée, or the filete de ancho, a filet mignon served in an ancho chile reduction with mushrooms, mashed potatoes, and asparagus. Tomorrow we're going to bring the seafood ruckus, but tonight, we want you to refresh your taste buds with a watermelon-habanero margarita.

SUNDAY LATE NIGHT

Hop in the car (or better yet, ask someone to drive you) to **Samuel's Bar and Grill** (1160 Forest Avenue, Portland; 207-797-6924). In a town heavy with somewhat peculiar baked, breaded, and grilled preparations, Samuel's is serving, hands down, the best Buffalo wings in Portland, in a neighborhood bar that is so unspoiled, I almost don't want to tell you about it. Samuel's wings are the real thing: patted dry and then fried, with crispy skins and nasal-passage-clearing hits of vinegar from the sauce. Best of all, the kitchen stays open until 1 AM, so there's always time for one last round and a basket of food.

MONDAY BREAKFAST

Let's start light this morning. **Coffee By Design** (67 India Street, Portland; 207-780-6767) is operating their own micro-roastery, toasting their own beans into perfect cups of coffee. Grab a cup and hoof it over to the **Standard Baking Company** (75 Commercial Street, Portland; 207-773-2112) for a warm, buttery croissant or a morning bun and a walk along Commercial Street, where you can check out the biggest, laziest seagulls on the planet. Not exciting enough? Take your breakfast up to Monument Square or walk along Congress Street to watch people instead of gulls. Or you can take the railroad walkway to Munjoy Hill park and sit with your face in the sun.

MONDAY LUNCH

For lunch on your last day in Portland, you're going to have to make a decision based largely on your appetite for more seafood. If you still have room for one last cup of clam chowder, get thee to **Gilbert's Chowder House** (92 Commercial Street, Portland; 207-871-5636). Why? Because Gilbert's is a Maine institution, a holdover from the days before the words "Portland" and "foodie" could be combined in the same sentence. It's light on atmosphere, but you can get a Styrofoam cup of classic, thick clam or fish chowder for less than five bucks. Need a break from the briney stuff? Forget what you know about pizza and head to **Micucci's Italian Grocer** (45 India Street, Portland; 207-775-1854) for a hard-fought slice of their Sicilian Slab pizza. The super-thick but surprisingly light, cakey focaccia supports a startlingly sweet sauce and a light marbling of pleasantly salty mozzarella, making it well worth the wait in line. See the "April" chapter for a review of Micucci's.

MONDAY DINNER

Given all the time you've been spending on Commercial Street, you are bound to have noticed **DiMillo's,** the car ferry-turned-restaurant. It floats. The lobsters are $30. It's for tourists (though we do admit to loving every visit we make to DiMillo's in the winter). Instead, hang a left, and if the wait isn't too long, try **J's Oyster** (5 Portland Pier, Portland; 207-772-4828). You can sit outside on the patio, which is right on the dock, but the real action is indoors, where the bulk of the dining room is taken up by a giant, wood-paneled bar populated mostly by locals. The sticky tables are almost an afterthought, leaving just enough room for the sometimes short-tempered waitstaff to walk. It never fails to remind me of the Maine of my memory, as it existed (perhaps too perfectly) in the 1980s; it's as if Hank Chinaski's dive bar from the movie *Barfly* (based on Charles Bukowski's semi-autobiographical screenplay) came to life and also sold seafood. It doesn't smell like cigarette smoke, but you kind of wish it did. Don't get distracted by the dollar-a-piece raw oysters: They're small, gnarled, and often muddy. The real star here is in the battered tin buckets of steamers, the mussels (be sure to ask for some soft potato rolls to sop up the broth), the wide selection of local beer on tap, and the no-frills, reasonably priced lobster dinners. For a review of J's Oyster, see the "February" chapter.

MONDAY LATE NIGHT

For your last stop, don't miss the selection of over 500 bottles of beer (including some hard-to-find Belgians) at **Novare Res** (4 Canal Plaza, Suite 1, Portland; enter through the alley by the Key Bank sign on Exchange Street; 207-761-2437), a bar in the Old Port with a large outdoor space made intimate by the surrounding buildings. If the heavy-duty binder that serves as a beer listing is intimidating, don't be shy about asking your server for advice; the staff is stunningly knowledgeable without showing even a flicker of pretension. And if you get snacky later in the evening, you can pick and choose from a list of $3 portions of cheese, prosciutto, and mortadella.

There you have it: our recommendations for three all-too-short days in Portland. This list is by no means exhaustive; there are many, many more options to suit almost any craving. There's as much good food in this town as there are opinions on where to find it. Use our list as a guide and then forget everything we said. On a bright, sunny, cloudless Maine spring day, sometimes it's much more fun to hit the pavement and let the day take you where it will. Wherever you decide to eat, whether it's a tourist trap or a locals-only dive, it's ultimately up to you to discover your favorite spot for lobster, chowder, or mussel—all the things that Maine does best.

Food for Upta Camp

- Homemade Bacon Jam
- Haddock Chowder
- Coffee S'mores Pie

INGREDIENTS

1 pound bacon

1 medium yellow onion, chopped

4 cloves garlic, chopped

⅛ teaspoon cayenne pepper

¼ cup apple cider vinegar

½ cup packed brown sugar

½ cup brewed coffee

Deep-rooted Mainers have a reputation for being solitary and connected to nature. In April and early May they shake off their winter torpor like a bear emerging from a cave to blink in the sunlight, and with the approach of Memorial Day Weekend, while the oncoming hordes of summer visitors are still milling around south of Boston, they get an urge to head for camp. As Maine natives know instinctively and the rest of us come to learn, a camp is a dwelling capable of supporting basic life functions if your tastes aren't too refined. It's usually uninsulated and is heated either by wood or propane. It may have running water if its owner remembered to drain the pipes last October. It's almost always rustic, requires minimal maintenance, and does not have a lawn to mow. More often than not it's located even farther north than the owner's primary home, preferably near a lake to ensure nearby habitat for wave upon wave of blackflies and mosquitoes. Modest or grand, a camp is a family retreat, a place in the woods where Mainers can escape Portland's bustling rat race while New Yorkers and Philadelphians are escaping to Portland.

The recipes that follow are a nod to camp. They will work anywhere in the great outdoors, whether in Baxter State Park or your own backyard.

Homemade Bacon Jam • *Malcolm*
Makes about 2 cups

With the economy circling the drain, home canning and preservation has seen a huge revival in the last few years. Although I'm all for homemade jellies and jams, I can't help but wonder why they always seem to be made with fruit. Raspberries and blueberries are full of antioxidants and taste like little bursts of summer, but is there some divine law against putting bacon in a jam? And where is it written that spices, bourbon, and chiles have no place here either?

Before you dismiss me as a lunatic, whip up this sweet-salty-spicy-porky bit of heaven and spread a dollop onto thick, crusty bread. Just be sure to save a little. You'll be glad you did. It should keep a few weeks in the refrigerator, but there's no way it will last that long.

Method

1. In a large, deep skillet over medium heat, cook the bacon until brown and crisp. Remove the cooked bacon to a paper towel or paper bag–lined plate to cool and drain. When cool, cut the bacon into 1-inch pieces.

2. Pour off all but one tablespoon of the bacon fat from the pan. Add the onions, the garlic, and the cayenne. Cook until the onions begin to turn translucent.

3. Add the vinegar, the brown sugar, and the coffee. Bring to a boil.

4. Add the cooked, chopped bacon. Turn the heat to low and allow the mixture to simmer about 45 minutes, stirring every few minutes, until most of the liquid has evaporated and what is left is syrupy.

5. Transfer the cooked mixture to the bowl of a food processor, and pulse until the consistency of a chunky jam is reached. To serve, spread on crusty bread.

Haddock Chowder • *Jillian*

Serves 6

The first time I ate haddock chowder was on a Christmas trip home to New England while Malcolm and I were living in Mexico. We booked a room at the Samoset Resort in Rockport, overlooking a snow-spackled golf course and Penobscot Bay. It was a divine break from the heat and vividness of Mexico. On Sunday, we went downstairs to brunch. The restaurant was toasty warm, while the wild outdoors shone picturesquely in the low winter sun. We began with mimosas, then glided toward buffet tables laden with meats, fruit, chafing dishes, and stacks of warm-from-the-dishwasher plates. And then, from across the room, I spied a bubbling tureen of soup—chowder, to be exact—creamy and clearly of the sea.

I ladled the liquid into my bowl without paying attention as I learned its great and glorious name: haddock chowder! In a tone more guttural than mellifluous, a kindly, elderly lady said, "Yah spillin' yah soup, deah." I thanked her politely, not wanting to waste any of the heavenly broth. Carefully, I made my way back to our table, where I proceeded to devour the richest yet lightest, most fragrant fish soup I have ever in all my days tasted.

INGREDIENTS

4 strips thick-cut bacon, chopped

1 yellow onion, diced

½ leek, chopped

1 celery stalk, chopped

2½ cups red potatoes, cubed

1 cup clam juice

1 cup white wine

1 cup water

2 tablespoons thyme, chopped

1 pint half-and-half

Salt and pepper, to taste

2 pounds whole haddock fillets

8 tablespoons (1 stick) unsalted butter, cut into pats

Chives, chopped

Method

1. In a large pot over medium heat, cook the 4 strips of chopped, thick-cut bacon over medium heat for about 15 minutes. Transfer the cooked bacon to a paper towel to drain.

2. Add the onion, the leek, and the celery to the bacon fat. Cook until the vegetables soften.

3. Add the potatoes, the clam juice, the white wine, and the water. Bring to a boil, then reduce to a simmer. Add the thyme, the half-and-half, and the salt and pepper, to taste.

4. Add the whole haddock fillets (the fish will break up as the soup cooks), and cook until the fish turns opaque and breaks apart, about 5–10 minutes.

5. Just before serving, add the butter and the chives, and stir well to combine. Top with the reserved chopped bacon and serve.

Coffee S'mores Pie • *Jillian*
Serves 8

Juliette Low founded the Girl Scouts of America on March 12, 1912. On September 15, 1985, I joined their illustrious ranks as a member of Troop 207. Those early days of scouting were building my character, I was told. Mostly I was bored and wished I could bring a book. Forced to craft an orange while perched on a vinyl sit-upon one afternoon after school, I was incensed. I had two couches, a bed, and a Cabbage Patch Kid bed tent at home to fully satisfy my sitting/reclining needs. What possible use could I have for an uncomfortable cushion made of plastic?

But worse was to come in the form of Girl Scout camp, which was held, of all places, in the great outdoors—an entire weekend without television. Still, there was an upside. At age seven and a half, I was planning to use this rare opportunity to run away from home (through the wild woods of Niantic, Connecticut) to meet circus-performing gypsies and begin my rightful existence. I had long been convinced that I was not my parents' child, and I knew that everything would be all right if I could just find more interesting people with whom to live. But my mother, as usual, foiled my plans for greatness and escape. She insisted on coming along.

As it turned out, however, she did prove useful. She showed us a very cool flashlight game we could play in our tent after lights out; she taught us silly songs that seemed bristling with innuendo to sing around the campfire; and she knew how to make s'mores—how to properly impale a marshmallow on a clean stick and keep it hovering just above the flame, turning it slowly, so that it toasts but does not burn, with the perfect ratio of chocolate

to graham cracker to golden, oozing marshmallow. I never did run away—not that weekend anyway. Camp turned out better than anticipated, and my mom, I was beginning to suspect, had more than a few tricks up her sleeve.

This pie is incredibly easy and delicious. The chocolate ganache is rich, dense, and decadent. The meringue is more like grown-up fluff, if there is such a thing, and the crust is made with Nutella. What could be better than that? Bring this the next time you're invited to a picnic, a cookout, or camping in a friend's backyard. S'mores make us nostalgic for simpler times, childhood, summers long past. This dessert will make everyone at your party feel dreamy and content.

Method

For the graham cracker crust:

1. Mix the ingredients in a small bowl. Press the mixture into a 9-inch metal or glass pie dish. Chill until the crust is firm, about 30 minutes.

For the coffee ganache:

1. Combine the chocolate and the butter in a large bowl.

2. In a small saucepan, bring the coffee, the cream, and the 2 tablespoons of water to a boil. Remove from the heat, cover, and let steep for 5 minutes. Strain the cream mixture through a sieve into the bowl of chocolate and butter. Stir until the mixture is melted and smooth. Pour into the crust and smooth the top. Chill until set, about an hour.

For the meringue:

1. Use beaters to blend the egg whites until light and frothy. Add the sugar in four parts, beating for one minute after each addition. Continue beating until the egg whites are stiff and glossy. Spoon the meringue over the ganache, smooth, and swirl. If desired, use a kitchen torch to toast the meringue to a golden-brown. This pie can be made 8 hours ahead. Keep chilled.

INGREDIENTS

For the graham cracker crust:

9 whole graham crackers, ground in a food processor

2 tablespoons heavy cream

2 tablespoons Nutella

1 ounce semisweet chocolate, melted

1 tablespoon unsalted butter, melted

For the coffee ganache:

12 ounces semisweet chocolate chips

2 tablespoons (¼ stick) unsalted

butter, cut into ½-inch cubes

2 tablespoons finely ground coffee beans

1¼ cup heavy cream

2 tablespoons water

For the meringue:

2 large egg whites

½ cup granulated sugar

JUNE

Summer Solstice Celebration Menu

- Sweet Corn and Poblano Chowder
- Gluten-Free Corn Spoonbread with Tomatoes
- Cochinita Pibil
- Mexican-Style Chocolate Cake

The sun doesn't set until eight-thirty on the longest day of the year, and we make the most of the warmth and light of its vitamin D–laden rays. When night finally sets in, we catch fireflies in jars and hang paper lanterns from the trees. Under a canopy of stars we take a deep breath of sweet summer air and bask in the glory of nature. We love to gather friends for a good, old-fashioned outdoor supper.

In the state of Yucatan, Mexico, cochinita pibil is a pig that's been cooked in a pit. We have modified this classic for home cooking, wrapping the roast in banana leaves. It pairs so well with other flavors of summer—corn and tomatoes, and chocolate cake. In Maine in June, it still gets chilly when the sun sets, so we zip up sweatshirts and gather around the fire pit for a spicy, Mexican-inspired dessert.

Sweet Corn and Poblano Chowder • *Malcolm*

Serves 10

The weather may be getting warmer, but it's never too warm for a delicious corn chowder. Our version uses half-and-half in lieu of heavy cream to lighten it up a bit, and the poblanos provide a nice, spicy heat. After chopping and adding one, check the heat level; poblanos vary in potency, and you don't want to make the chowder too spicy. The sweetness of the corn will temper things nicely, though, so if it seems too spicy at first, don't worry, it will calm down. We make this chowder all summer long, even in the dog days of August, when the air may be hot and sticky but the local corn is ripe and irresistibly sweet.

Method

1. In a soup pot, sauté the onion, garlic, and poblano peppers in the butter and olive oil until all the vegetables are soft and the onions are translucent, about 10 minutes.

2. Dust the sautéed vegetables with the flour and toss or stir to coat. Add the vegetable stock, and bring to a boil. Add the half-and-half, potatoes, and crumbled bacon, reserving 2 tablespoons of the bacon. Bring to a boil and boil hard for about 7 minutes, until the potatoes break down. (This will help thicken the soup and give it a good texture.)

3. Cut the kernels off the corn, saving as much of the "milk" that comes off the cob as possible. (This will impart a very rich, strong corn flavor.) Add the kernels and the "milk" to the soup. Season with salt and pepper, and simmer until the corn is soft, another 10 minutes.

4. Ladle the soup into bowls, garnish with a sprig of parsley and the reserved crumbled bacon, and serve.

INGREDIENTS

2 tablespoons unsalted butter

Extra-virgin olive oil

1 medium white onion, diced

2 cloves garlic, minced

1 to 2 poblano peppers, seeded and chopped

¼ cup all-purpose flour

6 cups vegetable stock

2 cups half-and-half

2 potatoes, cleaned, peeled, and diced

3 slices bacon, cooked and crumbled

6 ears corn

Salt and pepper

Parsley to garnish

Gluten-Free Corn Spoonbread with Tomatoes • *Jillian*
Serves 6

Last summer I stopped at Fresh Off the Farm, a wonderful farmstand on Route 1 in Rockport, and filled my basket with a bounty of beautiful vegetables, including sweet corn from Beth's Farm Market in Warren and a bulbous, gargantuan heirloom tomato. Beth's corn is so sweet, so bursting with flavor and ripe and delicious, you can almost eat it straight from the cob without any cooking. We sautéed it ever so quickly with a little butter, and it was the best thing I ate all week.

A mouthful of this spoonbread imparts creaminess and a touch of sweetness. The addition of acidic tomatoes with fatty, fruity olive oil creates a perfect summer supper side dish. (And locally grown hydroponic tomatoes are available year-round now in Maine.)

Method

1. Preheat the oven to 375°F and prepare the ramekins with butter and a dusting of cornmeal.

2. In a large bowl, beat the eggs by hand or with a mixer until thick and airy, about 5 minutes. Set aside.

3. In a large pot, combine the cornmeal, milk, corn, and a pinch of salt over medium-high heat. Whisk continuously until the mixture thickens, about 15 minutes. Stir in the chives and ¾ cup of the cheese. Slowly fold the cornmeal batter into the whipped eggs.

4. Pour the mixture into ramekins and top with the remaining cheese. Place the ramekins on a baking sheet and bake until puffed and set, 20 to 25 minutes.

5. Toss the tomatoes with the olive oil, salt, and pepper. Top the spoonbread with the tomatoes and serve warm.

INGREDIENTS

½ cup cornmeal, plus more for the ramekins

Butter (to prepare the ramekins)

4 eggs

2 cups milk

1 cup corn kernels (from two ears of corn)

Kosher salt

2 tablespoons minced chives

1 cup Parmesan cheese

1 large tomato, diced

2 tablespoons olive oil

Freshly ground black pepper

Cochinita Pibil: Mayan-Style Slow-Cooked Pork with Pickled Red Onions and Mellowed Habanero Peppers • *Malcolm*
Serves 8-10

The cuisine of Yucatan, Mexico, sometimes comes under fire from the uninitiated for being too subtle, too basic, and ultimately not Mexican enough. I disagree. Perhaps the pared-down ingredients of Yucatan cooking lack the in-your-face pizazz of a northern Mexico infant-sized burrito wrapped in a tortilla the size of a bedsheet (pizazz? Am I suddenly 80?), but so what? It is possible to enjoy a meal without being mugged by it. Yucatan food stands just fine on its own, but if that's not enough, it doesn't hurt that Yucatecans like to sprinkle habanero on almost everything, which brings the fire to more subtly seasoned, slow-cooked meats.

Cochinita pibil, or "baby pit pig," is one of our favorite examples of cooking from this part of Mexico. Cochinita is sold at food carts in almost every small Yucatan town on the weekends, either in tacos or in tortas, or sandwiches, topped with pickled red onions and diced habanero.

Our version assumes that you don't have access to sour oranges, the main component in the pork's marinade, but you do have access to a Mexican grocer or a mainstream grocery store with a healthy import section. Though our recipe for cochinita pibil doesn't contain any truly crazy ingredients, you may have to poke around your favorite grocery store to find what you need. Finally, we are assuming that you don't want to dig a hole in your backyard for roasting a whole pig, and will instead be tackling this dish in the comfort of your kitchen.

INGREDIENTS

1 package El Yucateco Achiote Red Paste (available in Latin groceries or on Amazon.com)

20 cloves garlic, peeled and roughly chopped

1 cup freshly squeezed lime juice

½ cup freshly squeezed orange juice

1 boneless pork shoulder (about 6 pounds)

1 package banana leaves, defrosted if frozen

Method

1. Preheat the oven to 300°F. Combine the first four ingredients in a blender or food processor, and blend until smooth. Cut the pork into 3-inch-square portions, cover with the mixture, and marinate in the refrigerator 12 to 24 hours.

2. Line a roasting pan with three banana leaves, allowing the edges to overlap on the bottom of the pan and hang out over the edges. Place the marinated pork on top and cover with the remaining marinade. Fold the edges of the banana leaves over the top of the pork, and place three additional overlapping leaves on top. Tuck these leaves in along the edges of the pan to form a tight seal around the pork. Cover the entire tray in aluminum foil for good measure. The goal is to let no steam escape.

3. Cook for 3½ to 4 hours. Carefully unwrap the pork, being careful of the escaping steam. Shred the meat using two forks.

This dish is best when served in tacos with pickled red onions and topped with habaneros. The combination of salty, sweet, and spicy is amazing!

2 red onions, cut in half lengthwise, with the ends removed

1 cup freshly squeezed orange juice

½ cup freshly squeezed lime juice

1 tablespoon salt

1 teaspoon granulated sugar

1 jalapeño, seeds removed, thinly sliced (optional, but recommended)

INGREDIENTS

5 to 6 habanero peppers, deseeded, deveined, diced

Water

White vinegar

Pickled Red Onions

Serves 8-10

Method

1. Bring a saucepan of water to a boil, and blanch the onions for 15 seconds. Drain thoroughly and add the remaining ingredients, stirring to coat the onions. Marinate for at least 1 hour (and preferably overnight) before serving.

The onions and the pork complement each other beautifully, but if you want to eat your cochinita pibil the way they do in the Yucatan, you'll want to add some heat from habanero peppers. We'll dial down the heat just a bit, but be warned—these peppers are spicy. And don't forget to wear gloves when working with habanero peppers; the oils can stay on your skin for a long time.

Mellowed Habanero Peppers

Serves 8-10

Method

1. Place the diced habaneros in a small bowl. Add enough water to cover and a splash of vinegar. Marinate for at least 1 hour before serving on top of the cochinita and pickled red onions.

Mexican Chocolate Cake • *Jillian*

Serves 8

Once upon a time in Mexico I got married in front of a fountain, a defrocked priest, and friends and family. We stood under a cloudless blue sky in the open courtyard of a colonial mansion. There was no aisle, no mass, no pews, no flower girl. No programs, no rice, no chuppah. There were, however, mariachis. And birds of paradise. And two cakes. And fake dancing. Later, at the Mambo Café, there was real dancing in this crowded, sweaty club. And bottle service. And late-night hilarity and hijinks. But back to the wedding cakes.

They weren't very good—more wet than moist. But the flowers and the food and the art of it were amazing. There was champagne, and a note from my groom before our vows, and so much happiness. I wish I could do it again right now. Being the bride among a crazy group of gringo wedding guests at a freshwater swimming hole and the greenest Mayan ruins in the middle of the Yucatan peninsula, talking too late by the pool and swinging in hammocks in cool rooms with old friends, drinking tequila, I had the time of my life. This cake has the classic Mexican combination of chocolate and spice, plus cinnamon. It would be fun for a Cinco de Mayo party, or any time of year. I like it in summer because a sweltering night will forever remind me of my time south of the border.

Method

1. Preheat the oven to 350°F. Prepare a Bundt pan with baking spray and a dusting of flour.

2. In a large pot over low heat, melt the butter. Whisk in the cocoa powder, coffee, and almond extract. Remove the pot from the heat. Add the eggs, sugar, Greek yogurt, and vanilla.

3. In a large mixing bowl, whisk together the flour, baking soda, cinnamon, chipotle powder, and salt. Sift the dry ingredients into the batter and stir until just combined. The batter may be lumpy. Pour into the prepared Bundt pan and bake, about 45 to 55 minutes, until a cake tester comes out with crumbs.

4. Cool the cake in the pan for 20 minutes. Turn over onto a large plate and top with your favorite brand of chocolate syrup if you like.

INGREDIENTS

1 cup (2 sticks) unsalted butter

½ cup unsweetened cocoa powder

¾ cup coffee

¼ teaspoon almond extract

2 large eggs

2 cups granulated sugar

½ cup Greek yogurt

2 tablespoons vanilla extract

2 cups all-purpose flour

1 teaspoon baking soda

1 teaspoon cinnamon

½ teaspoon chipotle chile powder

¼ teaspoon salt

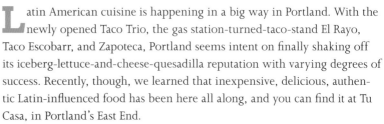

The Curious Collection of Authentic Latin American Cooking in Maine

There's a trend afoot in Maine that catches many visitors to the state (or anyone "from here" who may have been away or hibernating for a while) completely off guard. What's the big surprise? It's that somewhere along the line, a state whose collective Mexican restaurant scene seemed to lean heavily on molten Jack cheese, bottomless-well margaritas, and guacamole from a Sysco can started producing inventive, authentic Latin American cooking with an identity all its own.

Even more surprising, much of this cooking didn't originate in Portland or Bangor. While Portland boasts two of our favorite sources for fiery, exciting food, the other two come from a hole-in-the-wall in Brunswick and a converted barn in Sedgwick, near Blue Hill.

A perfectly respectable taco al pastor being served out of a barn down east? Only in Maine.

TU CASA • *Malcolm*
70 Washington Avenue, Portland, ME 04101; (207) 828-4971

Latin American cuisine is happening in a big way in Portland. With the newly opened Taco Trio, the gas station-turned-taco-stand El Rayo, Taco Escobarr, and Zapoteca, Portland seems intent on finally shaking off its iceberg-lettuce-and-cheese-quesadilla reputation with varying degrees of success. Recently, though, we learned that inexpensive, delicious, authentic Latin-influenced food has been here all along, and you can find it at Tu Casa, in Portland's East End.

We started with cheese pupusas ($1.75 each), flat corn masa cakes filled with herbs and cheese and pan fried. The national dish of El Salvador, pupusas are topped with a slaw of quick-pickled cabbage and as much hot sauce as you can muster. The corn exterior stays fluffy and ever so slightly crisped, with a warm, soft inside. The texture is similar to the hand-shaped cakes used in a Mexican sope, or like a really tight corn polenta. The crunchy cabbage provides a perfect contrast in texture, and the chewy melted cheese (Oaxaca?) inside bursts through the outside here and there, crisping and browning in the pan.

Next, we tried the taquitos de lengua ($6.95), small, soft corn tacos filled with lightly crisped, fried pieces of flavorful beef tongue, topped simply with lettuce, tomato, and cilantro. I was pleased to see that Tu Casa

was doubling up on its store-bought white corn tortillas, which helped prevent the dreaded "taco blowout" of wet ingredients ripping through inferior tortillas and ending up all over your plate. And with homemade salsa this delicious, lending fresh vegetable flavor and layers of heat to anything it touches, things could get messy otherwise. This is salsa to apply using a ladle, and it complements the salty meat perfectly with a freshness that is surprising and delicious.

While the tacos and the papusas were delicious (not to mention head and shoulders better than anything similar in town), it's the Plato Montanero ($11.95) that I know will get in my head and keep me going back again and again. This "mountaineer's platter" combines a thinly cut grilled rib eye, sliced avocado, a fried plantain, and a hard-cooked fried egg and is served with rice and pinto beans. The rice and beans alone would keep me going back: wondrously fluffy, cilantro-scented grains with a background heat that comes out of nowhere and keeps you shoveling spoonful after spoonful into your mouth like a greedy street kid. The pintos were delicious, adding a mellow, mildly seasoned contrast to the rest of the dish. The beans were more similar to a frijoles charros than to typical Mexican refried beans, and it was only the attention I was paying to the rest of the dish that kept me from finishing them.

The steak, thinly cut and tenderized to melt-in-your-mouth perfection, is grilled simply. Combine a bit of steak on a fork with a piece of creamy avocado, a slice of the fried plantain, and a bit of the hard-cooked yolk from the egg, and you've got a perfectly balanced mouthful of flavor. It was one of the best things I'd eaten in weeks and may represent one of the best single forkfuls of food you can eat in Portland.

Tu Casa is the kind of place that would be easy to overlook. Tucked among other businesses fronting Washington Avenue (a Thai place, a laundromat, an Asian market, etc.), the unassuming, pale green little clapboard building doesn't reach out and grab you. And for the uninitiated, the siren call of Salvadoran food may not incite a ton of enthusiasm. Though it may be similar to some Mexican dishes you've tried, a lot has been cut out that you don't need: there's no guacamole that you won't eat anyway, and a lot of the staples of Mexican cooking are served a bit more simply (though, we suspect, with no less pure lard used in the process). The atmosphere in the dining room may seem a little basic, though spotlessly clean, and the service may seem a bit on the slow side. Try it, though, and you'll find some of the best cooking of its kind anywhere in the area . . . and you can get in and out for less than ten bucks.

ZAPOTECA • *Malcolm*
505 Fore Street, Portland, ME 04101; (207) 772-8242; zapotecarestaurant.com

When I hear about a new restaurant that hopes to specialize in an "elevated" form of traditional Mexican cooking, I am filled with apprehension. I understand the intent—that is, to combine traditional Mexican ingredients and methods with modern cooking techniques and interpretations, producing new dishes at a premium price in an upscale setting. What happens much, much too often, however, even in Mexico, is that these enhancements add nothing to the original dish.

Unfortunately, many reinventions of classic fare lean toward rather grotesquely Americanized versions of Mexican cooking as they might have appeared in an upscale kitchen of the 1980s. Instead of a well-executed 30-ingredient mole or a pork shoulder that has been lovingly cooked in the ground in banana leaves for two days, you instead are confronted with sloppy tri-tip chipotle chili tacos with cilantro-scented crema, or tuna tartar taquitos with a side of ranch dressing, or—you get the idea. Such dishes don't improve on traditional methods and certainly don't elevate Mexican cuisine. Instead, it's as though Rick Bayless had been forced to cook with the ingredients from a Chili's restaurant in a *Top Chef* challenge (brought to you by GLAD® ForceFlex® Tall Kitchen Drawstring Trash Bags).

It was with a healthy dose of skepticism, then, that I approached dinner at Zapoteca, Portland's newest spin on Mexican-influenced cuisine. Occupying the former Siano's pizza restaurant at the intersection of Fore and York streets (Jillian swears she could still detect a faint hint of pizza inside . . . it must get infused in the brick), Zapoteca has been transformed into a slick, sophisticated restaurant space. The interior is dominated by brick walls and polished wood floors, with soft, punched-tin lighting and tasteful Mexican thematic elements. The owner greeted us at the door, welcomed us warmly, and sat us at a booth. I had a moment of panic at this seeming clash; the upscale decor didn't jibe with sitting in a straight-backed booth, and I wondered if this was a sign of a potential identity crisis.

We needn't have worried. Our server's breezy conversational tone combined perfectly with a well-trained, open-handed service style that was comfortable, accommodating, and easy to be around. She explained a few of the drink options, including a good selection of Mexican beer (such as Bohemia and Pacifico in bottles), as well as full tasting flights of tequila. I stuck to the draft Dos Equis as we went through the menu.

The appetizer section held a few pleasant surprises. In addition to the expected guacamole preparation and Jalapenos Rellenos de Queso, which sounds suspiciously like a jalapeño popper, we were happy to see local ingredients mixed in, including mussels and chorizo simmered in a white wine broth and a few creative local spins on ceviche featuring lobster as well as crab cake tortas made with Maine crab. We settled on the Tres Salsas sampler ($7), a tasting of the three house salsas, and the Queso Fundido con Champinones.

The three salsas were delicious and fresh. There was a cool tomato-serrano pico de gallo as well as a warm green tomatillo salsa and another warm red salsa Mexicana. While they were all delicious, cooked salsas aren't my favorite; I look to salsa for brightness, tartness, and heat, and I think many of those characteristics are lost when a salsa is cooked. But that is a quibble that stems from personal preference. We were pleasantly surprised by the warm, glowing heat the salsas contained; Zapoteca isn't afraid to use chiles, and we took that as a great sign that the flavor of the rest of our dishes wouldn't be washed out to appeal to the broadest number of diners.

The queso fundido was the first example of Zapoteca's creative approach to Mexican classics. In Mexico, an order of queso fundido in most

WHAT ABOUT CEVICHE?

Yucatecan Mexicans have an unrelenting love for eating quantities of ceviche of questionable pedigree. I once attended an afternoon party of six or seven husbands in Progreso, a small port town, where we all sat around a plastic table in the sun eating from a 24-inch aluminum steam tray that was overflowing with a ceviche made of raw white fish, shrimp, and octopus "cooked" with what must have been buckets of lime juice. I ate what I thought was a polite pound and a half of the stuff before my host looked right at me and in a deadpan tone asked, "What's the matter? You don't like fish?" The experience may have provided me with my lifetime allotment of ceviche.

casual restaurants will bring you a bowl of warm, melted Mexican Manchego that must be attacked quickly and voraciously with scraps of tortilla because you have only moments before it hardens into a giant, clumped mass. That's not to say that it isn't delicious, but a sophisticated dish it isn't. Zapoteca approaches the dish a little differently, making it a perfect example of the care and thought they are giving to the classics. Monterey Jack cheese is slow roasted in their ovens and tossed with several varieties of mushrooms, grilled onions, fresh tomatoes, and a dash of Mexican beer. The result is a dish that is much lighter than traditional queso fundido (that is, as light as a pan of melted cheese can be), with wonderfully satisfying slices of earthy, meaty mushroom in every bite and enough other flavors to keep each bite interesting.

For our main courses, Jillian chose the Relleno de Champinones ($16), a poblano pepper stuffed with mushrooms, jalapeños, tomatoes, roasted pumpkin seeds, and goat cheese. Served wrapped in a corn husk, the pepper offered a comforting smokiness and a mysterious tartness in its filling that I quite enjoyed. I ordered the Carnitas de Puerco ($22), a combination of shredded, locally raised pork shoulder with tomato chile sauce, pickled red onions, avocado, and black beans. I expected these to arrive already assembled into tacos but was pleasantly surprised to be served a platter of the promised elements along with a basket of warm corn tortillas. While assembling little tacos a quarter of a torn tortilla at a time, I was delighted by the pork: slow-cooked, shredded, then pushed into a mold and grilled in a hot pan so that a golden crust formed on the entire surface, only to be broken apart by my fork and scooped up with tortillas. The tomato chile sauce was pleasantly spicy, while the pickled onions added a nice crunch and acidity and the refried black bean purée was perfect, topped with a rustic (cotija?) cheese. Because I am a filthy little taquería rat, I could have used a wedge of lime to squeeze over the whole thing. Also, I would have loved to see homemade tortillas used; the perfectly round shape of our tortillas gave them away, though they were at least three times thicker than normal, falling somewhere between a tortilla and a sope shell. Our waitress let me know that homemade tortillas are in the restaurant's future; for now, these manufactured versions will do just fine.

The inevitable success of Zapoteca spells the end of careless, cartoonish, bottomless-margarita, kid-friendly Mexican cuisine in Maine. Each dish we tried included an unexpectedly sophisticated, delicious surprise, whether it was in the use of additional ingredients or in the way those ingredients were assembled and presented. Zapoteca is the first New Mexican restaurant that we have tried—in Mexico or the United States—that perfectly delivers on its "new" promise, producing dishes that honor and respect the flavors of the originals while sending them off into glorious new directions that you just want to keep tasting and tasting.

HACIENDA PANCHO VILLA • *Malcolm*

164 Pleasant Street, Brunswick, ME 04011; (207) 729-0029

As we sat munching on a basket of piping hot corn tortilla chips, still shimmering from the oil bath they had received only moments before, we tried to figure out why the back booths in this restaurant felt exactly like being in Mexico. Hacienda Pancho Villa's decor doesn't go completely over the top. The waitstaff aren't wearing holsters filled with hot sauce, and there are no gigantic luchadores anywhere or pinatas hanging from the ceiling. It might be this very sparseness that makes the place feel so much like a family restaurant south of the border. There are a few sombreros and a few pieces of talavera pottery on one wall; another is filled with a gallery of the kind of faux-antique black-and-white portraits of Pancho Villa that you find in tourist traps up and down the Pacific Coast. The concrete walls are textured and grooved as if by trowel-wielding albanile and are painted a bright rusty orange that casts all the customers in a lovely, warm light. Though there were a few other people in the dining room at lunchtime, the waitress made sure to warmly greet each person who came through the door, mostly in Spanish, even as she zoomed back and forth between the kitchen and her waiting tables. It felt good.

Jillian: Hacienda Pancho Villa is not a lonchería or a cocina economica, which are tiny, three- or four-table home-based businesses in which the specials change daily and are served by the silver-toothed women of the house. When you take your early meal at one of these, inevitably sweating into your steaming bowl of nose-to-tail soup, sipping your glass-bottle Coca-Cola through a straw, and swabbing yourself with dozens of single-ply napkins, you can sigh and say contentedly, "Ah, now this is authentic." But Hacienda Pancho Villa is very, very good.

After greedily munching our way through most of our chips and salsa (which may have come from a jar, though a fresh pico de gallo is available for just $2.99), we moved on to the enormous menu. There were a few surprises there, including an enchiladas con mole ($11.99), camerones a la diabla ($14.49), and a torta made with either chicken or carnitas ($8.49), alongside more standard Tex-Mex offerings, including a gigantic $16 Burrito Macho that the restaurant dares you to finish.

Because I wouldn't have time for a three-hour nap that day, I steered away from the burritos and tried the Tacos al Carbon combination plate ($13.49), selecting pastor as my taco filling. Minutes later, the waitress reappeared with a dinner plate the size of a truck tire, covered in refried beans, rice, three tacos, and scoops of guacamole and sour cream. The corn tortillas for the soft tacos were dipped in some sort of salsa roja prior to assembly, which added flavor but made them somewhat difficult to handle. The pork inside was delicious and well-seasoned with a few bits of crunchy skin and succulent fat, even if it didn't bear any resemblance to a typical pastor preparation. The lack of pineapple, orange, and achiote flavors made this pork preparation seem more like carnitas, but getting hung up on this minor detail didn't stop me from finishing all three tacos in just a few seconds. The giant pool of pinto bean refritos was excellent, oozing slowly over the warm plate and mixing well with the lightly seasoned rice and guacamole. Spice levels were low across the board, but a sidecar of pickled jalapeños perked up the flavors considerably.

Just as she does when overwhelmed with a large menu in Mexico, Jillian defaulted to an order of chicken fajitas ($9), served at half-size for the lunchtime crowd. A large sizzling cast-iron skillet overflowing with strips of marinated chicken, onion, and peppers, more beans, and more rice were ideal for folding into the warm flour tortillas that accompanied the dish.

Jillian: Ordering fajitas is the lunchtime equivalent of taking your cousin to the prom. You know exactly what you're getting, you'll have a few laughs, you won't get groped slow dancing to "Wonderful Tonight," and you'll be home by eleven. And a safe choice isn't always a bad thing. My plate of fajitas arrived sizzling hot, accompanied by a brave little tortilla warmer that was red, plastic, and practically smiling. The refried beans on the side, a soupy slurry, blended into the yellow rice. I was pleased with my order; nobody cried in the bathroom, drank a pint of Southern Comfort, or slept in a sequined dress alone on a beach. Not that that ever happened to me.

We sipped $2.50 bottles of Corona, a beer that my dad would have teased us for ordering, particularly because Hacienda Pancho Villa has a wide selection of other Mexican varieties available. Two-dollar beer is two-dollar beer, though, and we joked that for him, value often trumped quality when it came to beer drinking. If paying two dollars for a Corona instead of four dollars for a Sol was a little bit less authentic, then so be it.

The notion of "authenticity" gets thrown around a lot, particularly when it comes to Mexican restaurants or Latin American dishes. Americans in general seem to have agreed to equate "authenticity" with "quality," and we use the terms almost interchangeably. For a Mexican restaurant to be good, it had better be authentic. Hacienda Pancho Villa challenges this equation somewhat. The food is absolutely, unquestionably authentic and exactly like meals we have enjoyed hundreds of times in family restaurants in Mexico.

That's not to say that Hacienda Pancho Villa is necessarily the best Mexican restaurant in the Brunswick environs. Other Mexican restaurants in the area sometimes use better ingredients, preparing Mexican food in a studied, intellectual way that can often taste better even if it isn't quite as "authentic." Hacienda Pancho Villa is preparing honest Mexican food the way it is prepared in Mexico, not in the way a classically trained chef with a passionate interest in New Mexican cooking might prepare it. Thus, there is unquestionably no more authentic Mexican cuisine than that being served at Hacienda Pancho Villa anywhere nearby, even if there may technically be better food elsewhere.

Jillian: I ate this meal a thousand times in Mexico, at a restaurant called La Parilla that was nestled within a palapa in a touristy pueblo where we'd go to swim. In fact, fajitas were the first thing I ordered on the day we arrived there, and I remember thinking that I'd get more adventurous in the future and that we must have chosen a very silly eating establishment because we were green foreigners. Restaurants like La Parilla were so much more common in Mexico than we knew then. And so it was comforting and delightfully surprising to find this totally unassuming place on Route 1 in Brunswick.

When I am craving Mexican food, it's not because I have a sudden hankering for melted cheese and tequila. Okay, sometimes. Usually, it's because I want to be in Mexico, and in this way, Hacienda Pancho Villa delivers a better experience than any other Mexican restaurant we have tried in Maine. As we sat waiting for our check, a middle-aged man came in with his brother (wearing a black cowboy hat) and a young, pigtailed daughter. They spoke in rapid-fire, Northern-style Spanish to the lone waitress and whoever was manning the kitchen, explaining that the daughter, born in the United States, spoke only English. The waitress teased the girl good-naturedly, in the easy, casual way that many Mexicans seem to adopt with children, and the little girl smiled and laughed. After they took an order to go, the waitress returned to our table, offering a "gracias" of her own to our repeated "thanks" and telling us about the party she was planning with her three children, complete with pinata. For just a moment we felt like family, and it's this kind of warmth and atmosphere that will carry us back to Hacienda Pancho Villa the next time we long to be in Mexico.

EL EL FRIJOLES • *Jillian*
41 Caterpillar Hill Road (Route 15), Sargentville, ME 04673; (207) 359-2486; elelfrijoles.com

We drove about 50 miles to have lunch in a barn. On a desolate-feeling peninsula that is empty of apparent industry or populace, where great swaths of blueberry barrens are studded with glacial erratic boulders as if ancient giants are emerging from the mantle, you will find a big barn with a bright yellow sign and an interior filled with happiness.

El El Frijoles represents everything we love about Maine. Owners Michele Levesque and Michael Rossney met in the Bay Area, arguably ground zero for Mexican food in the United States, and now run a Mexican restaurant in Sargentville, on the Blue Hill peninsula. It's in the middle of nowhere and the center of the universe. That's how it is when you find where you are supposed to be, even if it is not where you planned or expected to land. We were knee-deep in interesting conversation before we knew what was happening, learning their backstories, which only made the tacos more delicious.

Michele and Michael are witty, effusive, and talented. From the loteria logo to the clever name, they are keeping it light, making Mission-style Mexican on a road through pastoral Maine. And it's their humor and self-awareness as much as their excellent food that we appreciate and admire. Michael acts as host and auctioneer, salesman, huckster, showman, and independent politician, a genuinely nice guy who ran a photography shop and continues to work in that medium. Michele was a private middle-school art teacher with a storied history in kitchens. They didn't want to linger too long, to burn out or become aging hipster parents, all style and lacking in substance, so they moved back East, where his family lived

and hers soon followed, and now they're raising a kid of their own among the colorful chaos. There are sculptures and picnic tables at the edge of the woods, and a screened-in shed with five or six tables and Ikea high chairs. The decor is taqueria casual without being kitschy or obvious. It all somehow looks like it should be there, an extension of their experience, home, and personalities.

Malcolm: As with many people drawn to Maine, Michele and Michael are pioneers. They didn't arrive in the area intent on finding work; instead, they made it. It's easy to imagine them in their gigantic, then-unrenovated, unused barn, wondering what to do next, referring to El El Frijoles (get it?) only in the abstract at first. A love for California-style Mexican and the urging of relatives led them to open the restaurant, which quickly became the only place in town to eat out and the center of the local social community.

We sampled a side of their famous organic black beans, which were creamy with a whisper of smoky sweetness. We tried their corn chip triangles with four fresh salsas, carnitas, and one of the day's specials, a crab-meat quesadilla. I also couldn't resist trying a spoonful of El El Frijoles' rajas y papas—strips of wilted poblano pepper and chunks of toothsome red potato in a cream sauce with just enough heat—a very satisfying vegetarian option and one of my favorites.

Malcolm: In addition to the couple's homemade salsas, which are all outstanding, the pork carnitas tacos ($8.95) were a standout. Slow-simmered all day in a mix of spices and studded with a few chiles japoneses, the pork imparted big punches of flavor while staying succulent and moist. A light bit of crunch from the cabbage slaw, cool guacamole, and a squeeze of crema were enough to balance the tacos perfectly. The pork is served on a bed of three made-to-order corn tortillas. If I had to stretch to find a criticism, it might be that the tortillas could have used another moment or two on the griddle, but I am so falling-down overjoyed that a Mexican restaurant in Maine is finally (FINALLY!) taking the time to press tortillas to order that such a criticism hardly makes sense at all. There's nothing like freshly made corn tortillas. Nothing in the whole world. It may add a second to a restaurant's prep time, but it's the single most important step in great Mexican cooking, and Michele knows it.

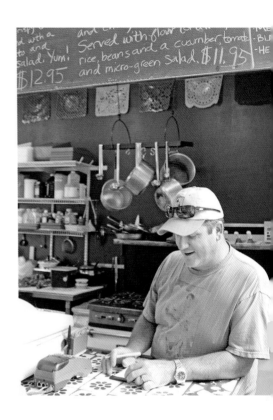

The crab quesadilla ($12.95), a menu item I would not ordinarily think to order, was incredible, and it got better with every bite. The meat was sweet and complemented by creamy cheese and a scoop of guacamole, not overwhelming, overspiced, or in any way wrong. Instead of "Let's jam up a perfectly nice and melty tasty tortilla with crab, of all things, because, you know, it's Maine and we have some lying around," the Deer Isle fresh-caught crabmeat is there because it's beautiful and enhances the dish. If it's on special when you visit, get it. And get it with an agua fresca. Mine was lime/mint, the most hydrating combination of fruit and herbs that exists, though Malcolm's blackberry version was also outstanding.

This is not Tex-Mex, New Mex-Mex, or the Yucatecan food I am most familiar with. Michele makes her own corn tortillas, thick and earthy, and fills them with wonderful, aromatic things like stewed meats and grilled veggies. It's all very accessible and simple, not to mention handmade, slow-cooked, and locally sourced. Though I've never had a Mission-style burrito anywhere near the Mission, it's just what I would expect, and it feels exactly right.

Malcolm: I think that's the area in which El El Frijoles most excels. For whatever reason, taquerias with a focus on simplicity and someone's notion of "authenticity" continue to be trendy and multiply, with new outposts of Mexican street food opening around the state. The mistake many seem to make, however, is that classic taqueria fare is only deceptively simple. Someone's vacation photo of seared meat piled on a tortilla with a few onions, a few snips of cilantro, and a squeeze of lime may seem like the simplest thing in the world, but a few tastes of most

local pseudo-taquerias' wet, sloppy, run-together flavors will prove that it's harder to get right than many people think. Mexican taqueria cooking relies on careful balance and on coaxing massive amounts of flavor from just a few humble ingredients. It's easy to make everything taste like cumin (for days) or to completely obliterate a customer's mouth with chiles. It's much more difficult to cook elegantly and with restraint. El El Frijoles manages both admirably.

The couple works with local fishers and farmers. The organic black beans, for example, are grown just for them on a nearby farm that never imagined they'd be turning part of their crop over to growing black beans.

If you love what El El Frijoles is doing, you can get on their winter supper club mailing list and enjoy whimsical, slightly dressed-up theme dinners during the long cold months. "The Supper Club reservations fill up fast," Michael explained. "I send the email out announcing the supper, and the phone starts ringing immediately."

Michele and Michael are making out-of-context fare that somehow feels totally authentic—as in true to themselves and sincere, the thing itself and not the idea of the thing. Maine needs more restaurateurs like them—people who grew up nearby and feel compelled to come back and cook, or people from away who can't seem to leave—good folks making good food and art while making the neighborhood a better place. El El Frijoles is well worth the time it might take you to get there.

Meals to Enjoy on Long Days and Cool Nights

This is the time to dust off the wicker chairs and funky floral pillows and bring the grill out of the shed. We string lights across the yard and set out candles in tall, steel lanterns. It is a wonder to be outside in the dark under a great canopy of stars. The night in Maine is darker than in other places and still seems full of mystery. As the sun sets, eat dinner outside and breathe in air that is sweet with fresh-cut grass. There are meals that just taste better when you're sitting above a valley, where eagles soar.

- Fried Oyster Po' Boy Sandwiches with Spicy Remoulade
- Haddock Ragout with Mussels, Bacon, and Peas
- Broccoli Rabe, Spicy Sausage, and Ricotta on Garlic-Rubbed Bread

Fried Oyster Po' Boy Sandwiches with Spicy Remoulade • *Jillian*

Makes 2 sandwiches

My first visit to New Orleans was on my twenty-something birthday. Malcolm and I were living in New York and in the process of getting back together after an awful/awesome summer apart. He wanted to impress me, and so he surprised me with a weekend stay at a fancy New Orleans hotel where we could fill the jetted tub with soap bubbles and drink champagne on the balcony. We strolled in the Garden District, made plans to live in a storied house, drank hurricanes and French 75s in the French Quarter, listened to jazz in the dark, danced in the streets, rode the trolley, visited the cemetery, and did all the other things you do on a first visit to that haunted, sinking city. We ate étouffée followed by celebratory Bananas Foster and got into a terrible fight for reasons I can't quite remember. It was a marvelous, fabulous, dramatic, romantic adventure. We ate beignets at the airport with one last tipple before boarding our plane home. Oh, but we never got around to ordering po' boys. The first time I had one of those was a different trip altogether.

On that occasion we were staying with Malcolm's parents at their house in Florida's panhandle. It was one of those great little Southern houses that have been known to disappear into the swampy earth. It was charming, lovely,

INGREDIENTS

For the remoulade:

1¼ cup mayonnaise

1 tablespoon Dijon mustard

1 tablespoon capers

1 tablespoon pickle juice

1 teaspoon prepared horseradish

1 teaspoon ground mustard seeds

1 garlic clove, smashed

⅛ teaspoon paprika

⅛ teaspoon cayenne pepper

½ teaspoon Crystal brand hot sauce

For the oysters:

12–16 shucked oysters

1 cup, plus 1 tablespoon milk

2 eggs, lightly beaten

1 tablespoon water

Continued on page 134

INGREDIENTS

Continued from page 133

½ teaspoon white vinegar

1 cup all-purpose flour

½ cup cornmeal

1 teaspoon kosher salt

½ teaspoon ground black pepper

⅛ teaspoon cayenne

Vegetable oil

2 hoagie rolls

Mixed lettuce greens

Lemon wedges

and warm. Mostly, we sat by the pool, watched the dogs frolic on the lawn, sipped Bloody Marys, and read and ate and ate. One afternoon we picked up a Santa-sized sack of oysters from a roadhouse. Malcolm's dad immediately used the knife on his hip to open one, wordlessly daring me to eat it. I swallowed the slimy bivalve and asked for another, quivering. We went on to have many dozens of Gulf oysters on that vacation, and by the time I was done, I think I liked them best raw, with Saltines and lots of hot sauce.

But a fried oyster is a truly splendid thing. You use cornmeal and flour to achieve a crunchy exterior, and thus coated and cooked in very hot oil, the slippery shellfish becomes creamy and rich. You need a roll that is soft with a slight crunch to its crust.

This particular remoulade is awfully good. I love whipping a bunch of salty, spicy, strong condiments in mayo and slathering the end result on everything. You could dip your shoes in this stuff. I buy already-shucked oysters from our local fish market. Po' boys are a perfect way to celebrate nothing and everything. And when you want somebody else to do the prep work for you, try Po' Boy and Pickles Restaurant on Forest Avenue in Portland. (See our review in the "May" chapter.)

Method

For the remoulade:

1. Whip all the ingredients together in a food processor and chill for at least an hour before serving.

For the oysters:

1. Drain the shucked oysters before soaking them in 1 cup of milk for 15 minutes and draining. Set aside.

2. Meanwhile, in a medium-sized bowl, combine the eggs, the tablespoon of milk, the water, and the vinegar.

3. In a large brown bag, combine the flour, the cornmeal, the salt, the pepper, and the cayenne.

4. In a medium-sized, heavy-bottomed pot over medium-high heat, heat the vegetable oil. Add the drained oysters to the liquid mixture. Use a fork to transfer the coated oysters to the bag of dry ingredients and shake.

5. When the oil has reached 360°F, carefully submerge 4 or 5 oysters in the hot oil. Do not overcrowd. Fry for 3 minutes, turning once. Drain on a paper bag or paper towels. Continue cooking the oysters in batches until all are done.

To serve, split open the hoagie rolls and spread both sides with the remoulade. Add 6 oysters to each roll and cover with a layer of lettuce. Serve with a squeeze of lemon.

Haddock Ragout with Mussels, Bacon, and Peas • *Jillian*

Serves 4—6

This is the consummate one-pot New England supper for serving the crowd at a party or community dinner. Salty, fatty, smoky bacon pairs so well with sweet fresh peas, briny mussels, and flaky haddock. It's not heavy like a stew, which makes it a good choice for this time of year, but it is warm and satisfying, because we all know that late spring and early summer nights in Maine can pack a chill, and for the love of everything, we are not turning on the heat in June. This ragout is quick, fresh, clean, and cozy, and I dare say this is what I'm making for dinner tonight.

Method

1. Season the haddock and set aside.

2. Combine the bacon, the olive oil, and the water in a saucepan and bring to a simmer over medium heat. Cover and cook for about 8 minutes.

3. Add the chicken broth, the shallots, the garlic, and the thyme and bring to a boil.

4. Add the mussels, cover, and cook until they open. Immediately remove the pot from the heat and remove the mussels. Return any juices from the mussels to the pan. Set the mussels aside.

5. Add the wine to the pan and bring to a simmer. Add the seasoned haddock and the peas. Cover, turn down the heat, and let cook for about 7 minutes or until the fish is firm and opaque.

6. While the fish is cooking, shell the mussels and rinse them well under tap water.

7. Adjust the seasoning of the ragout if needed. Stir in the mussels, the butter, and the parsley. Serve in shallow soup bowls with crusty, buttered bread.

INGREDIENTS

1½ pounds haddock, cut into chunks

¼ pound thick-cut bacon, cut into thin strips

1 tablespoon olive oil

2 tablespoons water

¼ cup minced shallots

1 huge garlic clove, minced

2 thyme sprigs

1½ pounds mussels

½ cup white wine

2 cups chicken broth

1 cup frozen peas

2 tablespoons unsalted butter

2 tablespoons parsley (I use the curly kind)

Salt and pepper

Crusty bread (optional)

Broccoli Rabe, Spicy Sausage, and Ricotta on Garlic-Rubbed Bread • *Malcolm*

Serves 2

INGREDIENTS

1 head broccoli rabe

2 links spicy Italian sausage

3 tablespoons olive oil

3 cloves garlic, 2 thinly sliced, 1 halved

Red pepper flakes

1 cup ricotta

¼ cup whole milk

Toasted slices of crusty bread

Kosher salt and freshly ground pepper

Parsley

Squeeze of lemon

In this dish, the creamy ricotta cools the heat of the sausage, and the broccoli rabe falls somewhere between healthy and heavy. In short, this is a perfect dinner for early summer. Eat this one outside on the patio.

Method

1. In a large pot of salted, boiling water, blanch the broccoli rabe, about 5 minutes. Drain in a colander.

2. Meanwhile, in a deep skillet, cook the sausages in a little olive oil and remove them to a plate. Add a little more olive oil to the same pan over medium heat, and infuse with the sliced garlic cloves and the red pepper flakes. Add the broccoli rabe to the infused oil and sauté very quickly, about a minute.

3. In a small bowl, combine the ricotta and the milk, season with the salt and pepper, and drizzle in a little olive oil.

4. Slice the bread. Rub each slice with the halved garlic clove, and spread the ricotta mixture on top. Squeeze a little lemon juice over the broccoli rabe, and garnish the ricotta-covered bread with parsley. Serve with sausages.

JULY

For our first Fourth of July back in the States after four years in Mexico, we jumped on the Vespa in search of a rocky coast, a lobster roll, and leafy green, breezy, shaded roads. We found our heart's desire in lovely Cape Elizabeth and fell madly in love with America again. Maine is perfect on this day, which may be why the Fourth has always been Malcolm's favorite holiday. The weather is usually hot and sticky. Everything is abundant. Cold beer and sweet lobster are abundant, and fireworks rise and fall through the pine-scented night over the Damariscotta River—a perfect venue to cheer for the land of liberty—and in a hundred towns across Maine.

Our Independence Day menu is a little more daring than the traditional fare of hot dogs, hamburgers, potato chips, macaroni salad, and ketchup, but only by a smidge. We keep it simple, as always, so the focus can be on friends, kids splashing in the kiddie pool, and the sparklers we wave in the long midsummer twilight.

Successful cooking on the Fourth of July needs only to meet a few requirements: Do not heat up the kitchen too much; turn out enough food to satisfy a crowd; and allow ample time for socializing with your guests.

Fourth of July Menu
- Lemon Meringue Jello Shots
- Tomato Pie
- Orecchiette with Yellow Squash, Corn, and Bacon
- Manchego Lamb Burgers with Fried Potato Chive Cakes
- Fourth of July Ice Cream Pie

Lemon Meringue Jello Shots • *Jillian*

Serves 6

I'm somebody's mother now, so I'm not supposed to do Jello shots. I'm somebody's mother, so I go to bed at 10 o'clock, wear sensible shoes, and never dance in fountains anymore. These are the rules of adulthood that are only occasionally meant to be broken.

Spending time with college friends is one of the best excuses there is for acting like a kid again, once the actual kids are in bed asleep. And nothing says summer and silly and reckless abandon quite like jellified alcohol. I recommend trying these Lemon Meringue Jello Shots as soon as you possibly can. What time do you get off work? What are you doing right now? They are prettier than a faceted topaz, twice as intoxicating, and totally easy to make.

Method

1. Prepare the Jello according to the package directions, replacing half of the cold water with vodka.

2. Cut each lemon in half lengthwise. Use a paring knife to trace carefully around the white perimeter and remove the fruit without puncturing the peel. Discard the fruit. Use a muffin tin to stabilize the halves and fill to the brim with the liquid Jello/vodka mixture. Let set overnight in the refrigerator.

3. Slice the lemons into wedges (thirds) with a sharp knife, cut side down. Serve in the rind, with plenty of snacks and a designated driver!

INGREDIENTS

A 3-ounce package of lemon-flavored Jello

1 cup Whipped Cream–flavored vodka

1 cup cold water

6 lemons

Tomato Pie • *Jillian*

Recipe reprinted with permission from *RSVP: An Invitation to Maine Cooking*, by the Junior League of Portland, Maine

Serves 8

When does a vintage recipe require revision or reimagination, and when is it perfect as is? This is the question I asked myself as I unpacked the pie my mother-in-law made on Sunday. We had spent a gorgeous afternoon in Rockland—strolling down Main Street, popping into shops and galleries, having a fine, fried seafood lunch at a sidewalk café—and were piling a sleeping babe into the car when my mother-in-law handed me a foil-wrapped pie with instructions to bake until brown and bubbling. I was skeptical. A tomato pie made with mayonnaise and cheese? It sounded old-fashioned at best, and at worst inedible. She's a wonderful cook, and I trust her taste, but I had reservations. When I learned the recipe had come directly from the "RSVP cookbook," though, it all became suddenly clear.

RSVP: An Invitation to Maine Cooking was published in 1982, and its recipes reflect the transcendent spirit of that age. It's an instruction manual for elegant ladies putting on luncheons for one another, complete with menu plans and accompanying cocktails. There are various and sundry, somewhat dated but entirely delicious ideas here. The Mustard Ring, for example, which falls under the "Salad" heading, contains dry mustard as well as gelatin, turmeric, and whipping cream. This is garnished with greens and served with fresh fruit or coleslaw.

If I were to update and amend the Tomato Pie, I might recommend seeding or squeezing some of the liquid from the tomatoes. But we did

INGREDIENTS

For the crust:

1 cup all-purpose flour

½ teaspoon salt

¼ teaspoon granulated sugar

⅛ cup shredded cheddar cheese or grated Parmesan cheese

1 cup unsalted butter

Squeeze of lemon juice

½ to 1½ tablespoons cold water

For the filling:

4 to 5 ripe tomatoes

Salt, pepper, basil, and chives, to taste

1 cup mayonnaise

1 cup shredded Cheddar cheese

not. We followed the instructions as typed by Mary Louise Meyer Dyer (Mrs. Ralph). I wonder if Ralph himself ever enjoyed the pie on a hot summer Saturday or if his missus only made it for company—say, when the girls came over to play cards and drink a perspiring pitcher of daiquiris. I might consider using a different cheese, like gruyère, or adding a couple of strips of bacon. While the notion of hot mayonnaise is still upsetting to me, I would be lying if I said I didn't enjoy it. The pie is a bit unkempt at its molten core, and I would advise allowing it to cool a bit before serving.

Adapt as you see fit, but I say make it according to the ladies of the Junior League of Portland.

Method

For the crust:

1. Preheat the oven to 350°F. In a bowl, sift the flour, salt, and sugar together. Stir in the cheese. With a pastry blender, work in the butter. Add the lemon juice and gradually blend in the water until the mixture holds together.

2. Gather the dough into a ball. Roll out on a floured surface and place in a 9-inch pie plate. Crimp the edges of the dough.

For the filling:

1. Peel and slice the tomatoes. Layer the tomatoes in the pie crust and sprinkle the herbs on top of each layer.

2. Combine the mayonnaise and cheese and spread on the top layer of the tomatoes. Bake for 35 to 45 minutes. Cool on a wire rack before serving.

NOTE: *It is acceptable, and even encouraged, to use a premade pie crust.*

Orecchiette with Yellow Squash, Corn, and Bacon • *Jillian*
Serves 4

It was the summer before seventh grade. I had just made my Clinton Town Hall stage debut as Moth in a professional production of *A Midsummer Night's Dream.* I had a crush on blond Lysander and longed to be as elegant as the dancer who played Titania. After the last performance, a cast party was held at a house on High Street in the lavender garden. I had never seen anything so lovely. The grand old house was white and gauzy with its doors flung open to the outside. Effortless art was everywhere—so many rich, beautiful objects, living together, surrounding lucky, lovely people. Most players/revelers were already outside, since we were all immersed sylvan creatures after months of rehearsals and a week of performing Shakespeare's green world tale of confusion. I loved everything about this sparkling, silver night.

This pasta dish is like that night, perfect for an outdoor gathering of friends when all the produce is gorgeous and only requires the heat from the pasta, salt, and fat from the bacon and cheese, and the acidity of the lemon. It cooks in its own juices—simple, elegant, magical.

Method

1. In a bowl, sprinkle the salt on the grated squash and toss. Let sit for approximately 20 minutes in a strainer while prepping the other ingredients.

2. In a large skillet over medium-high heat, cook the bacon and smashed garlic cloves until the fat has rendered and the bacon is crisp. Discard the garlic (optional).

3. Bring a large pot of salted water to a boil; cook the pasta until it's al dente. Drain, but not thoroughly, and return the pasta to the pot.

4. Squeeze the squash to remove any excess liquid and combine it with the pasta. Incorporate the corn, basil, shallot, bacon, and olive oil. Toss with the Asiago cheese and ground pepper. Squeeze a little lemon over the top before serving.

INGREDIENTS

1 teaspoon kosher salt

1 large yellow squash grated into a bowl

4 strips thick-cut bacon, diced before cooking

2 cloves garlic, smashed

½ pound orecchiette

2 ears of corn, kernels removed from the cob

1 cup roughly chopped basil

½ shallot, minced

2 tablespoons olive oil

Asiago cheese

Freshly ground pepper

Lemon

LAMB BURGER INSPIRATION FROM MCDONALD'S?

To give this burger a little extra crunch, I include a quick hash brown layer, an idea I have become obsessed with since I first read Internet rumblings about the McDonald's "10:25" burger, which you can only get by visiting a McDonald's drive-through when breakfast transitions into lunch. During this magical 5- to 10-minute window at the window, it becomes possible to order breakfast and lunch, allowing you to mix and match components from a Quarter Pounder and an Egg McMuffin. While the idea of eating one of those lifeless little McDonald's white egg discs on a burger doesn't seem too appealing, the notion of a crispy hash brown layer seemed like something I urgently wanted to replicate at home.

Manchego Lamb Burgers with Fried Potato Chive Cakes • *Malcolm*

Makes 3 to 4 burgers

INGREDIENTS

1 large russet potato, peeled and grated

1 teaspoon kosher salt

½ teaspoon pepper

2 tablespoons chives, chopped

Vegetable oil

12 ounces ground lamb

4 ounces ground pork

3 cloves garlic, minced

4 slices Spanish Manchego cheese

1 teaspoon parsley, finely chopped

3 tablespoons mayonnaise

2 teaspoons dijon mustard

4 leaves of butter lettuce

4 onion rolls

I've been having a love affair with my crumbling grill. It's an old three-burner inherited Brinkmann that, even at its newest and best, was a $200 grill styled to look like a $600 model. It leaks gas. The electric ignition is shot, requiring the operator of the grill to frantically fling lit wooden kitchen matches at the open grill top in order to ignite it. The gas line to the side burner is dangling under the shelf. The heat dispersion panels are rusted out and falling into the bottom of the grill. To get the third burner to light, you have to make whooshing-to-the-left motions with your hands, then close the lid and hope for the best. But I'll be damned if it doesn't still work, cranking out consistent, even-enough 650°F temperatures that put one hell of a sear on anything you throw at (on) it.

Today I made cheeseburgers using ground lamb that boldly proclaimed its "Raised in the USA" status. The domestic origin did seem to drive down the per-pound cost, which is great in the case of lamb burgers, because nobody wants to grind up a beautiful $50 Australian lamb shoulder to make burgers. Domestic lamb also seems to have a slightly stronger "lamb" flavor, which I like in a burger to which we are going to be adding lots of other flavors. I make these burgers thicker than I would a beef burger, about 5 or 6 ounces per patty, because of lamb's tendency to dry out on a grill. A thicker patty will ensure that our burgers stay moist and juicy.

Method

1. Soak the grated potatoes in water for a few minutes to rinse off any excess starch. Drain. Toss with the salt, pepper, and chives. In a large frying pan, heat the oil over high heat. Drop spoonfuls of the potato mixture into the pan and flatten with a spatula into patties. Cook until very brown on both sides, about 6 minutes total. Drain on paper towels.

2. Combine lamb, pork, and parsley in a large bowl, and mix well. Form the ground meat mixture into 3 or 4 thick patties. Cook over high heat on a grill or in a frying pan, turning occasionally, about 3 to 4 minutes per side. Top with the sliced cheese and cover until the cheese melts. Remove from the heat and let the burgers rest while you assemble the other ingredients.

3. In a small bowl, combine the mayonnaise and dijon mustard.

4. Split an onion roll, and toast if desired. Place a leaf of lettuce on the bottom bun, followed by the grilled lamb burger. Top with a fried potato chive cake and about a teaspoon of the dijon mixture. Serve immediately.

Fourth of July Ice Cream Pie • *Jillian*

Serves 8

Celebrate Independence Day the way our forefathers intended, with cake-flavored ice cream and syrupy fruit. Berries are abundant, ripe, and tart this time of year and make perfect complements to the sweet dairy and the crumbly graham cracker crust of this red, white, and blue frozen confection. I wish you all a wonderful, safe, gleefully excessive Fourth. Have a blast and eat pie until you feel like bursting.

Method

1. Soften the ice cream on the counter. Meanwhile, bring the blueberries, sugar, and water to a boil. Turn down to a simmer and reduce the fruit, about 5 minutes, stirring occasionally. Add the lemon juice and allow the mixture to cool.

2. Spread the ice cream into the pie crust with a rubber spatula and freeze. When the blueberries cool, spread them over the ice cream and place the pie back in the freezer, about 3 hours. Top with the whipped cream, fresh strawberries, and raspberries, and serve.

INGREDIENTS

3 cups strawberry ice cream, softened

2 cups blueberries

¼ cup granulated sugar

¼ cup water

1 teaspoon fresh lemon juice

1 graham cracker pie crust

Whipped cream

Strawberries and raspberries, for garnish

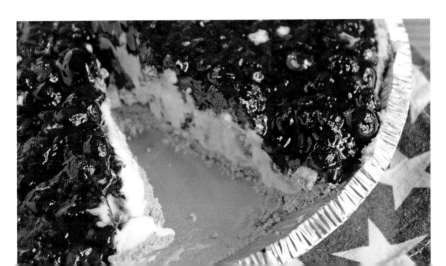

SEASONAL INGREDIENT: LOBSTER
Featuring recipes for Lobster Tom Kha / Warm Maine Lobster Dip / Lobster Fra Diavolo/ Lobster Macaroni and Cheese

Lobster Tom Kha • *Jillian*
Serves 6

INGREDIENTS

2 tablespoons Thai red curry paste

A 14-ounce can lite coconut milk

2 cups vegetable stock

2 stalks lemongrass, chopped into 4-inch pieces and pounded flat

Two 1¼-pound lobsters, steamed 6 minutes, shelled and cut into bite-size pieces

1 to 2 tablespoon(s) fish sauce

1 teaspoon granulated sugar

2 tablespoons lime juice

4 ounces shiitake mushrooms, roughly chopped

Cilantro, for garnish

Rice noodles (optional), cooked according to package directions and tossed with a bit of vegetable oil

The recipes I consulted for making tom kha coconut soup (all of which were for versions containing gai, or chicken) called for galangal and kaffir lime leaves, neither of which I could find locally. So I made do with a little pot of prepackaged Thai red curry paste made by Thai Kitchen, which contains both, as well as garlic and chile. It turns the soup a satisfying orange-red and adds a bit of heat. I could and perhaps should have used the lobster shells to make a rich stock, but the soup didn't suffer much. Adding nam pla (fish sauce) imparts that certain something inherent in Asian cuisine. Also, slowly warming the stock and coconut milk with the aromatics helps deepen the flavor. I undercooked the lobster by maybe a minute so that it wouldn't get gummy when I later added it to the soup. This soup requires a bit of tasting and adjusting of seasonings as you go. I use "lite" coconut milk because the full-fat version freaks me out.

Whenever I get tom kha at my favorite Thai place, it is full of oddly buoyant mushrooms that bob and float and somersault. In this recipe I used sliced shiitakes, which add a good earthiness. And finally, noodles! Hooray, noodles. About the lemongrass: I used a meat tenderizer to smash it, which was both fun and fragrant.

Method

1. In a large soup pot over low heat, whisk the red curry paste into the coconut milk and vegetable stock. Add the lemongrass, and let the mixture steep while you prepare the lobster. Turn up the heat, an bring the soup to a boil. Add the fish sauce, sugar, and lime juice, tasting and adjusting seasoning if necessary. Add the mushrooms and reduce the heat to low. Add the lobster meat and cook until just warmed through, about one minute more.

2. Garnish with cilantro. Serve with rice noodles if using them.

Warm Maine Lobster Dip • *Malcolm*

As an appetizer, serves 4–6

There's a delightful 1950s vibe about this dish, a certain something that makes me want to put on a ruffled apron with a pair of high heels, pop a Benzedrine, and wait patiently for my husband to get home to discipline the children. And what is that something? It's cream cheese—specifically, cream cheese mixed with seafood and served hot.

I know, I know. It's hardly haute cuisine. The first time I ordered it, at the sea-level dining room of **Cook's Lobster House** on Bailey Island, it was mainly out of morbid curiosity. The term "lobster dip" on its own isn't terrifically appealing, but nor does it sound like something that could be truly bad. Their version is served in a bread bowl, and like most things at Cook's, is excellent exactly half the time you order it. That first batch was a winner, a combination of succulent Maine lobster swimming in a thick cream sauce that bubbled and dripped over the edges of a crusty bread, which we tore apart and hungrily devoured.

It wasn't until my second exposure to this dish, served to me by a dear friend well-versed in classic Maine cooking, that the pieces began to fall into place. "Cream cheese," he explained, absentmindedly flipping a beer cap onto the kitchen counter with a heavily tattooed hand. "It's a huge pan of lobster and cream cheese."

INGREDIENTS

Two 1½-pound live Maine lobsters

16 ounces cream cheese, softened

2 shallots, minced

1 clove garlic, minced

1 tablespoon horseradish

1 tablespoon Worcestershire sauce

⅛ teaspoon cayenne

1 teaspoon Sriracha or other hot sauce

Salt and pepper, to taste

I'm ordinarily not crazy about using lobster as an ingredient, preferring to enjoy it naked and on its own. In this case, though, a 13-inch by 9-inch glass baking dish of the stuff, along with an entire sliced baguette, vanished in minutes, leaving the four of us standing around his midcoast kitchen mopping the inside of the tray with any last scraps of bread we could find.

We've tweaked the recipe slightly, adding a tiny bit of crunch and warm background heat while still allowing the flavor of the lobster to be the focus. The hot sauce adds a touch of light pink color and spice, but by all means, you can leave it out. It's a great way to stretch the meat from just a few lobsters into enough food to serve with a loaf of bread at your next swingin' party.

Method

1. In a large stockpot, bring an inch of salted water to a boil. Add the lobster and steam, covered, until the shells are deep red, about 10 minutes. If the pot boils over, leave the lid off a crack to allow some steam to escape. Let the lobster cool, then crack the shells and remove the lobster meat, including the tails, claws, and knuckles. Tear or chop the lobster meat into small pieces, and set aside.

2. In a small bowl, combine the cream cheese, shallots, garlic, horse-radish, Worcestershire, cayenne, Sriracha, salt, and pepper. Add the lobster meat and mix well to combine. Transfer to a glass baking dish and refrigerate for at least 2 hours.

3. Preheat the oven to 375°F. Cook uncovered about 25 minutes or until the lobster dip is hot and bubbly. Serve with bread, crackers, vegetables, or right off your finger.

Lobster Fra Diavolo • *Jillian*

Serves 2

The landed value of Maine's lobster harvest was $350 million in 2012. The groundfisheries are gasping; shrimp are on the ropes; scallops and urchins have been overfished; green crabs, warm-water invaders, are decimating the clam flats. Without King Lobster, it seems, Maine's outport coastal villages would shrivel and die. All hail *Homarus americanus*; long may he crawl. Have we artificially inflated the pleasure we take in eating such an ugly bug? Not on your life. You may have heard the story about how the Maine State Prison was at one time enjoined from feeding lobster more than a few times each week to the poor prisoners. Apparently, meal after meal of steamed, succulent lobster was considered inhumane treatment. Silly humans. Let's dispense with economics and history and eat. But how shall we prepare our favorite local delicacy?

We've steamed lobster, of course, and served it straight up with drawn butter, corn on the cob, clams, and a baguette for numerous dinner parties. Last Labor Day, we baked them in the ground. This was only a partial success culinarily, but as an event, a performance piece, it was quite a sight to behold. We've made lobster clubs, a lobster dip, and Maine lobster rolls complete with homemade buns.

For a special evening's feast for two, however, we went with Lobster Fra Diavolo. Fra Diavolo is Italian for "Brother Devil" and refers to one of the ways in which medieval monks self-flagellated during Lent. Really, though, it just means "spicy bits all up in yo' mouth."

INGREDIENTS

¼ cup extra-virgin olive oil

1½-pound lobster, tail cut into 4 pieces, claws cracked, knuckles separated from body

¼ cup all-purpose flour

1 teaspoon crushed red pepper flakes

1 teaspoon dried oregano

3 cloves garlic, finely chopped

1 tablespoon tomato paste

¼ cup white wine

½ cup fish stock

14-ounce can whole peeled tomatoes in juice

1 bay leaf

Kosher salt and freshly ground black pepper, to taste

½ pound angel hair pasta, cooked

1 tablespoon chopped parsley

This dish turned out to be magic for a number of reasons. You know how sometimes the sauce and pasta remain separate and distinct, but occasionally they unify with a harmonious and mystical alchemy? This was most definitely a case of the latter. It was buttery (though there was no butter) and creamy without any cream.

The lobster is sweet, which complements the heat, and the angel hair is appropriately delicate. The sauce seeps into the lobster, and the lobster imparts its flavor to the sauce. It's symbiotic like that, and wonderfully, artfully messy. You're enjoying this marvelous pasta with lots of hunks of garlic and spice, and then you have to dig in with your hands to crack open the shell to access the meat. And there's red sauce on your face and wine glass and napkin and somehow your ear, and you are so incredibly happy and grateful for this dinner at your own dining room table.

It's a little retro, like sitting in Little Italy in the 1960s, a Chianti candle slowly catching its death on the straw, and discovering a new world—from the Old World—of flavor. Sophia Loren should be there, wearing a ridiculously risqué peasant top and looking for all the world like a shifty gypsy mermaid while you eat this saucy dish. There's something sexy—and spicy, messy, and decadent—about Fra Diavolo.

Method

1. In a stockpot or Dutch oven, heat the olive oil over high heat. Dispatch the lobster by driving a knife straight down through its head, between the eyes. Remove the tail, claws, and knuckles. Cut the tail into four pieces, twist the knuckles to remove from the claws and bodies, and strike the claws with the back of a knife to crack the shell. Toss the lobster pieces in flour, shake off the excess, and add the meat to the pot. Cook until the shells turn red, about 4 minutes. Transfer the lobster pieces to a plate; set aside.

2. Add the red pepper flakes, oregano, and garlic to the pot; cook until the spices bloom, about 3 minutes. Add the tomato paste; cook until lightly caramelized, about 2 minutes. Add the white wine, and cook until almost evaporated, about 2 minutes. Add the stock, the tomatoes, and the bay leaf, and bring to a boil. Reduce the heat to medium-low, and cook partially covered until the sauce thickens, about 20 minutes. Return the lobster to the pot, and cook until the lobster is cooked through, about 5 more minutes. Add the pasta and toss with the sauce. Transfer to a large serving platter; sprinkle with the chopped parsley.

INGREDIENTS

16 ounces cavatappi pasta

6 tablespoons unsalted butter, divided

8 ounces fontina cheese, shredded

4 ounces sharp white cheddar cheese, shredded

4 slices white sandwich bread

¼ cup all-purpose flour

4 cups milk

8 ounces mascarpone cheese

3 tablespoons brandy or cognac

¼ teaspoon cayenne pepper

¼ teaspoon freshly grated nutmeg

Salt and freshly ground black pepper, to taste

16 ounces cooked lobster meat, cut into 1-inch chunks (meat from approximately five 1¼-pound lobsters)

3 tablespoons chives, minced

2 scallions, sliced

Lobster Macaroni and Cheese • *Malcolm*

Serves 8 to 10

I've never been one to fall all over myself at the mere mention of lobster mac and cheese. Maine lobster doesn't need to be dressed up or have its flavor improved, and a combination of lobster (or clams or oysters) with cheese doesn't appeal to me. Mainly, though, rich chunks of sweet lobster meat covered in a heavy, sticky, gluey cheese sauce just seems too excessive, too decadent, too much. Combining lobster with mac and cheese often works to the detriment of both dishes; the flavor of the lobster meat is masked by the thick cheese, and the simple comfort of mac and cheese is overly fussified with lobster meat.

Not long ago, however, after a weekend of hosting family from out of town, we found ourselves with a surplus of leftover lobster meat chilling in the refrigerator. What's more, an unseasonable storm came to town, turning

the week cool, gray, and rainy. Suddenly the occasion seemed perfect to cook a decadent macaroni and cheese with plenty of big chunks of lobster.

My go-to mac-and-cheese recipe, which uses a combination of sharp cheddar and gruyère, wouldn't do for making lobster mac and cheese. Those strong cheeses would bury the flavor of the lobster, and the sauce is just too heavy. I eventually settled on a combination of white cheddar, fontina, and mascarpone. The fontina melts beautifully and has a mild flavor that doesn't compete with the lobster. The mascarpone adds silkiness and just the lightest touch of sweetness. Finally, finishing the dish with lots of big, buttery, fresh breadcrumbs and another layer of cheese ensures lots of golden-brown crunchy bits after baking. The resulting lobster mac and cheese is light and creamy, and allows the flavor of the lobster to shine through just as it should. It's one of the best I've ever made.

Method

1. Preheat the oven to 375°F. Bring a large pan of salted water to a boil over high heat. Add the pasta and cook, stirring occasionally, cutting the cooking time on the package in half. Drain the pasta and set aside.

2. Combine the shredded cheeses in a bowl, and toss well to combine. Set aside.

3. Melt 2 tablespoons of the butter in a microwave or in a pan over low heat. Remove the crusts from the bread and discard. Tear the remaining bread into tiny bits and place in a small bowl. Add the melted butter and toss to coat the breadcrumbs evenly. Set aside.

4. In a large saucepan or stockpot, melt the remaining butter over medium heat. Add the flour and cook, whisking constantly, until the flour mixture is smooth and just starting to darken.

5. Slowly whisk in the milk and simmer, whisking frequently, until the sauce has thickened, about 10 minutes. Remove the pan from the heat, and stir in 2½ cups of the shredded cheese mixture, the mascarpone, and the brandy.

6. Add the cayenne and nutmeg. Stir until the cheese is melted and incorporated. Adjust the taste with salt and pepper as needed. Add half the lobster, half the chives, half the scallions, and the cooked pasta to the cheese sauce. Stir well to combine.

7. Transfer the mixture to a 9-inch by 13-inch baking dish.

8. Sprinkle with the fresh breadcrumbs and the remaining shredded cheese mixture. Bake until golden-brown and bubbly, about 30 minutes. Let cool for a few minutes, and finish with a sprinkle of the remaining lobster, chives, and scallions.

HOSS AND MARY'S • *Malcolm*
27 W Grand Ave, Old Orchard Beach, ME 04064; (207) 934-2411

During the summer, an influx of tourists from Maine and Quebec blankets Old Orchard Beach in acres of pale white skin, Marlboro Light smoke, airbrushed T-shirts, and thumping dance clubs. Dozens of mostly seasonal food stands and restaurants spring up in their wake around The Pier, the amusement area's spiritual center, slinging their versions of typical boardwalk fare: pints of fried clams, soft-serve ice cream, candy apples, cotton candy, fried dough, and, inexplicably, some remarkably good oversized slices of cheese pizza. Within this smash-and-grab food culture, where a limited few months of warm weather and a near lack of repeat business can mean focusing your business on volume rather than quality, Hoss and Mary's is nestled like a diamond in the rough. Owners Brian "Hoss" Coddens and Deena "Mary" Eskew first gained national attention in their previous restaurant, the Tradewinds Cafe in Arundel. There, the Travel Channel's "Man v. Food" filmed host Adam Richman's dominance over the

restaurant's "Manimal" challenge, downing an eight-patty cheeseburger, two coleslaw-topped hot dogs, an order of fries, a Moxie, and a coffee cake–infused one-pound milkshake in under 20 minutes. The national exposure and positive press exploded the small restaurant's customer base, and soon, Coddens and Eskew relocated to a larger space in the shadow of Palace Playland in Old Orchard Beach. Husband-and-wife team Hoss and Mary first met in Key West, and the couple's new Old Orchard Beach location reflects the breezy, coconut, rum-soaked culture of the Florida Keys. Bright yellow and red hand-painted signage advertises "tasty grub" and "local color," and the theme continues right through the small restaurant, all the way to Mary herself, laughing with regulars and taking orders behind the front counter. It was the first surprise of the day; rather than staffing their restaurant with an army of surly minimum-wage teenagers, Hoss and Mary are right there behind the counter every day, taking orders and making food for their hungry customers. This kind of attention and care made it immediately clear that we weren't in for a typical beachside afternoon of preformed, artificial smoke–flavored hamburger patties and flavorless Sysco coleslaw.

Jillian: Hoss and Mary's is a bright spot, an ambassador of the Conch Republic in New England. It's cheerful inside, and we found it impossible not to feel embraced by the silliness, the signage, the excess, the milkshakes, and most of all, the friendly, happy, hang-loose owners.

We were a little overwhelmed by the massive menu, featuring dozens of special combination hamburgers, hot dogs, seafood, and sandwiches. Hoss and Mary's signature offerings read like the doodled munchie-dreams from the back of a stoned college student's notebook. The Foghorn Leghorn, a cheeseburger topped with chicken fingers, and the Bride of Frankenstein, a cheesesteak topped with clam cakes, immediately caught my eye. After talking with Hoss, though, who took a quick break from his station behind the grill to recommend I try a cheeseburger, I settled on the Land 'n' Sea burger, a $4.95 "crossover burger" topped with a deep-fried clam cake, spicy tartar sauce, lettuce, and tomato, with a side of onion rings.

After stepping outside to eat at the outdoor counter, I unwrapped my cheeseburger to find a store-bought hamburger bun stacked to overflowing. The hamburger patty was well done and well seasoned, if a little on the small side at just two or three ounces. Hoss and Mary's hamburger patties are treated almost like condiments; you can find eight griddled hamburger patties stacked into a single burger, and breakfast sandwiches that combine an entire bacon, egg, and cheese atop a junior cheeseburger. Most of the hamburgers include other ingredients for inspired combinations. In my

Land 'n' Sea burger, the patty combined perfectly with the deep-fried, golden clam cake, and the spicy tartar sauce bound the couple together in a marriage that made sense. Actually, it didn't just make sense; it was so jaw-droppingly delicious that halfway through, I put my burger down on the wooden counter to pause and catch my breath before ducking back inside to order another of the restaurant's divine creations.

Jillian ordered the day's special, a Cuban Haddock Sandwich ($8.95), a monstrous, foot-long toasted submarine sandwich roll filled with three enormous pieces of crispy fried haddock, coleslaw, onion, and Sriracha-infused mayonnaise. We were amazed by the quality of the fish, the creamy crunch of the coleslaw (why hasn't someone thought to add coleslaw to a haddock sandwich before?), and the spicy kick from the mayo, and even the roll was excellent: soft, but with a kind of crackly, shellacked outside that provided just enough structure for containing the delicious ingredients within.

Jillian: We took our food outside to eat on the deck across from one of those double-decker OOB motels from the 1950s that never stops wrestling with erosion, depression, and disrepair. And sweet lord, I loved that sandwich. A foot-long loaf of good, crusty bread jammed with super-fresh haddock, coleslaw that cools while contributing crunch, and rooster sauce for a tangy, orange kick. I had to do a little dance after every bite, insisting that each would be my last, but it never was—not until the last lovely bit was down my gullet. I felt full but not defeated.

After finishing the Land 'n' Sea burger, I circled back for another of the day's specials, the Flaming Moo burger ($5.95), which turned out to be two griddled cheeseburger patties dipped in Buffalo wing sauce and topped with bacon, nacho cheese, lettuce, and mayonnaise on a toasted bun. It was named via customer suggestion on Hoss and Mary's Facebook page. Hoss spends the few remaining hours left after the close of business each day on the Internet, brainstorming new ideas and soliciting suggestions for his latest over-the-top culinary inventions. It's this "audience participation" aspect of Hoss and Mary's that makes eating there so much fun.

And the Flaming Moo burger is extreme, even obscene fun. A giant, towering quarter pound of beef piled, dipped, and drenched in every good-tasting thing that you might order after your sixth pint at your favorite pub, this colossally messy, completely satisfying burger deserves a place in the restaurant's regular rotation.

We rounded out our meal with a few thick slices of Hoss and Mary's

famous Muther Futcher's coffee cake, Mary's grandmother's special recipe coffee cake that can be eaten plain, blended into a milkshake, or deep fried. It made me completely reconsider coffee cake; this wasn't the gritty, dry, stick-to-your-teeth version found in a box of Entenmann's. A Mother Futcher coffee cake is light, springy, and slightly elastic, with just the right amount of sweetness and a dark brown, caramelized, crunchy top. It perfectly rounded out an afternoon of gluttony that was nearly enough to make it unsafe for me to drive us home. Has anyone ever had to call a cab as a result of overindulging in cheeseburgers?

Writing about restaurants like Hoss and Mary's is easy. In fact, learning about places like these is one of the major joys of writing about them and a big inspiration for our own journeys into the world of food in Maine. At the core of the business are Hoss and Mary themselves, two fundamentally good people who "are just trying to have some fun with food," as Mary explains. "The Flaming Moo may be a little bit not-so-good for you, but what are you going to do, starve?" It's the attitude that permeates everything Hoss and Mary do, a shrug and a carefree, effortless ease that masks the difficulties inherent in operating a year-round business in a place whose population plummets during the unforgiving winter. If the menu were just wildly inventive, if the ingredients were only fresh and well prepared, if the space was just inviting and cozy, we would suggest that a place like Hoss and Mary's is worth a special trip. Factor in the genuinely warm, friendly personalities behind the counter and the loving care with which they craft their creations, and I simply must insist that you plan your next meal out around a trip to Old Orchard Beach.

Our Favorite Lobster Rolls

The sandwich seems so simple; how can there be so much debate about what defines a "real" Maine lobster roll? Most people agree on the basics: a New England split-top bun griddled in butter until golden-brown, then stuffed to overflowing with succulent, sweet, freshly caught Maine lobster. After that, things get a little trickier. Should the meat be served hot? (No.)

Should the lobster be naked or should there be mayonnaise, and if so, how much? Should there be a mix of lobster claw, knuckle, and tail meat spread on the inside of the bun or blobbed on top? Should the lobster be mixed with anything else, such as celery? (Also no.) Should there be spices or other flavorings? Should lettuce come into play, and if so, how much?

Ask ten different seafood-loving locals in Portland where to get the best lobster roll nearby, and you'll get ten different answers.

Some base their recommendations entirely on how much lobster a particular restaurant is cramming into their version of a lobster roll, but that has never struck us as the most important criterion. If quantity of meat were the chief concern, why not just eat a whole steamed lobster and forget the roll?

No, the difference between "good" and "great" lobster rolls is trickier to pin down. The best lobster rolls aren't just expensive, bready troughs full of lobster meat to shovel into the mouths of tourists. They are, instead, a careful balance of texture and temperature.

Something magical happens when a warm, soft-on-the-inside, crispy-golden-griddled-on-the-outside fluffy bun contrasts with the cool sweetness of the lobster with just a touch of lettuce for crunch. It's the interplay among those elements that make an outstanding lobster roll.

BITE INTO MAINE • *Malcolm*
Fort Williams Park, 1000 Shore Road, Cape Elizabeth, ME 04106; 207-420-0294; biteintomaine.com

Perched atop a grassy hill in Fort Williams Park, overlooking Portland Head Light in Cape Elizabeth, the Bite Into Maine truck serves some astonishing twists ($13) on the classic Maine lobster roll. After just two seasons in operation, their Maine lobster roll is one of the best we've tasted: huge, fresh chunks of cool, sweet Maine lobster tossed lightly with mayonnaise, exploding out of a warm, butter-griddled roll, optionally sprinkled with a few snips of chives. The options don't stop there; customers can also choose from five non-purist twists on the venerable sandwich, including versions spiked with wasabi or curry.

THE LOBSTER SHACK AT TWO LIGHTS • *Jillian*
225 Two Lights Road, Cape Elizabeth, ME 04107; (207) 799-1677; lobster-shacktwolights.com

The Lobster Shack at Two Lights feels idyllic. As you ascend the stone steps, white clapboard buildings come into view, a view that is completed by picnic tables perched between the lighthouses, metal sculptures spinning in the wind, and the ocean, wide and blue, spraying the driftwood-strewn rocks.

We recently found ourselves inside the narrow shack, placing an order, then sliding down past dessert and soda machines to wait for our number to be called. There were plenty of tables inside, but it was stuffy, and outside the sea beckoned. Malcolm's lobster roll was of the mix-the-blob-of-mayo-yourself variety, of which we had long been wary. But it was not so taxing a process as we feared, and the sandwich was buttery and delicious, filled with an appropriate amount of lobster meat.

My haddock boat was satisfying, though the fries were limp and the coleslaw too saccharine for my taste. The fish was tasty, though, firm and well battered. The tarter sauce was somewhat bland and lacking relish, but that didn't stop me from scraping my drugstore fries in the dregs of the plastic cup. And oh, the strawberry rhubarb pie. My sweet lord on a biscuit. Deeply candy-colored red filling, bursting with fruit, covered in fresh whipped cream on a toothsome crust, this was a hearty slice of pie damn good enough for Special Agent Dale Cooper. It tasted like America. Which tastes like freedom. And fruit. And summer.

What more could you ask for? What else can I say? It's all that I hoped it would be. Go today, go right this second if you can. Leave your home or office, flee swiftly to your car, and don't look back. Roll down the windows, let your left hand skim the wind, and sing out loud to radio songs as you drive toward the Atlantic. If you aren't in Maine or near it, I'm sorry. The Lobster Shack at Two Lights on the rocky shores of Cape Elizabeth is liberty with lobster for all.

PATTY'S SEAFOOD TAKEOUT • *Jillian*
Route One, Edgecomb, ME 04556

If you're driving north and east on U.S. Route 1 in high summer, destination Rockland, Rockport, or points east, you will inevitably be struck by a combination of interest and dread as you approach Red's Eats at the Wiscasset Bridge. Almost inevitably, you'll be stuck for an hour in Wiscasset's notorious traffic jam, idling in one of the most picturesque places in America. Having read all the articles in glossy periodicals, you know you should park, get out of the car, and wait in line at Red's (a long line) to try their brilliant take on the lobster roll. But you don't, because you are stubborn.

As you sail past the serpentine tourists sweltering in July, however, regret sets in. You're suddenly starving. Convinced there will never be another opportunity to eat, you sulk and look for Mentos in the glove compartment. But take heart. You will be rewarded for your impatience and impertinence. You just have to get to Patty's, and it's only a little farther up the road. After another mile or maybe two, you see a modest shack glimmering like mythic Brigadoon. Set back slightly on the left side of the road, surrounded by green trees and misty mountains, sits Patty's Seafood Takeout, a white wooden shack with shamrock accents and four picnic tables in front.

Patty isn't in the business of pleasantries, so don't be discouraged if she doesn't hold your hand and tell you what a darling boy you are. Ask her for a lobster roll. Don't dawdle. Pay what she asks, which is something like $17. It's worth it. Don't balk. Maybe, quickly, see if you can get a can of Mug root beer. Step aside and admire the lovely countryside. And then, at the second window to the right, next to napkins and straws, for you alone on a sunny summer Saturday, a vision of perfection will appear: the lobster roll.

Atop a buttered, toasted, New England–style split-top roll, the fresh flesh of a crustacean waits, dressed simply in mayonnaise and served with nothing but a small bag of Lay's potato chips standing sentry beside it. (The flaccid dill isn't worth a mention, sadly.) This is the platonic ideal of a Maine delicacy. It's like a Bodhisattva on a bun. I cannot express—and you may have noticed already that I am given to fits of description—how good this is. The meat is sweet. Whole claws are waving. The bun is overflowing with pieces of lobster that will spill onto your tray as you attempt to experience communion with the offering before you.

Close your eyes and take a bite. It isn't hyperbole to say that birds will sing blithely and northern breezes will pick up as you first taste this food of the gods. This is what they serve in Elysian Fields and Valhalla halls. In Christian heaven they do not eat this well. This lobster roll makes ambrosia seem sour, milk and honey curdle and separate. Crunch a salty chip, slug a slurp of syrupy soda, and go back again for more. It isn't something you'll want to share, in spite of your good upbringing. This is a piece of Avalon. And when you are done, you'll feel sated, impeccable, ecstatic. You won't have an ounce of compunction. Get back into your car and keep going to the wedding to which you were heading. Patty's is there. You will make this journey again.

Sweets

MILKSHAKES $6	GELATO $4.50
FLOATS $5.50	BEIGNETS $4
SUNDAE $6.00	CHURROS $3.50

SPECIALS

SOUP · ITALIAN WEDDING SOUP SM $4.50 LG $5.75

SALAD · CANDIED BACON, FRENCH FETA, PICKLED ONIONS GALA APPLES $8 · SPRING PEEPER DRAUGHT · GREENS & BROWN SUGAR VIN.

PANINO · NORTH CAROLINA BRAISED BEEF BRISKET W/MUSTARD BBQ SAUCE CHEDDAR & HOT PICKLED SWEET PEPPERS

ETC · MEXICAN SPICED SALAMI $8 (w) BLUEBERRY & LEMONGRASS · W/PICKLED VEGETABLES · ORANGE CREAMSICLE SHAKE $7 · GINGER ALE $2.50 · COLD BREWED COFFEE $2.50

DUCKFAT · *Jillian*

43 Middle Street, Portland, ME 04101; (207) 774-8080; duckfat.com

Duckfat is delicious, but it does make you sleepy. Because this restaurant is one of Portland's culinary destinations, a name that's mentioned whenever a writer from *Time Out Zeitgeist!* makes the harrowing journey north of the Hudson, we felt—what's the opposite of compelled? Repelled?—by the prospect of a meal there. Thus, we'd never been until recently. What a disservice to our senses. Because, as you might have read, it's very nice there.

It was a lovely late July evening, and all the townspeople were out and about, dining al fresco, walking in skirts with dogs and kids and balloons, breathing in the salty summer air. On the sidewalk a narrow bar rail and chalkboard sign beckoned us into the narrow space next to Ribollita. Inside, there is seating on bar stools at high tables along brick walls, in the window, or at the counter. The mason jar atmosphere puts you at ease, and we immediately ordered Brooklyn lager and lime mint soda. I felt that a preprandial milkshake would err on the side of lactic indulgence, but you could go that way if so inclined.

We were pleasantly unsurprised that the large cone of fries ($6.50) was as fantastic as we had been led to believe. Crispy without coating, crunchy burnt sienna in texture and color and not at all oily or heavy, with soft-as-mashed-potato centers, these fries are perfect without accompaniment but are enhanced delightfully by the dipping sauces served in pleasing little glass cups. Believe me when I say, try the curry mayo and truffle ketchup. That is all. If you submit to the cult of dipping sauce as I do, you may attain a state nearing nirvana here. All you need is this and a beer.

The paninis were good to very good—what one expects, buttery, crunchy with gooey goings on in the middle. I had the tuna melt ($8.50) and Malcolm the meatloaf ($9.25). Both come with thin and tangy pickle spears on the side of a rectangular wooden trencher. My chilled cucumber soup (cup, $4.50) was beautiful but not what I expected—neither thin nor creamy, with a sour herby bite, topped with cool yogurt and deep red harissa garnish. Akin to eating a bowl of finely chopped dill pickles, this was not what I crave in cucumber soup. We ended with beignets with cinnamon sugar ($4) also served in a proper paper cone, laced with orange zest and fried an earthy brown. I wish there had been a jam or cream or gelato. They had a heavy bitter taste, and while I get that they were going for a duck à l'orange doughnut thing, it didn't quite work for me.

Completely sated, we did not linger, as a family of unruly Belgians and/or Huns were waiting to take our seats. I like this place, and not because someone with credentials convinced me in advance that I would. It's another great neighborhood place, something Portland does really well. You go to Duckfat because it meets a standard of basic excellence that one expects in a city like this. The server kids are hip and sweet, other patrons seem equally content, and you can drink and talk and eat and laugh as if you were in your own, slightly cooler living room.

A Moxie Day Menu

- Moxie Cocktail
- Chicken and Corn Summer Chowder
- Atlantic Baja-Style Fish Tacos

In an old mill town on the Androscoggin River, every summer during Moxie Days, Mainers celebrate our great state's medicinal tonic, Moxie. When it comes to the taste of Moxie, ours is a house divided, but we are both big fans of small-town charm. If you too are a fan, and if you should ever find yourself in Lisbon Falls in July, you should get yourself to the two-square-block downtown for a celebration of Maine culture, heritage, and community pride. It's an excuse to parade, show off classic cars and juggling skills, highlight local dance schools and Boy Scout troops, eat barbeque, and get sunburned. It's tradition. Try a can of Moxie while you're there. You never know, you just might like it.

If you're elsewhere in Maine on Moxie Day, or any other slow, lazy July day, spice things up with this menu.

Moxie Cocktail • *Malcolm*
Makes one cocktail

INGREDIENTS

2 ounces Sailor Jerry's rum

4 ounces Moxie soda

For the uninitiated, Moxie is, as of 2005, the official state soft drink of Maine. It began as a patent medicine in the late 1800s, a tonic distinguished by the strong, sharp flavor of gentian root, and was used to treat everything from "nervousness" to "brain softening." Eventually, soda water was added, and Moxie was transformed into a curiously bitter soda. While it has fallen out of favor nationally, Moxie continues to be sold in the Northeast.

The taste is, at best, unusual. Earthy like a root, it's a bizarre combination of bitter and sweet that is sure to get in your head. It seemed awful when I tasted it as a child, but I thought everything that wasn't a hamburger tasted awful then. I now know that I've tasted far worse things, usually in alcoholic form. In fact, that's what Moxie reminds me of: Jägermeister without the annoying maniacal buzz. I set out to correct this oversight immediately with the creation of a Moxie cocktail.

The obvious choice, given their shared medicinal flavors, is to add Jägermeister to Moxie on the rocks. But I am not in a dorm room, am not seeking a fistfight, and do not consider myself a total lunatic, so Jägermeister is out. After trying a few other options, I fell in love with the following Moxie Cocktail.

Method

1. Combine the ingredients in an old-fashioned glass over cracked ice. Serve.

Chicken and Corn Summer Chowder

● *Malcolm*

Serves 6

The lure of a supermarket rotisserie chicken can be strong, particularly in the summer when the temperature rises. They're inexpensive (at around seven bucks), they're easy to prepare (once you manage to pry open the container), and best of all, they allow you to put a reasonably nutritious dinner on the table without spiking the already-sweltering summer temperatures to oven-like highs in the kitchen.

The downside? They're usually just not very good. They are hyper-moisturized and tender to the point that if you try to break the bird apart into recognizable breast, thigh, and leg portions, you're likely to end up with a pile of gristle and bones in one hand and a heap of shredded chicken in the other, with fat running down your arms and onto the floor. The finished product bears little resemblance to a home-cooked roasted chicken. The meat, while juicy, often doesn't have much flavor, but by the time you've reached 5 p.m. on a 95-degree day, you hardly care.

At the risk of venturing too far down the road of Sara Lee–style "semi-homemade" wizardry, we wanted a recipe that played to the unique qualities of the supermarket rotisserie chicken; something that uses its strengths (easily broken down, cheap, no cooking) while improving on its weaknesses (flavorless, shapeless).

This warm-weather version of chicken corn chowder fits the bill perfectly, offering richness and lightness at the same time. The avocado, tomato, jalapeño, and lime toppings are key, bringing a bright Mexican twist to the soup and making it more akin to a sopa de lima than a traditional chowder.

Method

1. In a large heavy pot or Dutch oven over medium heat, cook the bacon until the fat renders and the meat begins to turn brown. Add the onion and cook until soft, about 3 minutes. Sprinkle the flour on top and cook, stirring, until the flour barely begins to brown, about 3 more minutes.

2. Add the potatoes and the chicken broth, and bring to a boil. Reduce the heat and cook until the potatoes are barely tender, about 5 minutes. Add the chicken and the corn, and return to a boil. Reduce the heat to low, and stir in the cream to taste. Heat through, about 2 minutes.

3. Serve in soup bowls, garnished with the tomatoes, the avocado, the jalapeño, the cilantro, a squirt or two of lime juice, and black pepper to taste

INGREDIENTS

4 slices bacon, chopped

1 onion, chopped

3 tablespoons all-purpose flour

1 pound Yukon Gold potatoes, unpeeled and chopped

6 cups reduced-sodium chicken broth

Shredded meat from a 2½- to 3-pound roasted chicken

3 ears corn, kernels cut from the cob

¼–½ cup heavy whipping cream

2 medium tomatoes, seeded and chopped

1 avocado, pitted, peeled, and chopped

1 jalapeño, sliced

1 cup loosely packed cilantro leaves

2 limes, cut into wedges

Freshly ground black pepper

INGREDIENTS

1 cup dark beer

1 cup all-purpose flour

1 teaspoon salt

1½ pounds haddock fillet, cut into 1-inch-wide strips

Peanut oil (for frying)

1 small red cabbage, sliced thinly

1 cup cilantro, chopped

Juice from two limes

2 tablespoons vegetable oil

1 jalapeño, thinly sliced

2 tablespoons canned chipotle chiles, rinsed and seeded

1 cup mayonnaise

¼ cup pickle relish

½ onion, chopped

Lime wedges

Atlantic Baja-Style Fish Tacos • *Jillian*
Makes 6–8 tacos

We recently received a request from a landlocked friend somewhere in the mysterious Midwest, desperate for a good fish taco recipe. While we prepared and ate many fish tacos in Mexico (including, once, a memorable super-pink-tuna-and-wasabi-mayo version), our Yucatecan neighbors—despite the close-enough-to-feel-the-salt-spray Gulf of Mexico and myriad cement fishing boats bobbing in the waves—didn't specialize in the Baja-style fish tacos that most of us like best. They eat a lot of octopus in the Yucatan. Our Atlantic Baja-style fish tacos use haddock, but you can substitute any flaky, semi-firm white fish (such as cod or tilapia) that is readily available.

This is not a light lunch. There is a reason you typically eat these delicious calorie bombs after a day of swimming and getting pounded by the surf. And as lovely as it is here in July, a part of me longs for an ice-cold Pacifico, the siren call of "COCO!," and the loud, pungent, colorful mess of Mexico. These fish tacos transport me, if only for a moment, to a welcome vacation of the mind.

Method

1. Whisk the beer, the flour, and the salt in a medium-sized bowl until well blended. In a deep fryer or deep frying pan, heat the oil to 360°F. Dip each piece of fish in the batter and drain the excess. Slide the fish slowly into the oil, a few pieces at a time, and cook until golden-brown, turning if needed, about 4 minutes per batch. Transfer the cooked fish to paper towels to drain.

2. In a separate bowl, toss the cabbage, the cilantro, the lime juice, the vegetable oil, and the jalapeño until evenly coated. Set aside.

3. In a blender or food procesor, combine the chipotle chilies, the mayonnaise, the pickle relish, and the onion. Blend until smooth.

4. To assemble each taco, stack two warm tortillas, and top with a piece or two of fish. Top with spoonful of the cabbage slaw and serve with the chipotle tartar sauce on the side, with plenty of lime wedges to squeeze over the top.

AUGUST

Fat, ugly, many-hued, bursting, juicy, fragrant tomatoes. Enormous, almost lurid zucchini that neighbors leave early on the back porch. Sweet, perfect, adorable blueberries by the bushel. Fruits and vegetables are peerless in August in Maine, their flavors seemingly distilled and concentrated from an essence of life, sun, and earth, needing little enhancement. The last lingering memories of winter and cold are chased away by the delicious bounty at your fingertips.

Never mind that the nights are getting longer and the first frost may only be a month away. Banish such premonitions. August is August, and cooking should be done outdoors, either on the grill or with this neat trick for sun-cooked tomato sauce. We have lots of favorite recipes for the ubiquitous zucchini, but this one feeds a crowd for an impromptu feast and is super yummy. With the pimiento cheese, it makes a folksy and family-friendly meal, and all that's left is to lean back, face the sun, and sip a tall, icy daiquiri.

Dog Days of Summer Menu
- Zucchini Fritters
- Pimiento Cheese
- Sun-Cooked Heirloom Tomato Pasta Sauce
- Big Homemade Barbecue Burgers
- Blueberry Velvet Cake

Zucchini Fritters ● *Jillian*

Makes about a dozen

My Grandpa Jack was a plumber, steamfitter, and armchair theologian. He sat in a rocking chair, a most masculine nicotine-stained piece of furniture, or hunched over the kitchen table, dunking zwiebek cookies in instant coffee. I remember him reading the Bible and taking notes with his calloused, clean though not unstained hands. He was a large man, a working-class Democrat from the German-Italian ghetto, who played the saxophone and danced every Saturday night of his youth at a place called Pleasure Beach. That is where he met my Grandma Josephine. He swung her up perpendicular one night and then he left for The War—World War II, that is. In his garage he kept a phonograph, some screws and bolts in Maxwell House jars nailed to the wall, and a cast-iron pot that he used for Sunday dinners. The color of that workshed never changed, even after the house was re-sided for the twenty-first century. He planted beans, cucumbers, peppers, and zucchini in the garden until his mind was nearly gone, and always let me twist off the ripe tomatoes from their fragrant stalks.

Now is the time of year when zucchini are at their most abundant, and I remember my grandfather by cooking from our summer garden. These tasty fritters make a perfect weekday dinner, served with a salad and a cool glass of Vinho Verde.

Method

1. Grate the zucchini into a small bowl and squeeze out the liquid. Transfer to a large mixing bowl.

2. In a large skillet, cook the onions and peppers in the vegetable oil until translucent. Season with salt and pepper.

3. Combine the zucchini, onions, peppers, cheese, egg, and breadcrumbs. Form into patties.

4. Fry the fritters in olive oil on medium-high heat, about 3 minutes per side. Drain on paper towels or in a brown paper bag.

5. Combine the sour cream and Sriracha and serve as a dipping sauce with the zucchini fritters.

INGREDIENTS

1 large zucchini, ends trimmed

1 teaspoon vegetable oil

½ cup onion, diced

1 jalapeño pepper, seeded and diced

Kosher salt and ground pepper

1¼ cups cheddar cheese, grated

1 egg, beaten

¼ cup fresh breadcrumbs

1 tablespoon olive oil

½ cup sour cream

1 teaspoon Sriracha hot chili sauce

Pimiento Cheese • *Malcolm*

Makes about two cups

Visit nearly any home in the southern United States on a weekday afternoon, and it won't be long before your kindly host breaks out a bowl of pimiento cheese. This Southern staple, a simple mix of cheese, mayonnaise, and sweet peppers, is a quick, inexpensive snack for a group of good friends (the kind that you're not overly preoccupied with impressing) when served on crackers, corn chips, bread, pretzels, or scooped up with ribs of celery.

Though numerous brands of fluorescent orange, processed, pasteurized pimiento cheese are sold by the tub in supermarkets nationwide, why not just whip up a bowl from scratch? Some of the best pimiento cheese we've ever tasted is made from just a few ingredients—typically cheddar cheese, mayonnaise, salt, and pepper—though some people do schmancy the dish up with additional cream cheese, Monterrey Jack, or scallions. When you spread the premixed stuff on a cracker, you're spreading as many chemicals, sweeteners, and flavorings as real ingredients, and you won't capture the flavorful sharp cheddar bite and mild warming heat of a batch whipped up at home. Make it from scratch and it tastes almost like a cheese spread mixed with a fine alcoholic cocktail, a really, really dirty martini, if you will.

This recipe makes a large batch of pimiento cheese. What to do with the leftovers? It's a decadent addition to a cheeseburger, an incredible foundation for a grilled cheese sandwich (with bacon), and tastes great when baked into stuffed mushroom caps. Of course, you can always polish the leftovers off the way I do: straight out of the bowl in the middle of the night, fridge door open, spoon in paw.

Method

1. In a large bowl, mix all the ingredients together until well blended. Chill for at least 1 hour to let the flavors meld. Serve with crackers or bread.

INGREDIENTS

1 pound sharp cheddar cheese, grated

A 4-ounce jar of pimientos, drained and diced

½ cup mayonnaise

2 garlic cloves, minced

1 tablespoon Worcestershire sauce

1⅛ teaspoons cayenne pepper

Sun-Cooked Heirloom Tomato Pasta Sauce • *Jillian*

Serves 4-6

INGREDIENTS

3 misshapen red and yellow heirloom tomatoes

3 purple grape tomatoes

3 medium-sized spherical red tomatoes

2 garlic cloves, sliced thinly

A densly packed ¼ cup chopped basil

¼ cup fruity olive oil

½ teaspoon salt

½ teaspoon black pepper

Pasta of choice, cooked

Parmesan cheese shavings

It is high summer in Maine. Though the nights are cooling, our days are glorious, green, and breezy. Fields and farm stands are bursting with string beans, corn, tomatoes, and melons. Everything is ripe. On just such a day I was sitting in the grass, brainstorming ideas for dinner, and remembered—how could I forget?—one of the first meals Malcolm and I ever cooked together. It was his father's recipe. Make a pasta sauce from raw tomatoes, garlic, basil, olive oil, and vinegar; serve it over hot pasta to "cook" the sauce; and add fresh mozzarella cheese, and you have the most amazing simple summer dinner, a hit with absolutely everyone.

And then this idea struck like a lightning bolt: Cook a tomato sauce with the sun's light and heat, as in sun-steeped tea. How green an idea is this: a solar-powered sauce whose ingredients are all grown within minutes of where I live!

I am in love with how this came out, and it is wide open to interpretation and embellishment with whatever beautiful bounty you have sitting ripe on the kitchen counter. The result tastes like August—bright, clean, sweet, and nostalgic. It reminds me of family road trips to the Catskill Game Farm and Rhode Island beaches, when my parents would pull the family caravan into a rest area and unpack Italian bread, deli ham, and a container of tomatoes marinating in garlic and olive oil, piling it on, messy and fragrant. In those days I wished we could just get burgers and Frosties from Wendy's like everybody else. But clearly something important was embedded in my brain, because this dinner tastes like happy expectations and lazy summer. I only wish we could bottle this for February, to remind us of warmth and light when such reminders are needed most.

Method

1. Gently combine all the ingredients except the pasta and Parmesan cheese in a large bowl or jar, cover, and set in the sun for a few hours (five for us).

2. We cooked caponetti, a very thin spaghetti, just shy of al dente. Drain, but don't rinse. A little of the cooking liquid helps it all come together cohesively. Toss with the sun-cooked sauce and Parmesan shavings. Alternatively, slice a loaf of good, rustic bread.

Big Homemade Barbecue Burgers • *Malcolm*

Makes two big burgers

I'm not normally one for barbecue sauce, whether real or imitation. Not that I'm averse to condiments; I'll dump quarts of ketchup on macaroni and cheese or be the first in line to dip fries in mayonnaise. But rarely do I add barbecue sauce to anything, and BBQ-flavored potato chips are never my first choice (unless I am at the beach or attending a co-ed bikini pool party, both of which happen almost never). Unless I am eating actual barbecue, adding a bottle of sticky, sugary sauce to food simply isn't something that occurs to me.

Until it does, that is. Twice a year or so, I'm struck with a craving for barbecue sauce that borders on pathological. I want it slathered on everything, want it to run down my chin and pool into a greasy puddle on the plate. When the madness strikes, I'll even pound down liquid BBQ sauce straight from the bottle. This urge is without logic or lead time, which makes spending 10 hours smoking a pork shoulder (particularly in winter) an impractical response.

These burgers satisfy my barbecue sauce craving every time. You can cook them in a hot cast-iron skillet on the stovetop, or if your climate allows, outside on the grill. Cooking them on the grill allows you to baste your burgers with barbecue sauce as you cook them, which provides several layers of sticky glaze baked into the nooks and crannies of the burger. Don't do this on the stovetop; the sugar in the sauce will burn and smoke like crazy. If you're cooking indoors, add as much barbecue sauce as you'd like to the finished burger.

INGREDIENTS

⅔ pound 80/20 ground beef

Salt and pepper, to taste

1 ripe avocado, peeled and pitted

Juice from half a lemon or lime

4 strips thick-cut bacon, cut in half

4 slices sharp cheddar cheese

2 sturdy hamburger buns, split

½ cup barbecue sauce of your choice

½ cup packaged French fried onions

Method

1. Divide the meat in half and shape into patties about half an inch wider than the burger buns. Season generously with salt and pepper and set aside.

2. In a medium bowl, mash the avocado with a fork or potato masher until smooth. Add salt and pepper, plus the juice from a lemon or lime, and stir well to combine. Set aside.

3. Cook the bacon in a large skillet over medium heat until crispy, turning often. Transfer to paper towels to drain.

4. In a large cast-iron skillet over high heat, cook the burgers, flipping once, until the internal temperature reaches 130°F, about 5 minutes total. Top with the cheese and cover just long enough for the cheese to melt.

5. To assemble the burgers: Spread the bottom half of each bun with the barbecue sauce. Add the cooked cheeseburger. Top with the bacon, the mashed avocado, the French fried onions, and the top bun. Serve immediately.

Blueberry Velvet Cake • *Jillian*
Serves 8

INGREDIENTS

For the cake:

3 cups all-purpose flour

1 tablespoon unsweetened cocoa powder

1 tablespoon baking powder

½ teaspoon salt

½ cup (1 stick) unsalted butter

1¾ cups granulated sugar

4 large eggs, room temperature

2 teaspoons vanilla extract

1 cup buttermilk, room temperature

1½ pints blueberries

For the frosting:

½ cup (1 stick) unsalted butter, softened

8 ounces cream cheese

1 teaspoon vanilla extract

3 cups powdered sugar

Though I could have, I did not dye this blueberry cake blue. Is it color saturation that defines a velvet cake, or is it the hint of cocoa in the batter? I decided it was the latter. Yes, we use dye to make a red velvet cake red, but that's different. Red velvet cake is somehow sacrosanct, whereas a blue velvet cake sounds wrong, perhaps even a little creepy. And anyway, the plump, bold blueberries look gorgeous studding a dark yellow, dense, and homey cake. It looks like America to me, like something made by the Puritans or pioneers, like a cake the family cook Hannah would bake for the March girls in *Little Women*. Take this cake outside and sit on a blanket under a tree, smell the salt air, and bask in the sunshine.

Method

For the cake:

1. Preheat the oven to 350°F. Prepare two 9-inch round cake pans with butter and a light dusting of flour. In a large bowl, whisk to combine the flour, cocoa powder, baking powder, and salt.

2. In the bowl of a stand mixer, cream the butter, then beat in the sugar until fluffy and light. Mix in the eggs, one at a time, then add the vanilla.

3. Incorporate the dry ingredients into the batter in small batches, alternating with the buttermilk. Gently fold in the blueberries with a spatula. Pour the batter into the prepared pans and bake for 30 to 35 minutes. Let cool to the touch, then invert onto wire racks.

For the frosting:

1. In a stand mixer bowl, combine the butter and cream cheese. Add the vanilla extract and powdered sugar and blend.

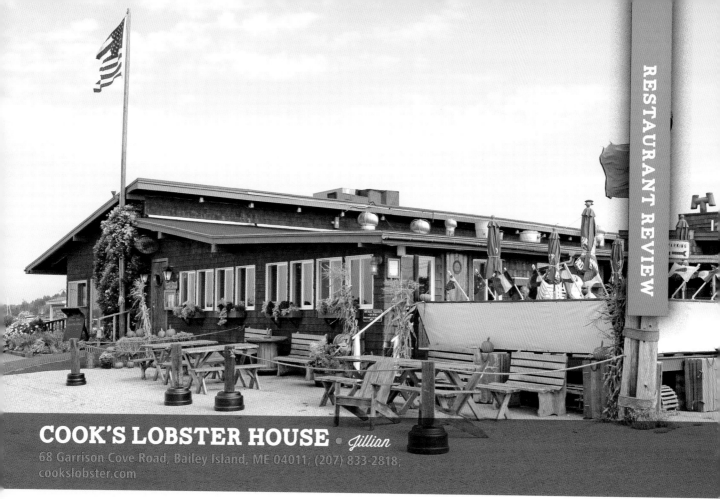

COOK'S LOBSTER HOUSE • *Jillian*

68 Garrison Cove Road, Bailey Island, ME 04011; (207) 833-2818; cookslobster.com

Determined to roll back our shared horizons, we set out for the islands—Orr's and Bailey, that is, south of Brunswick and Harpswell, pointing southward like a long, bony, finger into the waters of Casco Bay. What a stunning August day it is here in Maine. A cold front has chased away the dog days, and the air is shining and clear, the sky vivid, every leaf vein etched and highlighted. Here and there a patch of yellow-and-orange pre–Labor Day foliage—swamp maple perhaps—punctuates the greenery, reflecting the sun with heartbreaking intensity and reminding us that late summer in Maine is comprised of equal parts promise and nostalgia. We follow the signs to the rugged spit of land in Casco Bay. I hate to call it "quaint," but oh, it is so very! Churches and cemeteries from the nineteenth century, harbors mottled with boats and traps, and a storied, ghostly sort of quality you wish you could capture as art make this one of the most moving and picturesque places I have yet seen in this goddamn picturesque state. We drive all the way to the Land's End Gift Shop and stop to see the masculine statue commemorating those who have dedicated their lives to the sea, then double back on Route 24 toward Cook's Lobster House, which perches on a northward jutting point at the north end of Bailey Island.

I love Cook's from the moment we arrive. The waters of Harpswell Sound lap the parking-lot rock. Photographs of fishermen whose names adorn the local landscape line the dining-room walls. Ice-cold bottles of Maudite and Ephemera ale are available. I love this place to the depth and breadth and height of my soul. If you want lobster plain and simple, your wish is easily fulfilled here, and if you want to make it a four-pounder stuffed with seafood, you can do so for a tidy $87. We keep it modest: lobster dip in a crusty boule, a lobster dinner, a lobster roll, haddock chowder times 2, haddock nuggets, and a small order of mussels. Nothing fancy. Not too excessive.

The sign of a stellar bowl of mussels? Not feeling an ounce of embarrassment when you ask the waitress to bring more bread for bathing in your buttery broth. I am not ashamed to sop it all up. The mussels themselves are the sweet little Bang Island variety. All the food is the best we've had in days, whether fried, steamed, or floating in a briny broth.

I'm stuffed and happy. We don't always pick the right restaurants. We eat our share of merely adequate food. But we have stumbled into awesome in Cook's. It isn't problematic to make a lobster meet its maker here. This is a place to impress your guests—not as in, "Look at me on my yacht with my long-haired white cat and my cummerbund made of diamonds," but with how beautiful and good it is where you live, here in Maine in an August that will never end.

WEEKEND PROJECT:
Slow-Smoked Pulled Pork • *Malcolm*

Classic pulled pork is a perfect place to begin experimenting with a new meat-smoking hobby. It's an inexpensive cut (often under two dollars a pound) and a surefire crowd pleaser that leaves everyone fat and happy, and it's forgiving of errors in the cooking process. It's hard to make a mistake with a big pork shoulder; unlike ribs or a brisket, as long as you cook a big slab of pork long enough and slowly enough, it should turn out okay.

The only slightly unpredictable aspect of slow-smoking a pork butt is the time needed to cook it. Sometimes an hour and a half per pound at 225°F will suffice. Other times, for mysterious reasons, you need as much as two hours per pound. When planning your smoke, schedule two hours per pound to be safe, but the actual time might be less. One thing is constant: your finished pork shoulder must have an internal temperature of 190°F. This is the temperature needed for all the fat and connective tissue to liquefy and for your pork to fall apart easily. When it's ready, you should be able to reach into the butt with just two fingers and pull out the shoulder blade easily.

For a 5-pound pork butt, we're going to plan for about 10 hours of cooking at 225°F, though the meat may be ready sooner. You'll need an instant-read thermometer to check the temperature of the meat at the end of the cook, as well as a decent digital thermometer to measure the temperature inside your smoker. That little metal thermometer that's built into your grill or smoker is junk and can be off by as much as 50°F, which is a pretty huge potential swing when you are doing any cooking that depends on a constant, low, accurate temperature. Look for a digital setup that provides both a reading of the inside of your grill or smoker and a probe for checking the temperature of your meat.

Sauces Good pulled pork is about letting the flavors of the meat and the rub shine through; it is not about a heavy sauce. I am a recent convert to the North Carolina style: a light, thin, vinegar-based mustard sauce. It's sweet, sharp, and spicy all at once, and provides a bright complement to the heavy, smoky flavors of the pulled pork. Your pulled pork is going to turn out so well that I insist you try it first with no sauce at all. If it ends up a little dry, please give it a squeeze of our North Carolina sauce. You will probably also want to include a few bottles of the heavier, sticky, Kansas City–style, tomato-based sweet sauces for your guests, since many people won't accept barbecue any other way. You can feel free to mutter under your breath as your guests douse your beautifully cooked pork with the gloppy stuff.

Rubs Some recipes for pulled pork suggest that you coat your pork shoulder with mustard before applying your dry rub, ostensibly to ensure that the dry rub sticks to the meat. This is completely unnecessary. A big

INGREDIENTS

A 5-pound bone-in pork butt, trimmed of excess fat

8 hamburger buns, split

Cole slaw (optional)

For the North Carolina barbecue sauce:

2 cups apple cider vinegar

2 tablespoons molasses

½ cup (1 stick) unsalted butter

1 tablespoon ground dry mustard

1 teaspoon garlic powder

1 teaspoon onion powder

½ teaspoon cayenne pepper

1 tablespoon Worcestershire sauce

1 cup packed dark brown sugar

4 teaspoons cornstarch

For the dry rub:

3 tablespoons coarse-ground black pepper

3 tablespoons dark brown sugar

3 tablespoons paprika

2 tablespoons coarse salt

1 teaspoon cayenne pepper

pork shoulder will accept a dry rub just fine without a pre-coating. If you must, you can rub it with vegetable oil first; not only will this ensure that your rub sticks to your meat, but the oil will also break down the spices and carry them directly into the meat. Make sure to pat the rub thoroughly into the meat, working the mixture into cracks and crevices. To ensure a nice, thick crust on your meat, pull the shoulder out of the fridge about an hour before you put it into the smoker to allow the meat to come up to room temperature before cooking.

Mopping and Basting Some recipes recommend basting or mopping your meat as it cooks with either an apple juice or vinegar mixture. Don't. Pitmasters have a saying that goes something like, "If you're looking, you're not cooking," meaning that every time you open the door to your smoker to peek at your meat or apply a mop, you are rapidly dropping the temperature of the smoker, which is counter to your goal of maintaining a low, slow, even heat. Second, a crunchy, herbed bark is one attribute of a good pulled pork, and that bark is caused by dry heat driving moisture off the skin's surface, allowing the fat underneath to melt and baste the meat within. If you're constantly spraying your meat with water, you're inhibiting the formation of this bark. Put your pork butt in the smoker and leave it alone.

Wood chips Use wood from a fruit tree, like apple chips, soaked in water for 30 minutes before use. Start out by adding about 4 ounces of chips to your smoking tray (a big handful). Then add more soaked wood chips by the handful every 30 minutes for the first 2 hours or until you have used about 16 ounces of wood. Don't add any more wood for the rest of the cooking time. Meat will only accept smoke for the first couple of hours of cooking. After a certain point, no more smoke will penetrate the meat; instead, it will simply sit on top of the pork butt and turn bitter. You only need to keep adding chips for the first two hours.

Slow-Smoked Pulled Pork with North Carolina Barbecue Sauce

Serves 8-10

Method

For the North Carolina barbecue sauce:

1. In a medium saucepan, combine the vinegar, molasses, butter, dry mustard, garlic powder, onion powder, cayenne pepper, Worcestershire, and dark brown sugar, and bring to a boil. After the mixture boils, remove from the heat.

2. In a small bowl, dissolve 4 teaspoons cornstarch in 4 teaspoons cold water. Slowly pour the mixture into the hot sauce mixture, and stir.

The sauce will be thin, but it will thicken slightly as it cools. Transfer to and serve in squeeze bottles.

For the meat:

1. In a plastic bag, combine the dry rub ingredients. Shake until the spices are evenly blended.

2. About an hour before you begin smoking, remove the pork shoulder from the fridge to allow it to come to room temperature. Pat and rub the dry rub mixture onto the meat, working the spices into any cracks and crevices.

3. While you wait for the meat to reach room temperature, soak 16 ounces of fruit wood chips in a bowl of water.

4. Light the smoker and bring up to 225°F. If your grill or smoker has one, fill the drip pan with water. Place the pork butt in the smoker, directly on the rack, fat side up.

5. Add the soaked wood chips 4 ounces at a time (a big handful), every 30 minutes for the first 2 hours of cooking. Stop at 16 ounces of wood chips; no more wood is needed after the first 2 hours.

6. Check the smoker every hour or so to make sure your heat is remaining a consistent 225°F, but don't worry if your temperature goes too high. Pork butt is forgiving.

7. Check your pork shoulder after about 7 hours of cooking, though your particular pork butt may take longer to cook. Your pork should take 1½ to 2 hours per pound. When the internal temperature reads 190°F and the shoulder blade bone pulls out easily and cleanly, the pork is ready.

8. Remove the butt from the smoker and allow to rest for 30 to 40 minutes before pulling.

9. Using two forks, shred the meat into chunks, removing any obviously large chunks of fat. Pile onto buns, top with the North Carolina barbecue sauce, and, optionally, a scoop of cole slaw. Serve immediately.

EL CAMINO • *Malcolm*
15 Cushing Street, Brunswick, ME 04011; (207) 725-8228; elcaminomaine.com

Our first attempt to dine at El Camino was a bit of a bust. A bustling bar scene was not at all what we expected from this restaurant tucked away on a side street in Brunswick when we walked through the heavy door on a Saturday night. The restaurant is divided into three rooms, and the one you enter from the street is dominated by a huge, horseshoe-shaped bar. Everything glows a warm red from the numerous colored bulbs scattered through the space, and on this particular night, Brunswick hipsters (who knew Brunswick even had hipsters?) were clustered around the bar, jockeying for position and standing three rows deep. Our entrance went understandably unnoticed in the thick throngs of people; we had arrived during full-on drinking mode, not dinner mode. We spun around and scooted back out, vowing to return on a weeknight, when over-the-hill thirty-somethings and their expectant wives could presumably enjoy a midweek burrito and a mild "woohoo" instead of a full-on, tie-your-shirt-around-your-head "¡WOOOOOOOHOOOO!"

When we returned on a Thursday, it was to a much quieter restaurant. The bar was full, but there was ample room to maneuver, and there were several empty tables in the two adjoining dining areas. The restaurant is pleasantly dim and warmly decorated with a healthy sense of retro cantina style, including 1950s formica-and-chrome dining tables bathed in red Christmas lights, a few hubcaps on the orange walls, and colorful papel picado banners strung along the restaurant's dropped ceilings. Instead of the sprawling, 100-item menu so common in Mexican restaurants, El Camino focuses on a few key appetizers and regular dishes; some guacamole, some soft tacos, a few quesedillas, and a taco salad. Much more of the restaurant's attention and creativity is focused on their specials, written in chalk on a blackboard in the corner. That's where you'll find El Camino's bread and butter, wildly inventive dishes that may not be entirely authentic but are presented with enough imagination and enthusiasm that you'll hardly notice.

> *Jillian:* Sitting at a little table in the center room of El Camino, you are no longer in Maine, but neither are you in Mexico. An impossible border town of the mind, directed by Robert Rodriguez with rose-colored lighting and antique steering wheels driving the journey, this place transports you into the bleeding Jesus heart of all your romantic South of the Border fantasies. It's "the way" as well as the destination. Right now I wish I were bellied up to the U-shaped bar with red vinyl stools and a hibiscus margarita in my hand, even though I've sworn off tequila for life after too many Mexicans told me they respect it too much to drink it. There is a palpable drug-like quality in this atmosphere, which is appealing. Plus, the guacamole is delicious.

We started with the house guacamole and a basket of chips, one of the only starters at El Camino. Served with thick, crunchy corn tortilla chips and topped with a few stray beans, the guacamole was cool, smooth, and velvety, even if the presentation, made to appear more ample by being piled high on top of more chips, proved a little aggravating by the end. In order to put myself in the funky, festive mood the restaurant demands, I also tried an El Camino house margarita, an excellent $9 version of the classic served on the rocks, using top-shelf liquor.

I tried the Cider & Chipotle Braised Pork Belly Tacos ($15), one of the specials of the evening. The combination included two tacos, each wrapped in a dual layer of corn tortillas that may not have been made in-house but certainly had a lot more character than we are used to seeing in Mexican restaurants, as well as a pile of rice and a scoop each of refried pinto beans and black beans. The tacos were outrageously good, with huge, thick slabs

of braised pork belly covered with a quick salsa of diced apples and a sprinkling of red cabbage. "After they cook the pork," our server helpfully explained, "they drizzle the tacos with some of the braising liquid." The result is intensely flavorful without being clumsy the way this on-trend ingredient tends to be; the brightness of the fruit balanced the heavy, smoky, fatty pork beautifully. This attention to detail comes at a price; at around seven dollars apiece, these are not the least expensive tacos in town. I was less enthusiastic about the beans, which were seasoned a little too aggressively for me; I look to beans for some quieter counterpart to the raging flavors of the other parts of a Mexican dish. They were only okay—clearly made on-site by someone who really, really loves cumin.

Jillian ordered the pupusas ($13.50), another of the night's specials, served with more of the beans. The corn cakes were crispy on the outside but so thick that they were a little mushy and obscured some of the flavor of their fillings: fresh Mexican chorizo in one, and green chile in the other. I couldn't help but compare them with the (much superior) pupusas at Tu Casa in Portland, my only pupusa frame of reference, where they are flat, oozing with cheese, and the size of a salad plate, topped with a crunchy cabbage slaw. These pupusas proved to be more of a vehicle for crema and hot sauce, and I returned most of my attention to polishing off my tacos.

Jillian: My dinner was a many-textured thing, an oblong plate smothered in two kinds of beans, savory rice with carrots and onions, red and green salsas, cabbage shavings, a droplet of sour cream, and two dense pupusas, one filled with chorizo, the other with mild green peppers and cheese. I can't say it was unsatisfying, but I don't know that I'd order it again. There was a definite dearth of mouth-assaulting flavor—I wish the chorizo had been more potent—yet it all tasted good enough. But there was so much going on—on the plate, on the walls. And we had at least three servers, all of them fleet and helpful. Since the menu is brief, we stuck to the specials, many of which were vegetarian and sounded well thought out and intriguing.

El Camino is the kind of restaurant I could vividly imagine a past version of myself falling head over heels in love with. Ten years ago I would have practically lived here, seated on a vinyl stool at the end of the bar with other kids in self-consciously ironic T–shirts, drinking round after round of tequila as the dinner crowd thinned, broken up only by the occasional soft taco order and hilariously clumsy, unsuccessful attempts at flirtations with the bartender. By the end of the night I would do something wildly embarrassing and inappropriate, and maybe the owner would drive me home or at the very least call me a cab, only to welcome me back with open arms the next night. With those days (thankfully) behind me, I can still find lots to love at El Camino. The restaurant and the menu show a deep love and appreciation for Mexican flavor and culture, with nary a cartoon rendering of a luchador in sight. The restaurant's specials are all stunningly inspired twists on classic flavors, and not in that bumbling "let's-just-put-cilantro-scented-crema-on-everything" kind of way so typical in modern Mexican. Instead, local ingredients take center stage, and the flavors burst and combine in new ways that had never occurred to me. Maple chipotle marinated scallops? Squash and sage ricotta enchiladas? It may not be typical of what you'd find south of the border, but handled this expertly, that's fine with me.

Jillian: You will have fun at El Camino unless, upon drinking three strong cocktails and meeting a James Spader circa 1986 look-alike, you decide to flee your life and family and run away with his band to Canada, where he abandons you in the bathroom of a Tim Hortons and you can't even buy a box of Timbits because you lost your wallet and don't speak the language. If this exact scenario has been predicted by an oracle or sibyl, I exhort you to stay far away from Cushing Street and its exotic siren song of senoritas and swarthy men. The rest of you should go straight there. As the nights get colder, El Camino stays warm and lit from within. It's cinematic and cool and has tacos. What more could you ask?

NOTE: For a review of Brunswick's other great Mexican restaurant, Hacienda Pancho Villa, see the "June" chapter. One town, two noteworthy Mexican restaurants with wildly different approaches.

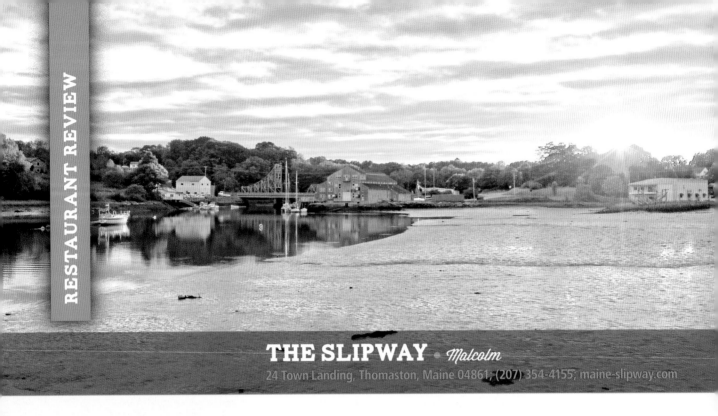

THE SLIPWAY • *Malcolm*

24 Town Landing, Thomaston, Maine 04861; (207) 354-4155; maine-slipway.com

I have a lifelong history with The Slipway in Thomaston. Okay, so it wasn't always The Slipway. For many years it was another restaurant altogether, located smack on the St. George River, and in the 1980s, it was the go-to option for dinner out for anyone living in the area. My earliest memories there include, in equal measure, a handheld ring-toss game to keep kids occupied while they sat patiently with their parents, a hot fudge brownie sundae served in an enormous brandy snifter that I had to stand up to eat, and my dad drinking terrifying amounts of gin and tonic.

These vague impressions make up some of my first memories of what it meant to be "out to dinner." They're mostly good memories, but certainly not appropriate to base a review on; a modern review of The Slipway should stand on its own, without being clouded by impressions of what came before. I'll do my best, but understand that I am operating from a base of fond memories.

After the restaurant at 24 Town Landing closed its doors in 2009, its future was uncertain until current owner Scott Yakovenko stepped forward and purchased the property. Yakovenko, who trained in fine dining in both New York and the Virgin Islands before moving to Tenants Harbor, spent years running both Cod End (in T-Harbor) and the famed Dip Net in Port Clyde. Both restaurants served world-class steamed and fried seafood in two of the most picturesque Maine environments imaginable. After Yakovenko's unceremonious ousting from the Dip Net, the funky dockside restaurant he had run for eight years, he searched for a new property where he could continue serving the kind of fresh, locally caught, rustically prepared seafood so dear to him. After extensive renovations, including a redesigned kitchen and the addition of a wet bar at the end of the 120-foot dock, Yakovenko reopened the restaurant in 2011 as The Slipway, an extension and evolution of his previous work.

Jillian: There may not be a better place to experience a summer evening in Maine than The Slipway. You can sit at one of the picnic benches over the water on a covered wooden deck that terminates in a bar. With a plastic cup of white wine in hand, you can watch seabirds flying overhead, solo kayakers paddling to the dock below, and incredible seafood being served all around you. I recommend arriving just before sunset, ordering the fried oysters and something sparkling, and breathing in the salty air; this, in my opinion, is the secret to happiness.

We visited The Slipway twice last summer, each time sitting out on the dock in the warm evening air, underneath huge tents strung with lights, listening to a three-piece band play lively jazz music. The huge communal picnic tables outside were full each time, with crowds of tourists sharing tables with locals, all happily munching baskets of fried seafood and drinking plastic cups of wine and beer. The menu features a mix of more casual fried fare served in cardboard baskets, along with more formal pasta and steak preparations. The Slipway uses as many fresh local ingredients as they can find; the majority of the seafood comes from Port Clyde Fresh Catch, while Warren's School House Farm and Beth's Farm Market provide the fruit and vegetables. Chicken and beef come from nearby Warren as well, from Maine-ly Poultry and Curtis Custom Meats, respectively.

Twin salad starters didn't disappoint. One featured a scoop of sweet Maine crab for $14.50, and another, two fish cakes with a lemon pepper aioli for $12.50. The seafood was fresh and sweet, served on a bed of interesting mixed greens, including yellow beets, radishes, and raw string beans.

Jillian: As interested as I was in the gorgeous three-tiered chilled seafood platter and the enormous portion of one of the best things on earth, linguine with clams, I went with the Lobster Bisque ($9.50). Until I am very old, shrunken, hunched, gray, and wrinkled, whenever I go out to dinner I'll feel like a greedy kid trying to have it all. I love to order lots of little plates to share. Appetizers forever! The first time we went to The Slipway was at the tail end of a seafood feasting weekend with friends from out of town. The only thing I had not had was

lobster bisque. I felt good about my order until it showed up, at which point, I have to say, I was a little saddened when I saw the color of the soup. Rust-murky is not one of my top five hues for food. But the flavor was lovely, velvety and deep without being heavy. Abundant pieces of lobster, rich broth, herbs, and crusty bread—there is nothing more I want from a bisque.

For our second visit to The Slipway, we ventured out alone, a blessed one hour alone, just us, away from Violet, our daughter, whom we love all day long with our whole hearts. We used to go out to dinner at least once a week, and we did it up, complete with drinks and appetizers, bottles of wine, and occasionally with room for dessert. Then we left Portland, had a baby, and for a year, we hibernated and cooked. We're both grateful for my mother-in-law, who lives nearby, so we can get back to looking at each other across a table and talking about nothing and everything. I ordered the mussels ($11.50), sautéed with garlic, wine, dijon, and fresh herbs. I admire what they were going for with the broth, something a little lighter and more elegant than gallons of butter and a whole head of garlic.

For four years I feigned vegetarianism, secretly eating salami at my grandparents' house and hot dogs with my dad at Duchess. These days I'm an open omnivore and enjoy meat in most of its forms, but maybe most especially, charcuterie. I love a rustic meat and cheese board dearly—meat that is cold, sliced, pressed, and cured, or pink, red, and mottled, and served with mustards or other bright condiments, crusty bread, pickles, and maybe a handful of capers. At The Slipway, the $10.50 charcuterie board combines speck, bresola, salami, Spanish chorizo, and paté. Elsewhere, these types of plates are getting really good, with DIY chefs doing the whole nose-to-tail thing on heritage pig parts. This wasn't exactly that. Not bad, but nothing special, with a bit of a prepackaged deli feeling. It's functional, but I'd say, stick with what they're doing best.

After nearly a decade overseeing the fryers at the Dip Net, Scott Yakovenko knows fried seafood. All of the fried seafood baskets at The Slipway are cooked in peanut oil, which is drained and filtered several times each day. The fried oyster appetizer ($8.50) is consistently the star of the show. The crisp, golden coating lightly covers the oysters, which practically explode with the briny essence of the ocean in each bite. Swabbed lightly in the accompanying bright beet juice–stained ginger shallot dipping sauce, the crunchy oysters taste like pure summertime. Order one, and then immediately order another. The fish and chips ($11.50) are also perfectly fried, top-quality thick chunks of fresh, flaky haddock served with crisp French fries. I wish there had been a little more fish; the portion of three small pieces of fish for eleven bucks seemed a little light. The fried calamari is also some of the best we've had recently, served hot, crisp, and with a lemon aioli.

The Slipway's wine and beer list is thorough and moderately priced. There are several wines served by the glass (or by the plastic cup), a selection of local taps, and plenty of imported bottles. In particular, the Slipway Sling, a distinctive mix of Jack Daniels, lemonade, and ginger beer, makes for the perfect accompaniment for fried seafood enjoyed dockside. The service can be a little absentminded, though well intentioned and cheery; it's the kind of place where the waitress may forget your drink, but the bartender will walk it over when she gets a moment. Besides, the bright smiles on everyone's faces make a few hiccups in service difficult to get cranky about.

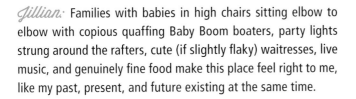

Jillian: Families with babies in high chairs sitting elbow to elbow with copious quaffing Baby Boom boaters, party lights strung around the rafters, cute (if slightly flaky) waitresses, live music, and genuinely fine food make this place feel right to me, like my past, present, and future existing at the same time.

The Slipway represents a remarkable dining opportunity in midcoast Maine, where diners choose from clam hut standards prepared with an atypically expert hand, sharing menu space with inventive upgrades of classic seafood entrees. Look at the smiling faces of the seated customers as you walk from the hostess station to your table; it will be enough to convince you what a special place this is, as what seems like the entire town turns out nightly to share in a local, finely prepared seafood feast cooked by a local hero. The sometimes spotty history of the old restaurant fades to just a memory, ghosts exorcised in a fine mist of peanut oil, oyster liquor, and citronella. It's a pleasure to once again see the banks of the St. George River filled with so much life, light, and great food.

FIVE FIFTY-FIVE • Malcolm
55 Congress Street, Portland, ME 04101; fivefifty-five.com

While you can almost always count on having a burger that has been cooked with care at a "fine dining" restaurant, there is the danger of having to endure a lot of "house-made tomato compote" and "Kobe beef sliders with tarragon aioli" nonsense. Not so at Five Fifty-Five.

Five Fifty-Five's signature hamburger is served only on the bar side of the restaurant. That can be a mixed blessing. While you can't expressly make a reservation for a bar seat, you can ask to have noted on your reservation that you would like to sit at the bar, and the staff will try to keep a seat open for you.

Five Fifty-Five changes its burger selection every few months, and the one being served these days is exceptional. For $12.95 you get a beautiful hamburger (we're guessing in the 10-ounce range) served on a brioche bun with melted Gruyère, horseradish aioli, and what the menu describes as "melted" mushrooms.

The first thing you notice about the burger is the thick slice of Gruyère that positively enrobes the burger in earthy deliciousness. The brioche bun is a soft, buttery, braided roll, almost like a slightly dense croissant. While delicious, after the first few bites, the bottom half tends to fall under the weight and juiciness of the burger itself and all but disappears into a gratifying wash of butter flavor, the sharpness of the horseradish aioli, and the hot, running beef juices. The top half stays strong, continuing to provide structure as you eat.

The hamburger meat itself is an excellent grind, with plenty of fat and strong, pleasantly husky beef flavors. It is cooked to the temperature you specify, and if not, wonderfully, a little under. Great care is clearly taken not to overwork the beef while the patties are formed; there are still intact tendrils of the ground meat, which provide great texture and chew (as opposed to the dusty little pucks common in inferior hamburgers). This is a simply seasoned hamburger for people who care about hamburgers prepared by a chef who likes them too. Fine attention to all aspects of preparation and cooking is shown—no tossing "hamburgers" on this fine-dining menu because they're hip, trendy, or wildly profitable.

The only thing that puzzled me were the mushrooms. Had the menu not referred to them as "melted," I wouldn't have given them a second thought. They were sliced so thinly as to barely affect the flavor of the burger and were not a huge contributor to the overall impact of the dish. That may have been the point: to shave slices of mushroom so thinly that they "melt" in your mouth. A nice idea; they just didn't influence the overall flavor of the burger.

Having a hamburger at the bar at Five Fifty-Five is a lot of fun. While the dining room is certainly more appropriate for "spendy" nights out or special occasions, the atmosphere on the bar side is much different. While service remains impeccable and attentive but not overbearing, there is the slightest hint of a more easygoing approach. The bartender will take your order with a smile, making conversation and generally paying the perfect amount of attention to you. The view from the bar is good, offering a great vantage point for people-watching, with just the right amount of friendliness from the staff. You will leave the Five Fifty-Five bar sated and sleepy, full of a great burger.

THE KOBE BEEF BURGER HOODWINK

Do you know why Kobe beef is prized? It's not just because the cows are given beer to drink. It's certainly not solely because of the profound beefy flavors of Kobe. It's because of the way the fat is intricately marbled throughout the meat. Its value comes entirely from its texture, from the way it feels in your mouth. You know what happens when you run that exquisitely marbled beef through a meat grinder, squash it into patties, and cook it medium-rare? You end up with a pile of under-flavored, offensive mush. It's a waste of Kobe beef, and the Japanese guy that spent months giving that cow massages and spoon-feeding it Cream of Mushroom soup would scream and commit seppuku if he saw what you were doing with it. The chef is shaking his head when you order it, though he is pleased to have charged you $26 for what essentially amounts to a catfood burger. Bottom line: Kobe beef is not for burgers.

A Maine Lobster Festival Menu

- Chilled Sriracha Lobster Salad Lettuce Cups
- Lobster with Sweet Corn Linguine

Eating locally is good—not just trendy or virtuous, but good, as in sweet, fresh perfection. And it doesn't get more local than snipping herbs from your backyard or windowsill garden. We chose basil, parsley, and dill for our Lobster with Sweet Corn Linguine, but sage, cilantro, or tarragon would also be interesting. Almost any herb will do! Our local corn is so sugary sweet in summer it almost doesn't need to be cooked. Don't boil the pants off it the way our parents used to do. These are perfect specimens of produce.

And finally, as always, lobster. We offer several lobster recipes in the "July" chapter, but there's always room for more. In Rockland, we kick off August with the Maine Lobster Festival, the best small-town event ever. Lobster tastes great any time of year, but Maine lobster in summer is an American rite of passage.

Chilled Sriracha Lobster Salad Lettuce Cups ● *Malcolm*

Serves 4–6

Method

1. In a large bowl, combine the first five ingredients and toss well to combine. Chill at least 30 minutes before spooning a third of a cup at a time into individual lettuce leaves. Serve.

INGREDIENTS

1½ pounds cooked lobster meat

¾ cup mayonnaise

1 tablespoon finely chopped chives

1 tablespoon Sriracha, or to taste

Salt and pepper, to taste

1 head butter lettuce, outer leaves removed

Lobster with Sweet Corn Linguine • *Jillian*

Serves 3–4

This dinner is the essence of August in Maine. The small ears of sweet corn are perfectly ripe and barely require cooking. The soft-shell lobster was not much more expensive than Spam, and I had lots of herbs in my backyard washtub garden to complete the trifecta. I bought butter and pasta and a bottle of wine from the grocery store, and it turned out to be the best thing we've made all summer. Sweet and bursty, salty and oceany, earthy, green, and savory.

Method

1. In a small saucepan over low heat, melt the butter with the garlic and the herbs. In a large bowl, toss the corn, the lobster, and the herb butter with the just-cooked linguine. Remove the whole garlic clove from the herb butter before serving. Season to taste with salt and pepper.

NOTE: The lobster can be cooked ahead. I used the same stock pot filled with a little more water to boil the linguine in a sea-salty bath. Use whatever herbs you love, and for that matter, any other sweet summer veggies you have on hand.

INGREDIENTS

8 tablespoons (1 stick) unsalted butter

1 big, fat clove of garlic

1 cup finely chopped parsley, dill, and basil

2 ears corn, kernels cut from the cob

Knuckles, claws, and tail meat of 2 steamed lobsters, chopped in smallish pieces

1 package fresh linguine, cooked according to package directions and drained

Kosher salt and freshly ground black pepper

SEPTEMBER

Back-to-School Menu

- Gluten-Free Two-Ingredient Banana Pancakes
- Homemade Marshmallow Fluff
- Chocolate Moxie Whoopie Pies with Allen's Coffee Brandy Buttercream

No matter your age, September is exciting—crisp apples ripening on the trees, a new school year and new beginnings, cooler nights but the days still warm and sweet, as if this year, in defiance of all previous history, summer won't end.

Our routines become more regimented after Labor Day. We need to plan more, packing snacks and trade-worthy lunches, making sure everyone has a nutritious breakfast in the 15 minutes before the bus comes. Finally, Mom and Dad get a much-needed break. Take a vacation day just for grown-ups to hang around the house eating chips and homemade salsa and sipping fruity drinks. When the whole gang is home from school and intramural sports, clarinet lessons and the debate team, gather around the dinner table to share the highlights of your day. Everyone deserves a nourishing bowl of chowder made with the last of summer's bounty and a comforting dessert before homework, bath, and bed, because it all starts again in the morning.

Gluten-Free Two-Ingredient Banana Pancakes • *Malcolm*

Serves 2

We spend more time sifting through Pinterest boards than most people, looking for inspiring new ideas to tackle. Pinterest is a great way to gauge reader reaction to our posts, but browsing through the site's "Food and Cooking" section can make us feel as if the world has gone stark raving mad. We see users frantically pinning and repinning cooking creations that range from "kinda gross" to "criminally insane."

What's more, these trends seem to hit Pinterest in waves. One week, every recipe is Buffalo-wing flavored. Buffalo chicken dip. Buffalo chicken tacos. Buffalo chicken pizza. Buffalo chicken donuts. Buffalo chicken soup topped with miniature buffalo chicken sliders. The next week, slow cookers might be the topic du jour. Slow cooker meatballs. Slow cooker pulled pork. Slow cooker Mexican chicken pockets. Slow cooker Mexican Buffalo chicken pockets! You get the idea.

We don't often get caught up in these food blogger minitrends. Okay, that's not entirely true; we've been known to make pull-apart bread from time to time or stuff Ferrero Rocher candies where they don't belong. For the most part, though, we resist these fits of food blogger mass hysteria, particularly when the recipes in question include terms like "gluten free" and "dairy free." Gluten and dairy are two of my favorite things, and it's tough to get too worked up about a new cooking project that tosses them into oblivion.

After reading about them at least a dozen times on the web, however, I couldn't shake my fascination with these two-ingredient banana pancakes. Two ingredients? That's right. Just mashed bananas and eggs. No flour, no grain, no gluten, no sugar. Mash well (or even better, give them a buzz with an immersion blender or food processor) and add a dab of (optional!) baking powder to give your batter a tiny bit more lift.

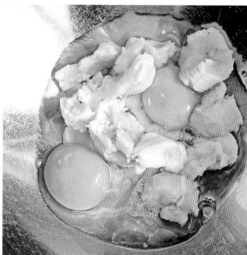

The resulting pancakes are light, fluffy, and healthy enough that, if you like, you can cover them with heaping fistfuls of bacon, chocolate chips, and Maine maple syrup. Because, hey, they're gluten free, right?

INGREDIENTS

2 large ripe bananas

4 eggs

¼ teaspoon baking powder (optional)

Method

1. Combine all the ingredients in a large bowl.

2. Mix well, or pulse with an immersion blender or in a food processor. Spray the griddle with nonstick cooking spray, and heat over medium-high heat.

3. Cook the pancakes in batches a ladleful at a time until they begin to bubble and hold their shape. Flip the pancakes, and cook for 30 seconds more. Serve with butter and syrup.

Homemade Marshmallow Fluff • *Malcolm*

Makes about two cups

If you harbor even a passingly fond memory of opening your lunchbox and finding a Fluffernutter, that classic sandwich made with peanut butter and smooth, spreadable marshmallow cream, you owe it to yourself to try making fluff at home at least once. And if by chance you were that spastic kid with the permanent ring of red Kool-Aid stain and dried bits of fluff around your mouth, you should carry this book into the kitchen right now to try this homemade version.

Homemade marshmallow fluff lives up to your fondest expectations and memories of this sandwich. Indeed, it delivers on a level that the commercial counterpart can't hope to meet. The homemade version is smooth, creamy, and flows and spreads easily. It can be used in any recipe that calls for store-bought marshmallow fluff (the best recipes always do), and pleasantly coats the inside of your mouth, not to mention every surface in your kitchen. It keeps in the fridge for about two weeks.

INGREDIENTS

3 egg whites at room temperature

2 cups light corn syrup

½ teaspoon salt

2 cups sifted powdered sugar

1 tablespoon vanilla extract

Method

1. In the bowl of a stand mixer, combine the egg whites, corn syrup, and salt. Beat with a wire beater on high speed for 5 minutes or until the mixture has thickened and doubled. Reduce the speed to low and add the powdered sugar and the vanilla. Stir until well blended.

Chocolate Moxie Whoopie Pies with Allen's Coffee Brandy Buttercream • *Malcolm*

Makes 8 big whoopie pies

When I was in high school, I don't think I ever went to a party in a gravel pit where there wasn't at least one handle of Allen's Coffee Brandy being poured into cartons of milk. For the uninitiated, Allen's Coffee Brandy is an exceptionally popular libation here in Maine, where over a million bottles are consumed each year; that's one bottle for nearly every man, woman, and child in the state. It's a syrupy combination of sugar and day-old coffee-ground flavor made by combining coffee extract with neutral grain spirits in a 60-proof cocktail that, if you drink enough of it, packs quite a wallop.

If the lies my high school friends told me were true, there are four main reasons for the drink's popularity:

1. Low cost. A gallon of Allen's Coffee Brandy will set you back around $20 dollars or less.

2. When mixed with equal parts milk (as in a so-called "Lewiston Martini"), the stomach-coating effects of the milk slow alcohol absorption, enabling immoderate drinkers to remain semi-functional longer.

3. There is a local legend that the drink smells like coffee and is therefore undetectable by law enforcement. In fact, nothing could be further from the truth. Allen's Coffee Brandy drinkers give off a fairly telltale odor.

4. And, of course, it's delicious.

INGREDIENTS

For the Chocolate Moxie Cakes:

½ cup (1 stick) unsalted butter

¾ cup granulated sugar

¼ cup light brown sugar

1 teaspoon vanilla extract

2 eggs

½ cup buttermilk

¼ cup Moxie soda

2½ cups all-purpose flour

5 tablespoons unsweetened cocoa powder

1 teaspoon baking soda

1 teaspoon baking powder

½ teaspoon salt

For the Allen's Coffee Brandy Buttercream:

½ cup (1 stick) unsalted butter

1 cup marshmallow fluff

4 tablespoons Allen's Coffee Brandy

2 cups powdered sugar

Such considerations no longer have more than academic interest for me, thank God. But I still enjoy a cocktail, and in an effort to drink my cocktails and eat my cake too, I set out to create one of the most Maine-centric desserts I could imagine. The result is the Chocolate Moxie Whoopie Pie with Allen's Coffee Brandy Buttercream. A little Moxie soda adds the mysterious herbaceousness of the fizzy drink to the chocolate cakes while lending tremendous lift, lightness, and rise to the batter. I really like the way the medicinal soda tempers the sweetness of the chocolate cakes; taste a cake by itself before filling the whoopie pies and you'll see what I mean. It's a good thing. The filling, a mixture of marshmallow fluff, powdered sugar, butter, and Allen's Coffee Brandy, is so excessively sweet that it would be almost unsuitable for a regular cake recipe. Eaten all together, though, this very lightly alcoholic dessert combines some of my favorite flavors of New England into an over-the-top twist on a Maine classic. Salud.

Method

For the Chocolate Moxie Cakes:

1. Preheat the oven to 375°F. Line two baking sheets with parchment paper and set aside.

2. In a large mixing bowl or stand mixer, cream the butter, white and brown sugar, and the vanilla for about 5 minutes or until fluffy.

3. Add the eggs, the buttermilk, and the Moxie, and mix for about 1 minute more.

4. Beat in the flour, cocoa, baking soda, baking powder, and the salt, and stir until well combined.

5. Drop by the tablespoonful onto the prepared baking sheets, leaving room for the cakes to spread out, and bake for 10 minutes. Transfer the cooked cakes to a cooling rack and cool completely.

For the Allen's Coffee Brandy Buttercream:

1. In a mixing bowl, beat together the butter and marshmallow fluff until light and creamy. Add the Allen's Coffee Brandy.

2. Slowly add the powdered sugar and mix until light and fluffy. Store in the refrigerator until you are ready to assemble the whoopie pies.

3. To assemble, sandwich a generous amount of filling between two of the cooled cakes. Refrigerate any leftovers.

MAINE FOOD ADVENTURE
A Weekend on a Maine Windjammer featuring the Angelique's Gingerbread Cake

Ready on the peak? Ready on the peak! Ready on the throat? Ready on the throat!

A tanned and sinewy crew member calls out and we respond, repeating the orders. Then we heave and pull the line as a team. I have signed up for a two-day sail, cruising the midcoast Maine waters on the windjammer *Angelique*. I understand now why there are guests who return every summer and fall. It's an escape and an adventure. You can mingle with your fellow passengers or stay solitary, pitch in as much as you like, walk, swim, row, or do nothing but read, eat, and sleep in the sun like a cat. The late summer sun shines every day over the sparkling ocean (on my trip, at least!), and all the stars come out at night. It's heaven.

We were scheduled to leave Camden Harbor on the early-morning high tide, so I arrived at 7 a.m. by taxi at the pier on Atlantic Avenue, just past the town library. All was quiet and pristine. There was no mistaking the *Angelique's* rust-red sails, so I hoisted my canvas and camera bags and walked the plank to the deck, where I was met by Eric, the first mate, who showed me the ins and outs of operating the head and took me to my stateroom, a tiny space all my own with a bunk bed, small sink, and a hatch that opened topside, which kept me from feeling claustrophobic. I threw my things on the top bunk and went topside to explore and mingle.

Most of the other guests had slept aboard the night before and were milling around, drinking coffee and looking pleasantly anxious, like kids on the first day of school. I assessed the group, as I always do in elevators or other close quarters, and decided that I could survive being shipwrecked with this cast: two families of four (children over nine are welcome aboard), single ladies traveling together, older men traveling alone, and young European-looking lovers, all clad in Sperry topsiders and wide-brimmed hats. Soon we were underway, and Sarah, the ship's CIA-trained baker, rang the breakfast (lunch, and dinner) bell, inviting us below for blueberry pancakes, Maine maple syrup, homemade sausages, and orange juice. We clustered around three bench tables and ate family style with our shipmates.

I heard that the cook had made the sausage himself; that's when I introduced myself to a bearded man in suspenders with tattoos on his knuckles and a warm chuckle. William (Bill) Howe is a Le Cordon Bleu–trained chef who has been working in fine restaurants around New England for over a decade, including a stint at one of our Portland favorites, Petite Jacqueline. When not using excellent technique and agility to cook in the cramped, narrow galley of the *Angelique*, he's a scuba instructor and Rumple Minze enthusiast, which means I can trust him with my meals and my life.

With the hills and sails of Camden in the middle distance, I see a man heading toward us in a dinghy. Captain Mike comes aboard and introduces cast and crew, which includes Bill and Sarah in the galley and mates Eric, James, Zach, and Meara. He then tells us that our destination is Camden, meaning that we'll wander aimlessly around the spruce-flecked Penobscot Bay for two days until Sunday morning, when we return to our homeport. Whether this rhetoric is part of the theater of the sea or not matters little. It's thrilling to feel that we're without itinerary, free from phones and Facebook and email. And with that, we set sail with the wind.

This is when the crew enlists volunteers to unfurl the mizzen and hoist the mainsail and perform all sorts of other nautical-sounding tasks. I am otherwise occupied, however—sleeping under a book, watching the clouds go by, chatting up other passengers, and waiting for my next meal. I take my role as resident food blogger and writer seriously, eating everything that is offered and going back for seconds. More on this later. I have not been without my tiny, adorable companion—my baby girl—for the last seven months (and really, for the nine before that), and I plan to bask in sleepiness and solitude as a lady of leisure.

I eat, drink, tan, nap, make conversation, and swim without guilt or responsibility. It's glorious. And of course, I take photos and scribble copious notes in my journal. A few short hours after breakfast, lunch is served on deck: an incredible fish chowder, green salad, and flaky biscuits. I'm beginning to realize that meals on the *Angelique* are going to be memorable.

No one is using a rusty can opener to feed us Hormel chili with a side of hardtack. The food is fresh, bright, and elegant. I really want to get an interview with the chef, but first, another nap under my straw hat.

The afternoon grows long, and we drift stagnant on windless water. It's hot and I'm restless, ready for a change of scene, some land under my feet. At four o'clock we climb down the ladder backwards, into the ketch's rowboat, taking ourselves to shore at Pond Island Wildlife Refuge for a hike and a lobster bake. I have changed into my suit, determined to swim in the calm waters. When I take the plunge, the water is as chilly as one expects Northern Atlantic waters to be, but I don't mind. I feel free, weightless, blissful. When my fingers start going numb, I swim toward the others who have braved the bracing sea, float a bit, and emerge refreshed and renewed. Thank goodness it's time for supper.

Cheese and crackers are served at the water's edge as the sun sinks toward the horizon. Someone opens a bottle of Ketel One and we mix vodka tonics, so civilized that the ghost of E.M. Forster hovers above us, whispering a benediction. Then it's time for the main event: lobster cooked in seaweed that one of the mates has gathered ashore, a three-bean salad dressed in olive oil with poblano peppers, and plastic cups of white wine. I eat my meal while seated on a piece of driftwood, chatting with an older gentleman from Florida. The sweet meat is plentiful, and we are all encouraged to have at least two lobsters, but I'm saving room for s'mores toasted over the open fire. For those not interested in lobster (yes, they do exist), there are also hot dogs and Boca burgers. Then we row back to the *Angelique* in the gathering dusk for hot showers and stargazing in sweaters.

I wake at 9:30 the next morning to the sound of Sarah announcing a breakfast of quiche made with lobster, Canadian bacon, and fruit salad. This is the latest and longest I've slept in over a year, and it feels delicious.

We are anchored near Castine, about an hour and a half from my home by slow boat, but it feels worlds away. The air is crisp and pine scented as we sail to our next destination, Holbrook Island Sanctuary State Park, where I walk alone in the woods, noticing the first fire-colored leaves of autumn. Then I join a small, brave group who have decided to dive from the anchored ship into the ocean, encouraging each other to find pockets of warmth. Once again, I feel elated to be swimming in Maine's icy waters.

Then it is time to eat again. We have been so well fed on this trip that we are starting to wonder if we're being fattened for market. Lunch is tarragon-curry chicken salad wraps with olive oil, lemon, chives, a touch of mayo, honey, pickled grapes, and a crisp pink apple salad. Bill the chef uses a standard pickling blend plus cloves, red wine vinegar, garlic, and sage to pickle grapes, and the result is a taste sensation that is totally unexpected and totally great.

A real camaraderie has developed among the passengers, one I've never experienced during vacations on land. Unrelated adults indulge the whims of children who do not belong to them, even mildly reprimanding the kids when necessary. There is casual conversation between naps, crossword puzzles, and snacks, and a feeling of peace blankets our afternoon cruise in calm waters. By dinnertime we are all starving, and salivate in Pavlovian fashion at the sound of the dinner bell. Tonight's offerings are marinated steak tips with creamy garlic mashed potatoes, roasted squash, and chocolate chip brownies for dessert.

After dinner we take our places around the ship as if we've done this a thousand times. One of the older women helps Sarah with the dishes while the young Swiss lovers practice tying knots on each other's wrists. In the deckhouse, members of the crew (have I mentioned how cute and helpful they all are?) play the banjo and guitar until quiet hour at eleven o'clock. I listen to a few songs, from "Good Night Irene" to "Wagon Wheel," and then retire to my bunk to read. I fall asleep to the sound of mingled voices of song and sea.

Sunday morning dawns clear and bright. We can see Camden Harbor, but the trip isn't over yet. On deck, the mess mates present breakfast: Bill's impressive cured gravlax (equal parts brown sugar and kosher salt, lemon juice, and dill, wrapped and pressed for three days) with bagels, cream cheese, onions, capers, and cornichons. Other offerings include a homemade granola, yogurt, and sliced fresh fruit. I savor this meal in silence, knowing it is my last on the *Angelique*. I am truly, vividly happy, and ready to go home.

Tears roll down my sunburned cheeks when I catch sight of Malcolm and Violet waving from the dock. My very own family has missed me and is awaiting my return. Everyone is exchanging phone numbers and email addresses, signing posters, and snapping photos while I run down the white gangway into the arms of my husband and daughter. This has been the best two-day vacation for a woman traveling alone, a new mom, a food lover, a lady in search of a small piece of sanity, a world watcher and amateur naturalist. I loved getting to read, write, talk, and photograph all by myself in such good company. I cannot imagine a better host than the *Angelique* and her crew.

The *Angelique's* Gingerbread Cake

Adapted from *The New England Cookbook*, by Brooke Dojny
Serves 8

Method

1. Preheat the oven to 350°F. Grease an 8-inch by 8-inch baking pan with butter and flour.

2. In a large mixing bowl, whisk together the flour, baking soda, ginger, cinnamon, nutmeg, and salt.

3. In the bowl of a stand mixer, cream the butter and sugar. Add the molasses, corn syrup, eggs, and orange juice.

4. Stir in the dry ingredients until just combined. Fold in the ginger candy and pour into the prepared pan.

5. Bake 45 to 50 minutes, until the cake is deep brown and a toothpick comes out clean. Pour maple syrup over the still-warm cake and top with the unsweetened whipped cream to serve.

INGREDIENTS

1¾ cups all-purpose flour

1½ teaspoons baking soda

1½ teaspoons ground ginger

1 teaspoon cinnamon

½ teaspoon nutmeg

¼ teaspoon salt

6 tablespoons unsalted butter

½ cup brown sugar

½ cup molasses

½ cup light corn syrup

2 eggs

¾ cup orange juice

¼ cup ginger candy

Maple syrup

Unsweetened whipped cream

COD END SEAFOOD · *Jillian*
Commercial Street, Tenants Harbor, ME 04860; (207) 372-6782; codend.com

I have an imagined history in Tenants Harbor, a tiny, pretty town that inspires quasi-mythic reverie. I can almost remember jumping into the bracing sea from a swing hanging by the edge of the pier and scrambling around the rocks to poke at small crabs and other sea life. I feel like a kid, free of worries, consumed with snail-shell treasures and other sensory adventures. Some of this fiction comes from memory superimposed on this picturesque place. My first-ever high school boyfriend worked at the gas dock at the marina in my hometown, so I spent every day of that summer hanging out in my bikini and jean shorts, getting thrown into the oily water.

Small boats bob in the mid-distance, and the foreground is a pile of line, traps, and the other odds and ends of a working harbor. Here, there is a restaurant you really should visit.

Cod End is a fish market serving super-fresh seafood. You walk through the store/seating area, around the lobster tanks, and pull the knotted door handle that takes you back outside to the cookhouse, where you order at the window a round of the usual suspects of fried goodness and plastic cups of Geary's cold ale from the tap. In warmer weather, we have sat outside and watched the water lap against the rocky shore. But it was too cold for that during our recent September visit (which may be why Cod End closes early to mid-September—call and check to see if they're still open before you make the drive down the St. George peninsula).

Malcolm: I have an actual history with Cod End that is very similar to what Jillian imagines growing up in Tenants Harbor to be like. Located in my hometown, Cod End is tough for me to be objective about, so entwined is it with my childhood. My older sister spent a summer as a teenager behind the counter there, and the place serves as the backdrop for a lot of memories. Like the time I was climbing on the pilings at around eight years old; the tide went out, stranding me at what seemed a dizzying height but was in fact a few feet in the air until someone from the shop came out in a rowboat and rescued me. Or the time in third grade when I jumped off the dock into the freezing water in late November in exchange for half of a Twix candy bar, then walked home shivering to get scolded by my parents, who just couldn't understand the compelling allure of a free candy bar and neighborhood glory. Or in the summer, the way my older friend Jake, who ran a grocery delivery service for the harbor's maritime population using his very own dinghy, would clear a path through the sheen of floating maggots that were sometimes rinsed out of the bait holds of arriving lobsterboats so that I could go swimming. Cod End is as familiar to me as anyplace in the world; it just never dawned on me to actually eat there until now.

We were with friends visiting from out of town who needed fried fish and beautiful views. The air temperature on the peninsulas was a cool 61° thanks to a brisk breeze off the chilly Gulf of Maine. We'd done the obligatory stroll around Marshall Point Lighthouse and sniffed the sweet salt air. We'd filled up glass bottles and jars with sweet, cold water from the spring at Wiley's Corner. We'd driven down to the quarry, past belted cows lying under trees with views of the St. George River. It's becoming a familiar tour, something to do with family and guests on funny-weather days. At this point, we were all starving.

We ordered a fried trifecta for the table: haddock, clams, and oysters, plus a small container of mussels and steamers. It was all very good if not outstanding food with a few excellent touches. Number one, the coleslaw. I am not usually inclined to take more than a polite bite of slaw, which I typically find either unremarkable or somewhat gross, like wet yarn. This particular little plastic cup of cabbage was perky, finely shredded with a pepperiness I could not quite name. It complemented the fried fare nicely. I also enjoyed the two cups of drawn butter that were served with the steamed bivalves, one plain and the other jammed with chopped garlic. Brilliant.

Malcolm: The fried oyster and fried clam rolls were outstanding—ample amounts of fresh oysters and clams, expertly fried golden, nestled into butter-griddled split-top hot dog rolls. The huge haddock fillet shared the same excellent batter and crisp exterior with a few handfuls of (frozen) French fries. I also really enjoyed my split order of steamers and mussels, a lunch-time portion served with both plain and garlic-infused clarified butter. The clams were meaty and sweet, without a hint of mud, and the mussels were perfectly plump, briney vehicles for repeated dunks in garlic butter.

There's lot to like about Cod End. Getting there via the winding woodsy roads leading back from a visit to Port Clyde is the prologue to its charms. Then descending into the parking lot and crossing your fingers that it will be open. Their season seems short—mid-June through early September—but I've been cold there at both ends, so it makes sense to keep it brief and sweet. It is a little pricey, especially if you live in the area and contemplate repeated visits. But I haven't had seafood fresher or sweeter than the stuff I've been served at Cod End. In fact, I think I enjoyed the plump, light sienna-colored mussels and the clean clams that undulate obscenely from their springy black necks as you let them linger in the liquid butter the most.

Malcolm: Locals may balk a little at some of the prices, but for anyone visiting the St. George peninsula, Cod End is worth a stop. They're open well into the evening, and it's hard to imagine a more picturesque place to slow down with a cold Geary's and a basket of fried clams and watch the sun set over the harbor while the ocean laps the hulls of the numerous fishing boats moored there. (It's the Lobster Shack at Two Lights conundrum: Does a lobster roll taste better when the scenery is straight out of a postcard? Yes. Yes, it does.) Cod End is also a full-service fish market with reasonable prices, making it a fine choice for picking up a few (dozen?) lobsters to take home.

But there's almost no reason to end up there, which is what's so cool about it. There are no Ferris wheels, funnel cakes, or spray-painted booty shorts inline skating toward the sunset. There's no sand on which to spread your sunning towel, and it's practically never warm enough to swim. You can kayak or paint with watercolors, go out on a puffin watch, or eat the most amazing fruits of the sea. That's about it. It's a contemplative spot for quieter tourists who aren't seeking thrills or the exotic. It's simply a nice piece of America, and I feel lucky to live a short drive away.

WEEKEND PROJECT: A Scratch-Made Ultimate Cheeseburger, or the Cheeseburger We're Eating When We're Eating Cheeseburgers at Home • *Malcolm*

Makes 3 big burgers

Organizing one's thoughts about the perfect cheeseburger can be more difficult than you might think. In our approach, we decided at the outset to forgo exotic toppings. While delicious, such ingredients aren't always accessible; a great burger should (hopefully) come together from what you already have in your fridge. Thus, we favor lettuce and tomato over foie gras and black truffles. When the cheeseburger craving hits, it's the meat and cheese that immediately spring to mind. Second, we considered each element separately, aiming for a harmonious design.

The Bun We considered several options. Store-bought hamburger buns are too cottony and small and wouldn't stand up to the beefy onslaught to come. Brioche is too delicate, gets obliterated by the juice from a burger, and tastes a little too sweet. We considered pretzel rolls but decided they would prove too chewy and would invite the toppings to end up on the plate rather than the burger. Ultimately, we settled on light rye hamburger buns, which are light and fluffy with just a hint of rye flavor to add a bit of depth.

The Cheese I am a firm believer that individually wrapped American cheese slices are the best possible choice for a cheeseburger, and I'll go to my grave defending that truth. While utterly lacking in flavor, the melt

INGREDIENTS

7 ounces beef sirloin tips

7 ounces beef brisket

7 ounces boneless beef short rib

Salt and pepper (to taste)

3 slices American cheese

3 slices cheddar cheese

3 light rye hamburger buns

2 tablespoons unsalted butter

Mustard

3 hamburger buns

3 leaves Romaine lettuce

Slices of white onion

3 slices tomato

Sliced dill pickle

Mayonnaise

Ketchup

and ooze of American cheese, which begins on contact with the sizzling patty, is immediately what I think of when I imagine a cheeseburger. It drapes the burger and fills in the nooks and crannies on the surface. Jillian, however, was unconvinced, thinking that we needed a cheese with more flavor—but what cheese could that be? Blue cheese, while delicious, overpowers the meat, and I don't like the way Swiss cheese turns plasticky and sweaty when it melts. Neither Muenster, Monterey Jack, nor mozzarella would impart the additional flavor "oomph" that we needed. In the end we settled on using two cheeses per burger: a slice of American for texture and a slice of cheddar for flavor. This decision helped shape another decision.

The Hamburger We would do our own custom grind (recipe follows), but we weren't sure what form the hamburger patty was going to take. I'm not crazy about huge hamburgers and am irritated when a restaurant sets a 10-ounce monster in front of me. Much of the joy of the burger comes from the exterior crust. Since we were using two cheeses, we decided to maximize the crust factor by opting for two 3.5-ounce patties instead of one larger burger. Two patties mean more surface area, more substrate for cheese, and more seasoned crunch.

The Toppings We wanted simple. Bacon, we decided, would make the burgers too meaty, and we had eliminated exotic toppings at the outset. We were tempted to include a fried egg, because you'd be hard pressed to find a more delicious topping for a cheeseburger. (Adding runny egg yolk to anything improves it by 200%; that's science—objective fact, not subjective preference.) Ultimately, though, we realized we had built an "ultimate fast food" burger, and a fried egg strayed from that theme. Since we were baking our own buns and grinding our own meat, we settled on using as many homemade ingredients as possible. Our burger is topped with homemade ketchup and homemade mustard, plus mayonnaise, Romaine lettuce, sliced tomato, sliced dill pickle, and sliced raw white onion. Classic.

A week's preparation, hours of brainstorming, and sheer minutes of analysis and discussion resulted in one of the best cheeseburgers either of us has ever tasted.

Method

1. Put all the knives, bowls, and the meat grinder pieces in the freezer to chill. Anything that touches meat should be kept as cold as possible. Cut the beef into 1-inch cubes and arrange on a baking sheet, leaving space between each piece. Put the baking sheet in the freezer and chill until the meat is cold but not quite frozen, about 10 minutes. Toss the partially frozen beef in a bowl to combine the meat. Push the beef mixture through the meat grinder using the coarse attachment. After all the meat is ground, grind again; this helps mix the different cuts thoroughly.

NOTE: You absolutely must grind your own beef. Do it once and you'll never buy a package of pre-ground hamburger again, that E. coli-tainted, ammonia-soaked meat slurry made from parts of hundreds of cows. Grind your own meat and you control everything from the fat content to the coarseness of the grind. The resulting hamburger treats beef with the dignity it deserves and has the pleasant side effect of being outrageously delicious.

2. Quickly and loosely shape the ground beef into six piles (approximately 3 to 4 ounces each), and press flat with the back of a spatula. Don't overwork or overshape the meat; you want loose, ragged strands, not a hard-pressed patty.

NOTE: Even though it's fun and awesome to press, mold, or shape ground beef or squeeze it between your fingers, don't. Hamburgers aren't supposed to be perfect little pucks. When you overwork the meat, you destroy the grain, and the heat from your hands starts breaking down the fat prematurely. That's how you end up with mushy little gray discs. If you like a thicker burger, use more ground beef. You'll have ragged edges (read: "crispiness") and an imperfect, cratered surface (read: "pools for cheese to gather").

3. Heat a cast-iron skillet over high heat until it's nearly smoking. (You want to get a great sear, and searing requires heat.) Season the patties heavily with salt and pepper. (Ground beef can take more of both than you'd think, and the seasoning will help form your perfect crust.) Place in the skillet, working in shifts if needed. Resist the urge to press down on your patties; doing so will release all their juices, and you'll end up with a dry burger. When the burgers release from the pan, flip and add the American cheese to three patties and the cheddar cheese to three patties. Cover and cook until the cheese melts, about two minutes. Remove from the heat and set aside to rest while you assemble the buns.

4. Split each bun in half. In a large frying pan, grill the halves in butter, cut sides down, until lightly browned. Remove from the heat and apply the mustard to the bottom half, then the lettuce (this will act as a barrier and keep the bottom half of your bun intact when you release the juicy fury of the burger). Add a cheddar-topped hamburger patty, then an American-topped hamburger patty. Top with the onion, the tomato, and sliced pickles. Spread the top half of the bun with mayonnaise and ketchup, and place on top of the burger. Eat immediately. Growl a little if you like.

Leaf Peeping in Northern Maine

● *Malcolm*

When I first started taking Jillian on long road trips north to my hometown in Maine, she was immediately charmed by the same version of the state that makes thousands of tourists visit again and again each summer; that is, the abundant lobster rolls, the easily accessible scenic lighthouses, and the picture-perfect summer weather. It was only after she agreed to move here that I explained that there is so much more to see, and that once you get out of southern Maine and off the coast, the feel of the state changes dramatically.

Drive north the 300 miles from Portland to northern Aroostook County, I explained, and the landscape changes from lobster traps and colorful fishing bouys to wooded timber lots and potato farms. There are great sections of the state that are vast unorganized townships, populated mostly by wild animals and pine trees, identified on maps not by name, but by number.

Popular media sometimes paint this vast region as the "Other Maine." In fact, it's just the opposite; more of Maine looks like the County than the Kennebunks. And there's no better time than leaf-peeping season to explore Maine's vast interior, with plenty of great stops to get a bite to eat along the way. Peak foliage in northern and western Maine occurs in a blaze of glory in late September and early October.

DYSART'S RESTAURANT AND TRUCK STOP
53 Coldbrook Road, Bangor, ME 04401; (207) 942-4878; dysarts.com

Any trip north through the interior of the state should make a stop at Dysart's, the renowned truck stop off Interstate 95 just south of Bangor. Dysart's is something of a Maine institution, serving home-cooked truck-stop food since 1967, when founder Dave Dysart designed the restaurant's first menu around his memories of the best foods he'd ever eaten in northern Maine logging camps. The menu reads like an ode to the red-suspendered set, with big plates of pot roast, dinner rolls the size of a logger's fist, and platters of crusty homemade corned beef hash with runny eggs, all fueled by unlimited cups of thin coffee served in thick, bottomless mugs. Everything is light on seasoning and leans toward stick-to-your-ribs, comforting classics.

I tried a bowl of Dysart's yellow-eyed baked beans with baked ham ($10.99), a dish so popular that Dysart's goes through over four tons of these beans each year. I was astonished by the pile of food placed in front of me:

a huge, thick slab of ham, complete with an anemic-looking slice of canned pineapple on top, a big bowl of creamy, classically Maine coleslaw, and a cup of beans. The ham was fine if a little boring; I chose to focus more closely on the beans, a thick, warm, not-too-sweet bowl of pure happiness. After dabbing on a little ketchup, I finished the bowl immediately and, ignoring the menu's request that I "ask for more if still hungry," swiped a huge buttered dinner roll through the remaining liquid in the bowl.

Jillian opted for the Grand Gobbler sandwich ($7.99), a huge platter that celebrated all that is starchy, refined, and processed. Thick slices of white bread hid piles of sliced roasted turkey and stuffing, with a paper cup of cranberry sauce on the side. One taste, and I regretted my order immediately; the assembly of her ingredients told me that the Hot Roast Beef Sandwich was the way to go at Dysart's, and I kicked myself the rest of the day for misordering. This was a mistake I would not make the next day.

Jillian: It is my new goal in life to make the perfect food order for the dining establishment I'm in. In Dysart's, "Get the Gravy" is practically stamped on the walls and the aprons of the surly waitresses. I almost ordered a burger—but a truck-stop burger, though bound to be greasy and good, seemed too close to a cliché, so I kept thinking. And obviously, no one dines at a truck stop for the salad. As I am not a fan of bottomless beans or roast beef, I found what made the most sense for the environment without stepping outside my personal comfort zone. Stuffing is maybe, secretly, my favorite thing in the world, and stuffing crammed between bread, making sweet carb-on-carb love, is almost too sensual to be true. The turkey, to me, is just gravy. Alas, there was no actual gravy. The Grand Gobbler is not a hot turkey sandwich, no sir. The turkey is cold. Let me say it again, THE TURKEY IS COLD. And therein lies its genius. Pile

hot (well, warmish) stuffing, cold turkey, mayo, and cranberry jelly on the whitest bread you've ever seen—thick, soft, and bearing little resemblance to the wheat from which it must have once, long ago, come—and get a sandwich that a person might compile at midnight, hours after a holiday meal. The stuffing gets zapped in the microwave, but you get impatient and slap the turkey on straight out of the fridge. I ate it all up, peering under turkey stragglers on my plate for any last remaining bits of wonderful, moist, pablum-ish stuffing.

There's something about being on the road, even an hour from home, that makes you crave a place like Dysart's. At any other opportunity, you might well turn your nose up at the short-tempered waitstaff or the communal seating, tables filled with fellow travelers on the road to somewhere, making a quick stop for classic Maine food. Ultimately, you don't come to Dysart's because you're craving a culinary experience; you visit because you want to feel, just for a few moments, like you're among friends and family. Dysart's makes you feel like you're sitting around the family dinner table. When you're just off the highway, it's a welcome relief.

GRAMMY'S COUNTRY INN • *Jillian*
1687 Bangor Road, Linneus, ME 04730; (207) 532-7808

I heard the record skip, but only for a moment, before the after-church crowd went back to their bulging breakfasts. The tractor boys at the counter pointed us to more tables in the back, but we seated ourselves on stools between the door and cash register, a great vantage point for viewing the action.

> *Malcolm:* We were quite taken with how patient and friendly everyone seemed. Grammy's can look from the outside like the kind of place where nonregulars might not be welcome, but nothing could have been further from the truth. While I'm sure it was a different story in the kitchen, where they must have been cursing our lunch orders at such an early hour, out front it was all smiles and warm nods.

Grammy's ceiling is low, and the walls are paneled in light wood—it must be a cozy refuge in the chasm of a bleak winter. Our courtside seats allowed us to contemplate the baked goods overflowing in front of us: whoopie pies as big as my face, hunks of yellow cake streaked with strawberry jam, chocolate-frosted peanut butter cookies (these rule), Brobdingnagian muffins and brownies, and I think pies. We'd read to be prepared for generous portions and already knew this was a place well chosen.

It was 10:30 in the morning, and Malcolm was single-minded in his quest for something smothered in gravy.

Malcolm: This doesn't begin to adequately explain my attitude that morning. I had spent the previous 24 hours quite literally kicking myself (this created quite the scene) over the previous day's misstep at Dysart's and had been mentioning my ordering mistake about every hour or so. After briefly considering a double breakfast in order to get an extra review in, I settled for one only on the condition that I get the biggest, graviest thing I could find.

I perused, pondered, and weighed all options, taking into account context and potential energy expenditure and caloric needs for the day ahead. (We would be in the Jeep from 11 AM until 6 PM.) My calculations led me in the end to what should have been immediately obvious: a fried egg breakfast sandwich ($4.79). Yes. Of course. This meant more of the whitest, squishiest bread on earth, bread I would be embarrassed to buy in daily life but which, the truth is, I love very, very much. It also meant two pristine fried eggs and, nestled between them almost invisibly, white American cheese. This was living. Freedom from foodie oppression. I almost wished I had a hangover. I could detect the essence of butter, golden fried butter, and heard a dim chorus sung by a lower order of angels. The hand-cut French fries were a low point, sadly, not quite crisp enough for my taste, but plentiful. More than sufficient, in fact. A ponderous pile of potato.

Malcolm: Jillian's fries were weak but plentiful. I blame this on us; the kitchen was not set up for full lunch service, in spite of our waitress's protests to the contrary. These seemed like fries that had been plunged desperately into oil that wasn't quite up to temp. My hot roast beef sandwich ($10.95), on the other hand, delivered on the restaurant's slogan: I really did "get more than [I] expect." A huge tower of thick, white bread, piles of roast beef, with two huge scoops of mashed potatoes and a big bowl of coleslaw. Everything was covered in thick brown gravy. It was an outrageous amount of food, and I loved every bite of it . . . when I finished it the next day.

Onward we drove, until finally we reached the northern entrance of Baxter State Park. The park is the legacy of Percival P. Baxter, the governor who carved out this plot of wild nature for the people of Maine and America. Entrance to the park is free for all Maine residents. We marveled at the sublime landscape, which includes majestic Mt. Katahdin. The road was in good condition, far less axle-breaking than described in the guidebooks;

we made the journey through in two hours, with a couple of lookout stops and a moment to dip our toes in the icy Allagash.

It was a spectacularly gorgeous afternoon, pine-scented and serene in the 200,000-acre woods. I'm glad I have seen more of Maine and glad to know there is so much left to discover. It is awesome to behold. We feel compelled to be back out there, to see more wildlife up close, walk into the woods, sleep under the stars, possibly touch a puffin (unless it's illegal to touch a puffin, in which case I shall not). We want to continue driving, eating, meeting, and making the most of this grand adventure. It isn't any more or less real than Portland, the midcoast, or the postcards. I have been to those places, too, and I can assure you they all have both weight and water. It is as idyllic as it seems in books, and I understand why there are so many storytellers weaving yarns about this magical state. We came home a little wiser, a little fatter, inspired and tired and happy to be home. It was the best kind of journey.

A Menu for Apple-Picking Season

- Smoky Lamb and Chorizo Chili
- Chicken Fricassée
- Hazelnut and Chocolate Chip Biscotti
- Baked Apple with Ginger Cookie and Whiskey Whipped Cream

Early autumn in Maine is homey, lovely, and magic. We like summer as much as the next person, but we never say no to September. Crisp air, the start of school with new shoes and schedules and pencils, wood smoke, colored leaves, a world full of promise—is it possible to emerge from a New England childhood, unless unusually deprived, without a fondness for September? Imagine yourself curled up on a window seat, on the couch, or at a snug kitchen table with a cup of coffee (cream and sugar, please) and a biscotti for dunking. Dunking just might be the reason for evolving opposable thumbs. Think about it.

Smoky Lamb and Chorizo Chili • *Malcolm*
Serves 6

After a chilly day of picking apples, this chili brings all the hearty, filling heat you want, with a slightly gamey, pleasantly funky flavor from the lamb. The toppings brighten up the smoky, rich flavor of the big bowl of meat, so don't skimp on the sour cream, cheddar, and chopped green onions.

If you've never worked with dried chilies before, they're fantastic. If you have trouble finding them, buy several bags at Whole Foods or your local Hispanic market, as other recipes in this cookbook use them, and they keep forever. To de-seed and de-stem, hold them over the garbage and start ripping them up; the seeds will fall away into the trash, and you can toss the stems (or better, compost them!).

Be sure to use Mexican-style chorizo rather than the cured Spanish style. The brighter red and more synthetic looking you can find, the better, as the oil that seeps out will be used for sautéing all the other ingredients. After all the ingredients have been combined, you can skim off some of the neon-orange oil, but this isn't usually a problem.

Method

1. Combine the first three ingredients in a saucepan. Cover and simmer until the chiles soften and the broth turns dark red, about 10 minutes. Purée the mixture in a food processor. Strain through a mesh strainer, pressing on any solids until all the liquid is drained. Set aside.

2. Cook the chorizo in a large pot over medium heat until the drippings flow freely. Add the onion, the garlic, the oregano, and the cumin, and sauté until the chorizo starts to brown and the onions soften, about 5 minutes.

3. Crumble the lamb into the pot, and add the salt and pepper. Sauté until the lamb is no longer pink. Add the chili liquid and reduce the heat. Cover and simmer for an hour.

4. Add the drained pinto beans and simmer until the mixture is thick, about 15 minutes. Serve with the grated cheese, the green onions, the sour cream, the pickled jalapeños, and the fresh cilantro.

INGREDIENTS

2¼ cups unsalted chicken broth

3 ounces dried ancho chiles

1 teaspoon cayenne pepper

1½ pounds pork chorizo, casings removed (about 4 or 5)

1 large red onion, chopped

1 ball of garlic, peeled and chopped

1 tablespoon dried oregano

1 tablespoon cumin

1½ pounds ground lamb

1 can (15 ounces) pinto beans, drained

Salt and black pepper

Grated cheddar cheese

Sliced green onions

Sour cream

Pickled jalapeños, chopped

Fresh cilantro, chopped

INGREDIENTS

1 whole chicken (3½–4 pounds), cut into pieces

Kosher salt and freshly ground black pepper

3 tablespoons unsalted butter, divided

1 tablespoon olive oil

1 small yellow onion, diced

½ cup carrots, diced

½ cup celery, diced

8 ounces crimini mushrooms, quartered

2 tablespoons all-purpose flour

⅔ cup dry white wine

4 cups chicken broth

2 sprigs flat leaf parsley

1 bay leaf

1 teaspoon fresh sage, minced

1 teaspoon fresh thyme, minced

1 tablespoon fresh rosemary, minced

2 egg yolks, room temperature

¼ cup heavy cream

2 tablespoons lemon juice

Chicken Fricassée • *Jillian*

Serves 4

Chicken fricassée is classic comfort food and absolutely ideal for fall. There are red leaves and political signs littering the lawns in the neighborhood, pumpkins and scarecrows and wood smoke in the air. It's my favorite time of year.

This recipe's result is velvety. Rich yet light. Creamy, lemony, and fragrant with winter herbs. I am pleased and proud to present my version of this ancient and wonderfully savory dish.

Method

1. Pat the chicken dry and season the skin with salt and pepper. In a large Dutch oven, melt 2 tablespoons of the butter with the olive oil. Over medium-high heat, brown the chicken on both sides, about 10 minutes total. Transfer to a plate.

2. Reduce the heat to medium and sauté the onion, the carrots, and the celery until soft, about 8 minutes. Scrape up any brown bits with a wooden spoon.

3. Add the mushrooms, cooking 4–5 minutes. Stir in the flour and cook about 1 minute or until all the liquid is absorbed.

4. Pour in the wine and bring to a boil, stirring until the liquid thickens, less than a minute. Then add the chicken broth.

5. Place the chicken, skin side up, in the pot, along with any accumulated juices. Add the herbs and bring to a boil. Reduce to a simmer, and cook, partially covered, 25–30 minutes.

6. Remove the chicken to a plate and simmer the liquid uncovered, about 5 minutes.

7. To thicken the sauce, whisk the egg yolks and the heavy cream together in a small bowl. Remove a half cup of the cooking liquid to another bowl and, one tablespoon at a time, temper the eggs and the cream. Slowly stir the thickener—called a "liaison"—into the pot.

8. Return the chicken to the pot. Add the remaining butter and the lemon juice. Bring to a simmer, stirring gently, and serve over rice or with bread.

Hazelnut and Chocolate Chip Biscotti • *Jillian*

Makes about a dozen cookies

It's possible that I've had more than thirty jobs in my thirty-four years. I just can't seem to figure out what it is I want to do all day every day for the rest of my life. Because I went to college in the late 1990s and wavered somewhere on the continuum between wing-wearing interesting and full-blown insane, I worked in a coffee shop off Newbury Street in Boston. We wore plaid, listened to moody or sprightly indie music, and drank thousands of cups of coffee. It was there that I first learned to bake biscotti between writing papers on Marguerite Duras and Anne Sexton and talking to the band boys from Berklee College of Music. I didn't much care for those carefully crafted, twice-baked Italian dunking cookies, but the truth is, I didn't like drinking coffee either. Don't tell Troy Dyer.

Method

1. Preheat the oven to 325°F. Spread the hazelnuts (also called filberts) on a baking sheet and toast 5–7 minutes. Allow them to cool completely, then rub between your palms to remove the skins. Chop roughly and set aside. Increase the oven temperature to 350°F.

2. In a large mixing bowl, whisk together the flour, the baking powder, the cinnamon, and the kosher salt.

3. In the bowl of a stand mixer, cream the butter and the sugars. Add the Nutella, then the eggs, one at a time, scraping down the bowl as necessary. Measure in the extracts, then beat in the dry ingredients until just combined. Use a spatula to fold in the toasted hazelnuts and the chocolate chips.

4. Halve the dough and roll each half into a 2-inch by 12-inch loaf. Bake on a parchment-lined baking sheet, 30–35 minutes, until the logs are firm to the touch and slightly golden-brown on the edges. Allow them to cool completely. Slice, slightly on the bias, into ½-inch pieces.

5. Preheat the oven to 275°F. Arrange the slices on the parchment-lined baking sheet and toast 30 minutes. Let cool. Store in an airtight container for up to two weeks.

Baked Apple with Ginger Cookie and Whiskey Whipped Cream • *Jillian*

Serves 4

This dessert is a bit of a hodgepodge. It's seasonal, it's boozy, and it's a delight for your mouth. You're gonna love it. It started with an apple. We also had this incredible heavy cream in a super-pleasing mason jar from Beth's Farm Market in Warren. I knew that ingredient had to be incorporated somehow. As I looked longingly at the bottle of Jameson on the bar, I was struck by a scathingly brilliant idea. Concoct a magical elixir. And

INGREDIENTS

1 cup hazelnuts

2¾ cups all-purpose flour

½ teaspoon baking powder

½ teaspoon cinnamon

¼ teaspoon kosher salt

8 tablespoons (1 stick) unsalted butter, room temperature

¼ cup granulated sugar

¼ cup packed light brown sugar

½ cup Nutella hazelnut spread

3 large eggs, room temperature

1½ teaspoons vanilla extract

½ teaspoon almond extract

1 cup chocolate chips

INGREDIENTS

Baked apples:

¼ cup brown sugar

¼ cup craisins (dried cranberries)

¼ cup chopped walnuts

1 teaspoon cinnamon

4 red apples

1 tablespoon unsalted butter

Ginger cookies:

¾ cup vegetable shortening

1 cup granulated sugar, plus more for rolling

1 large egg

¼ cup molasses

2 cups sifted all-purpose flour

2 teaspoons baking soda

1 teaspoon ground cinnamon

1 teaspoon ground ginger

½ teaspoon ground cloves

½ teaspoon salt

Whiskey whipped cream:

8 ounces heavy cream, very cold

2 tablespoons Irish whiskey

2 tablespoons granulated sugar

1 tablespoon vanilla extract

because this dish needed a base note, a platform from which it could sing, I baked ginger cookies—so-simple-it's-almost-embarrassing cookies.

Method

Baked apples:

1. Preheat the oven to 375°F. Combine the sugar, the craisins, the walnuts, and the cinnamon. Core the apples. (NOTE: I do not own an apple corer, but I found that a loose tea infuser worked exceedingly well for scooping out the apple's insides.) Pack the sugar filling into the hollow of each apple and top with a pat of butter. Place the apples in an oven-safe dish, pour in an inch of boiling water, and bake for 40 minutes.

Ginger cookies:

1. Preheat the oven to 350°F. Line cookie sheets with parchment paper. In the bowl of a stand mixer, cream the shortening and the sugar. Add the egg and the molasses and beat until completely incorporated.

2. In a large mixing bowl, whisk together the flour, the baking soda, the cinnamon, the ginger, the cloves, and the salt. Pour the dry ingredients into the creamed mixture and whisk until combined.

3. Roll the dough into 1-inch balls. Roll the balls in the granulated sugar and place them half an inch apart on the prepared cookie sheets. Flatten the balls slightly with the heel of your hand. Bake for 12 minutes. Cool on wire racks.

Whiskey whipped cream:

1. Combine all the ingredients in a stand mixer on high (or use handheld beaters) until a good, stiff whipped cream consistency develops.

To assemble this dessert, place an apple in a small bowl with a few cookies on the side. Top with the whipped cream. Each aspect of this dessert is easy. I first prepared the apple filling mixture, got to work on the cookies, and while it all baked, I whipped up the cream. The magic is in the combination, textures, temperatures, and sugars melting in your mouth in perfect bites. I have a feeling the spiked cream is going to be dolloped onto cups of coffee in the morning.

OCTOBER

O ctober in Maine is all about smoke from woodstoves drifting into jewel-toned leaves, walking through forests lit from within, appreciating your cozy indoor space, warming up with a big pot of soup and a knit sweater, and celebrating Halloween like a good New Englander with jack-o-lantern carvings, bobbing for apples, hot-spiked cider, and a spooky story marathon. Fall is a time to prepare and turn inward.

Though we can run out to the grocery store whenever we need to, unlike our forebears, there remains an ancient urge to stock the pantry and put up canned pumpkin and applesauce. Baking in October with apples and pumpkins, cinnamon and nutmeg just feels right.

Halloween Nibbles Menu

- The Scurvy and Spice
- Apricot-Shellacked Ghost Chile Chicken Wings
- Chinese Spare Ribs
- Lobster Noodles with Hot and Spicy Scallion Butter
- Apple Fritters

The Scurvy and Spice • *Jillian*
Makes one cocktail

For better or worse, spiced rum is tied to the Caribbean Sea. A vacation that takes you anywhere from New Orleans to Barbados will, if you are so inclined, have you sipping on some kind of fruity punch potent with the molasses-based spirit within minutes of arrival. Many years ago we spent a night in St. John in the U.S. Virgin Islands drinking Bacardi 151 and diving from the hot tub into the pool. The next day, a wild donkey challenged me to a fistfight and stole my wallet. At least, that's how I remember it. These days, I prefer to sip good rum poured over ice.

But when I'm throwing a party I love to have a punch, a cocktail with kick, something fun for the grown-ups while the kids are bouncing around on a Pixy Stix and Kit Kat high. This is the absolute perfect drink for your Halloween monster mash bash. I've concocted this cocktail from home-made ginger-infused simple syrup and lots of fresh-squeezed orange juice. Joining the illustrious ranks of The Hurricane and The Painkiller, I present my own creation, loosely based on one of my all-time favorites, The Dark and Stormy. Any dark rum with a salty name will work: Captain Morgan Private Stock, Kraken, or Sailor Jerry.

INGREDIENTS

Half of an orange, cut into thin wedges

½ ounce ginger-infused simple syrup

2 ounces dark spiced rum

Dash of Angostura bitters

Splash of seltzer water

Sprinkle of nutmeg

Method

1. In a cocktail shaker, muddle the orange wedges with a wooden spoon. Fill one-third of the shaker with crushed ice. Add the ginger syrup, the rum, and the bitters and shake. Pour the mixture into a highball glass. Top with a splash of seltzer and garnish with nutmeg and a thin orange wedge.

Apricot-Shellacked Ghost Chile Chicken Wings • *Malcolm*
Serves 6-8

When I think back on my history of eating spicy foods, a significant turning point springs instantly to mind. It was 2007, and Jillian and I were living on the Gulf Coast of Mexico. We were at one of our favorite restaurants, a few blocks off the zocalo in Merida. It was a bit of a tourist trap to be certain, but there were just as many hard-drinking expats lining the barstools on a Wednesday afternoon as there were smiling families posing for pictures with rifles and wearing multicolored sombreros. The Yucatan peninsula is a part of Mexico famous for its inclusion of sliced or diced habanero peppers, either raw or in a quick pickling solution, with every meal. On this particular afternoon I decided my lunch needed a little more fire, and I asked the waiter for an additional side of habaneros.

"Very hot," he explained in heavily accented English, setting the dish on the table. I assured him I understood, and began adding peppers by the forkful to my lunch. After a few bites and some spontaneous sweating, I saw that a small group of waiters had assembled off to the side, watching for any signs of weakness as I happily munched the peppers. I wonder if they were waiting to see if I would crack; I like to think that they were impressed by the heat tolerance (if not the language skills or common sense) of the pale extranjero.

As spice lovers like myself continue down the road of hot food, the danger is that food stops tasting like anything. Eventually, you are masking whatever you are eating with layers of heat that were never meant for human beings. Becoming comfortable with the heat of a habanero is enough, I think; it's a spicy chile, but still one that complements flavor rather than masking it. An orange habanero pepper weighs in at around 300,000 Scoville units (the scale used to measure heat in chiles), which makes a habanero about 60 times spicier than a jalapeño. That's enough heat for most people. Any hotter and chiles stop being mere ingredients

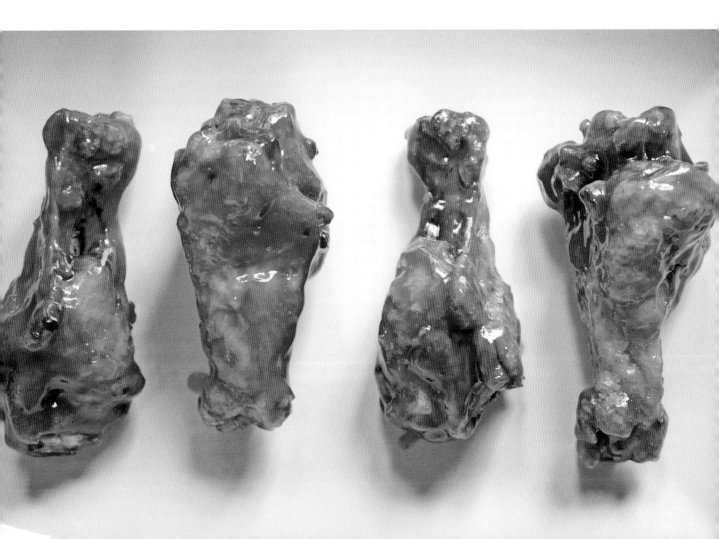

INGREDIENTS

3 tablespoons dark brown sugar

1 teaspoon honey

2 cloves garlic, minced

½ cup (1 stick) salted butter

½ cup ketchup

½ teaspoon ground Bhut Jolokia chile

1 cup apricot preserves

Pinch of salt

¼ cup bourbon

5 pounds chicken wing sections, room temperature and patted dry

Peanut oil, for frying the chicken

and become poison to the human body. That's where the Bhut Jolokia, or "Ghost pepper," enters the picture.

Until 2011, the Bhut Jolokia was recognized by the Guinness World Records as the spiciest chile pepper in existence. It registers up to 1,041,427 Scoville units, making it more than 200 times hotter than the humble jalapeño. The pepper grows naturally in the town of Tezpur in Northeastern India, but it's not widely used as a flavoring agent for food in that part of the world. Instead, mashed Bhut Jolokia is smeared on fences as a deterrent to wild elephants, or it is processed for use as a chemical agent in hand grenades and pepper sprays used by Indian authorities to control mobs and riots. It's not food. It's a toxin. Of course I had to try it.

After placing an order with a mildly sketchy online pepper dealer, I took delivery of a nondescript, unmarked plastic container of ground Bhut Jolokia and allowed it to sit in my pantry for several weeks while pondering how best to approach it. I could feel the heat from the pepper in my nose even through the sealed container; clearly some caution was in order. Though it is far, far too hot to be used by itself, ground Ghost chile is incredibly complex, with the taste of fruit bark and lots of roasted, earthy flavor behind the heat. It's not a one-note spiciness like the jolt you get from adding lots of Tabasco to your vegetable juice, but a round, flavorful, toasted heat that I was certain could be worked into a hot sauce that was plenty spicy but still edible and enjoyable.

My eventual solution was to balance the heat of the chile with an equal amount of sweetness—in this case, a whole jar of apricot jam, brown sugar, and honey with only a half teaspoon of the ground Bhut Jolokia. The first taste that your brain registers is fruity sweetness; it's only after you chew and swallow (and repeat) that the heat clings to the back of your throat and wraps itself around your tongue. As a sauce for Buffalo wings, it's a lot of fun to eat, and it creeps up on you with the startling suddenness of grain alcohol. Instead of tracing the progress of a creeping, building heat, the burn seems to come all at once, knocking you over the head and sending a rush of endorphins dancing merrily down your spinal cord. It's shocking and surprising. And delicious.

These chicken wings taste great any time of year. Cook them for Halloween, but remember them for your Super Bowl party as well. (And I promise you, they are memorable!) This recipe earned me an appearance on *The Today Show* on the Friday before Super Bowl 2013, where I competed in—and won—a Buffalo wing cook-off with two other finalists on Rockefeller Plaza.

Method

1. In a small saucepan over medium heat, combine the brown sugar, honey, garlic, butter, ketchup, chile, apricot preserves, and salt. Bring to a boil, stirring almost constantly. Reduce the heat to a simmer, add the bourbon, and stir. Simmer until the sauce thickens, up to one hour.

2. Pat the chicken wing sections until they are very dry. In a large sauce pan over medium heat, bring the peanut oil to 350°F. Working in batches, pat dry the chicken wing sections a second time and add them to the hot oil. Fry the wings, turning them occasionally, until golden-brown, about 10 minutes per batch. Transfer to paper towels to drain.

3. When all the wings are cooked, toss a few at a time in a bowl of the apricot Ghost chile sauce to coat evenly. Serve with a glass of milk, just in case.

DISCLAIMER: All those guidelines you read about safe chile pepper handling—such as wearing gloves and not touching your eyes—should most certainly be followed when working with Bhut Jolokia. Remember that this stuff is essentially poison, and doing something without thinking (such as taking a big whiff of ground Ghost chile) can destroy your airways and may even land you in the hospital. You've been warned.

Chinese Spare Ribs • *Malcolm*

Serves 4 as an appetizer

Chinese-style spare ribs are one of our fallbacks when dealing with an unfamiliar Chinese restaurant menu. Even when they're bad, they're pretty good—crunchy in some parts, chewy in others, and shellacked with a bright fire-engine-red sticky sauce.

Unlike many of our bastardized Chinese-American favorites (I'm looking at you, General Tso!), Chinese-style spare ribs can to some degree trace their lineage back to actual Cantonese cooking, where char siu is cooked hanging from the roof of a wood-burning oven. We've read plenty of stories about cooks using drapery hooks to hang the meat from the racks of their home kitchen ovens, but such elaborate preparation really isn't necessary; you can achieve similar results simply by roasting your ribs in a pan, then cranking up the heat at the very end to get some crispy caramelization on the honey-basted marinade.

A final note or two about the sauce: For maximum Chinese-style spare ribs, you can add a few drops of red food coloring to the marinade, but allow the ribs to soak in this marinade at least overnight, preferably up to a couple of days. Most ready-made hoisin sauce already contains some red coloring, so you may find you like the natural color just fine. We didn't add any for the photographs of this recipe. Also, this recipe gets a lot of its flavor from a dry rub of Chinese five-spice powder. If you can't stomach the idea of spending $8 on a tiny jar of spices that you may only use once, you can make your own by combining 1 teaspoon ground cinnamon, 2 teaspoons

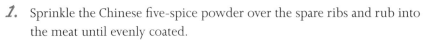

INGREDIENTS

1 tablespoon Chinese five-spice powder

1 full rack St. Louis–style spareribs, cut into individual ribs (about 3 pounds total)

½ cup hoisin sauce

¼ cup dry sherry

2 tablespoons soy sauce

¼ cup honey

2 cloves garlic, grated or minced

fennel, 1 teaspoon star anise, ¼ teaspoon ground cloves, and ½ teaspoon Sichuan peppercorns, and grinding them together in a spice grinder or mortar and pestle.

Method

1. Sprinkle the Chinese five-spice powder over the spare ribs and rub into the meat until evenly coated.

2. In a gallon-sized Ziploc bag, combine the hoisin sauce, dry sherry, soy sauce, honey, and garlic. Squeeze the bag a few times to mix the ingredients. Add the ribs and mix until evenly coated. Seal the bag, transfer to the refrigerator, and let the ribs marinate overnight or for a few nights.

3. When ready to cook, preheat the oven to 375°F. Remove the ribs from the bag, and reserve the marinade. Line a rimmed baking sheet with foil, set a wire rack in it, and spread the ribs evenly over the rack. Cover with aluminum foil and roast for 1 hour. Remove the foil, brush the ribs with the marinade, increase the heat to 450°F, and continue to roast until charred, glazed, and sticky, about 20 minutes longer, rotating the ribs and basting with the marinade once more during the roasting. Let rest 10 minutes, then serve.

Lobster Noodles with Hot and Spicy Scallion Butter • *Jillian*
Serves 2

I almost didn't buy the lobster for this recipe. Lobster wasn't cheap at the time, and I was feeling miserly. But you only need one lobster to feed two people with this dish, and I used pretty much the entire animal, like a plains Native American processing a buffalo. I'm glad I bit the bullet, because this recipe is awesome.

For kicks I made a lot of chile oil, but only used two tablespoons. You can absolutely skip this step or simply add red chile flakes to the vegetable oil in the skillet. If you don't feel like making lobster stock, you can substitute chicken broth, but the lobster stock really does add depth and makes you feel very chef-like. But also buy a scented candle (I like cinnamon-apple), because otherwise your kitchen will smell a little briny for a while. This brothy bowl has all the flavors I look for in an Asian-inspired dish. It's spicy, sweet, fishy, and herbal, with lots of slurpy, slippery noodles, which makes it a perfect post-trick-or-treating bowl of yum to slurp while still in costume.

INGREDIENTS

1 cup vegetable oil

4 dried red chiles, broken in half

A 1½-pound lobster

Kosher salt

½ box rice noodles

¼ cup onion, diced

2 tablespoons garlic, minced

2 tablespoons chile oil

¼ cup dry white wine

1 cup lobster stock

1 teaspoon Sriracha chili sauce

¼ teaspoon brown sugar

2 tablespoons unsalted butter

1 cup scallions, roughly chopped

1 cup basil, roughly chopped

Method

1. To make a chile-oil infusion: In a small pan, heat the oil and chiles over medium-high heat until the peppers begin to sizzle. Remove from the heat, cover, and let stand to steep for at least an hour.

2. Steam the lobster in a large stockpot in about 2 inches of salted water, 5 to 7 minutes. Remove to a cutting board and proceed to crack and extract the meat, reserving the tomalley. Return the empty shell to the stockpot, add enough water to cover the empty shell, and simmer the stock while you complete the next steps. Roughly chop the tail, knuckle, and claw meat, and set aside.

3. Cook the rice noodles according to the package directions and drain.

4. In a large skillet over medium heat, sauté the onion and garlic in the chile oil (the rest can be stored in the refrigerator for several weeks). Turn down the heat to medium-low, and add the wine, lobster stock, Sriracha sauce, brown sugar, butter, scallions, and basil.

5. Turn off the heat. Stir in the lobster meat and tomalley, then the rice noodles. Serve in shallow bowls, preferably with chopsticks!

Apple Fritters • *Jillian*
Serves 8

Late one Sunday afternoon, we went apple picking at Hope Orchards. With a warm sun on our backs and a crisp chill in the air, it was an idyllic hour of October. We put the baby in a backpack and went walking up and down the aisles between the trees, spying ripe fruit against a backdrop of bright blue. There were rows and rows of Cortland and Macintosh, small, squat, irregular, and tart. These are good snacking apples and even better for baking. Check the schedule for which varieties your favorite orchard will have in late September through October.

Because the weather was turning cool with gray skies overhead and a whipping wind, we thought of harvest-fair food, and most especially, we thought of fritters: fried, sweet, and scrumptious. These are awesome and easy, and they make a good after-school snack or Halloween party treat. Pop some popcorn, watch a scary movie, get cozy under a blanket, and eat apple fritters. Some people face fall with dread and bitter anticipation. Fall makes me feel nostalgic and hopeful, and especially excited to share my love of foliage, cider, gourds, costumes, giving thanks, boots, my birthday, wood-burning fires, and pies with Violet. Autumn in Maine is amazing.

Method

1. In a large mixing bowl, whisk together the flour, sugar, baking powder, salt, and cinnamon.

2. In a small bowl, whisk together the eggs, milk, vanilla, and melted butter. Stir the wet ingredients into the dry so that the mixture is just combined, then fold in the chopped apple.

3. In a deep skillet or pot, heat an inch and a half of oil. When the oil is quite hot (test it with a small scoop of batter) drop fritters by the teaspoon, about five at a time. Cook approximately 2 minutes, flip, then fry another 30 seconds to one minute until they are deep golden-brown. Remove to a paper towel and roll in cinnamon sugar or dust with powdered sugar when cool. Serve with hot coffee, tea, ice-cold milk, or brandy.

INGREDIENTS

2 cups all-purpose flour

½ cup granulated sugar

2¼ teaspoons baking powder

1¼ teaspoons salt

2 teaspoons cinnamon

2 eggs

¾ cup whole milk

2 teaspoons vanilla extract

2 tablespoons melted butter

2 cups chopped tart apple

Canola oil

Confectioner's sugar for dusting

Cinnamon sugar for rolling

Big G's

est. 1986

FOR TAKE-OUT ORDERS

581

DINING HOURS
6am-7pm

YES, We're
OPEN

BIG G'S DELI • *Malcolm*

581 Benton Avenue, Winslow, ME 04901; (207) 873-7808; big-g-s-deli.com

Big G's Deli is a central Maine institution, feeding class after class of Colby College students since 1986. What started as a small sandwich shop has evolved into a large, 200-seat cafeteria-style restaurant that takes up an entire vinyl-sided modular building, with a giant grimacing illustration of founder Gerald Michaud leering at you no matter where you sit. Boasting around 100 sandwiches, mostly named after celebrities, the restaurant's menu and interior are equally astonishing in scale. They are also completely insane. I'll try to elaborate.

To imagine Big G's, start with a famous NYC delicatessen—say Carnegie Deli or Katz's Delicatessen—where sandwiches are served with obscene amounts of freshly carved, fatty homemade pastrami piled eight inches high on hopelessly ineffectual, thin slips of rye bread; where the fatty parts of the brisket are as delicious as the half-sour pickles; and where a philosophy of glorious excess permeates every inch of the menu. Now strip away the long history and almost all traces of Jewish cultural influence from these delis, and replace the pounds and pounds of ingredients in their sandwiches with the most whitebread, suburban, commonplace sandwich items you can think of, such as bologna and ham salad. Pile these ingredients in crazy combinations on top of huge slabs of scratch-made bread and serve them in the bar section of a candlepin bowling alley to a crowd of tired-looking Colby students in matching sweatshirts, mealy-moustached townie teenagers, and, completely inexplicably, tables full of senior citizens eating plates of spaghetti that seem to have appeared from nowhere. If you're picturing all that, you're getting warmer.

Standing in line at Big G's, you're stunned by the efficiency of the operation. It's a mom-and-pop sandwich shop stretched to its greatest possible level of success. Every seat in the room is taken, and the line stretches a dozen people deep from the three cash registers, past the dinner plate–sized whoopie pies and the homemade silkscreened merchandise all the way to the front door.

After taking a moment to try (with only partial success) to make sense of the giant wall-hung menu behind the counter, we placed our order with an exceptionally patient counterwoman sporting several blown-out forearm tattoos. Not knowing that one whole sandwich at Big G's is plenty of food for four lusty people, we ordered four half-sandwiches in an effort to sample a wide array of options. The counterperson cocked an eyebrow, certain that we must be taking such a large order to go, but no, and a bag of Cool Ranch Doritos and a root beer as well, thank you. She gave us one of those chain restaurant sensors that lights up and goes berserk when your order is ready, and we snuck off to our booth to wait.

Jillian left the table to get a soda refill and came back peering over a stack of three plastic trays precariously balanced on her forearms, each holding the biggest "half" sandwiches I had ever laid eyes on. Most were made with the restaurant's signature freshly baked bread, a country-style white, each slice about as thick as three slices of bagged sandwich bread, with a fluffy, light chew and a light brown crust that stood up wonderfully to the chaos of fillings inside.

Jillian started with the Zeppo ($5.35/half), a combination of warm deli turkey, cream cheese, tomato, and onion, piled high on fresh pumpernickel. While tasty, with lots of big, fresh ingredients, and certainly enough food to feed two people, it didn't win the day; the onions overpowered the rest of the sandwich. We were much bigger fans of the Jack LaLime ($5.65/half), a mile-high hot sandwich combining tuna salad, melted cheddar cheese, huge slices of pickle, sliced onions, and a pickled spicy pepper relish. It's a sandwich I have made myself at home when I am alone and free to do what I like with tuna fish and spicy relish; I had no idea that the senses-destroying combination of fish, pickle, and spiciness was appealing to anyone else in the Free World.

Our final two half sandwiches, hastily ordered under the pressure of time, took a turn for the peculiar though still delicious. The Paul Harvey ($5.90/half) combines a huge portion of sliced deli turkey with a three-inch-thick stack of liverwurst and adds bacon, American cheese, and tomato for good measure. It's an outstanding sandwich for the three or four times per year that I develop an insatiable chemical craving for liverwurst. Combining it with turkey is an unusual choice, but it makes for a lighter(!) flavor. Even stranger was the Egg Macmahon ($5.60/half), combining egg salad, ham salad (which I don't think I'd even thought about for years), onions, lettuce, and pickles into a triple play of sogginess that has to be tried to be fully appreciated. Both the egg salad and the ham salad are finely chopped, making the entire sandwich a textural explosion of ham and egg and squishy bread that extends from your chin to the bridge of your nose. It needs another layer; the pickles, lettuce, and onions don't provide quite enough crunchy contrast to the four inches of mayonnaise-infused salad within, so we had to deduct 10 points from our rating. The fact that it is balls-out crazy was worth a bonus of 400,000 points, however, making this sandwich something to try at least once.

As it has for nearly 30 years, Big G's Deli is raising expectations for what sandwiches in Maine should be. From the more mild, mundane offerings such as the Dr. Seuss (ham and Swiss cheese) to the wild truck driver creations such as the Mystery Meat (liverwurst and egg salad), one thing is consistent in all of Big G's sandwiches: a dedication to fresh ingredients, scratch-made when possible, served in obscenely large portions for a low price. We were surprised, also, to find that most of the sandwiches err on the "healthy" side. Okay, so maybe liverwurst isn't high on anyone's list of healthy eating, but overall we found a wildly creative menu designed with an eye not just to lean meats and cheeses, but also to vegetarian options and far, far more avocado than we are used to seeing in Central Maine. Eating at Big G's is an endurance event; go and fill your table, as we did, with as many crazy sandwich combinations as you can carry, taking lots of pictures and attracting the eyeballs of the locals, or be much more sensible and quietly share a half sandwich and an enormous whoopie pie. No matter your approach, you are going to leave Big G's full and happy, with plenty of money left in your wallet.

The Best Drive-In Cheeseburgers in Southern Maine • *Malcolm*

I t's an unfortunate reality that independent roadside food stands are disappearing. Mom-and-pop joints are being replaced one by one by a never-ending chain of fast food restaurants. The resulting filmstrip-like repetition of McDonald's/Subway/Burger King/McDonald's/Wendy's/Taco Bell/Kentucky Fried Chicken/McDonald's that scrolls past our automobile windows as we travel down any road has robbed us not just of the unique possibilities for a great meal from the (usually strange) characters who staff the independents, but, slowly, of regional identity. As one fast food restaurant blurs into the next in today's landscape, Arkansas starts to look like Colorado, which starts to look like Minnesota, which starts to look like Puerto Rico, until the unique geography of place is lost in a blur of fat-laden disappointment.

Well, almost. In Maine, there are still plenty of places to get a great, quick cheeseburger served to you by someone who has been doing it his whole life and actually made your burger with his own two hands. That burger will blow the doors off anything being offered by the chains, and you'll usually leave with a story to boot. Here are our favorite drive-in cheeseburgers in southern Maine.

FAT BOY DRIVE-IN
111 Bath Road, Brunswick, ME 04011; (207) 729-9431

There's a peculiar stretch of Route 24 after you leave Bowdoin College but before you arrive in the gigantic, slowly dying 1990s-style strip mall that makes up nearly all of Cook's Corner. You feel as if you've driven through a time warp into the America of a half century ago. A short parade of autobody shops, marine supply stores, independent motor inns, and drive-in hamburger restaurants unfolds on sides of the road like a scene from the motoring heyday of the 1960s. Located across from the wide-open space of the former Brunswick Naval Air Station sits one of these restaurants, just as it has since the 1960s: Fat Boy Drive-In. The small building is dwarfed by a wraparound green-and-white fiberglass awning that casts a pale, cool green light on everything. From the moment you ease into an available parking space, the Drive-In starts issuing instructions: "Headlights on for service," one sign reads. Another urges you to "Try a BLT, made with Canadian bacon, and an order of onion rings." While I considered the hand-painted menu (with my lights off, no less), a carhop appeared to take my order. I must be exactly the kind of customer kids like this can't stand, with my obnoxious lobster vanity license plate and my endless questions. "Should I order the Royalburger or the Whoperburger?" My patient waitress explained that a Royalburger Basket ($3.50) was a regular 2-ounce cheeseburger with the addition of lettuce, tomato, mayo, and a side of fries, while a Whoperburger ($3.30) was a larger, 4-ounce burger that presumably was a knockoff of Burger King's famous burger. Does the single "p" indicate that I should be pronouncing the name of this burger like "Woe-per?" And finally, what should I choose for toppings?

The carhop walked me through the process, ultimately handing me a printed menu to show off the full width and breadth of what was available. I was surprised to see, in addition to the burgers already listed on the large outdoor menus, a wide variety of fried seafood options, including clamcake burgers, crabcake sandwiches, haddock sandwiches, and lobster rolls. There were sweet potato fries and chicken nuggets, grilled cheese and chicken salad, red-skinned hot dogs and egg sandwiches. I settled on a Whoperburger, an additional regular cheeseburger with grilled onions for good luck, an order of onion rings, and an order of fries. Total? Ten bucks.

Because everything is cooked to order, it took about ten minutes for my order to arrive. And that, immediately, is what sets these burgers apart from their fast food namesakes. The Whoperburger was like the freshest Burger King Whopper you've never had, with thoughtful, homemade details including some light crispy browning on the edges of the sesame seed bun, thinly sliced fresh tomatoes, shredded lettuce, and a river of mayonnaise. I wish there had been a slice of pickle, but this is probably something I could have specified.

The accompanying fries weren't worth ordering again: frozen, boring, crinkle cut, and a little on the limp side, they occupied space in my stomach that I would rather have reserved for something else, such as one of Fat Boy's famous blueberry 20-ounce thick ice cream frappés. The onion rings were better, with sweet flavor from the onions and seemingly homemade crunch and texture.

The real star, though, was the regular 2-ounce cheeseburger. After tasting it, I wished I had skipped everything else and ordered two or three of these instead. They come plain but can be topped with almost anything you'd like for little or no additional cost. I opted for cheese and grilled onions, and I dipped each bite into a side of ketchup. The small, steamed buns, melted cheese, and tiny little slip of beef all fuse into one tasty whole, and my extra burger was gone before I had time to realize what had happened.

The food is almost secondary to the experience. The Fat Boy Drive-In is doing today exactly what it has been doing for 56 years, and that's why you go. You can get a mushy, overwrought Wagyu burger served on a melted brioche bun almost anywhere these days, but eating piles of inexpensive and tiny, white paper–wrapped cheeseburgers that somebody actually made for you and placed on a tray that hangs off the driver's side window of your car is an experience more and more difficult to come by. That nostalgia is enough to make me pull into the Fat Boy Drive-In; that their burgers happen to be excellent is purely a bonus.

HARMON'S LUNCH
144 Gray Road, Falmouth, ME 04105; (207) 797-9857

I can't remember eating two cheeseburgers faster than I did at Harmon's Lunch. I even had the foresight to order two up front, so I wouldn't be delayed waiting for the second one. Come to think of it, maybe that was my mistake; maybe a forced intermission between burgers would have served me better.

Harmon's Lunch has been serving fresh, homemade cheeseburgers from their small roadside restaurant since 1960. The walls are lined with regional glass milk bottles, and tiny handwritten signs are scattered throughout the restaurant, correcting misbehavior on the part of Harmon's customers. "This cooler contains ice," one sign informs. "If you leave the lid open, the next customer will get water." Another reads, "We made a deal with the bank: They won't serve hamburgers, and we don't extend credit. Cash only." And a tiny sign over the ancient flattop grill, blackened with the remains of millions of hamburgers, reads, "This is not Burger King. You don't get it your way. You take it my way, or you don't get the damn thing."

Though founder Marvin Harmon passed away in 2003, the hamburgers being served from behind the tiny counter haven't changed. And for good reason: After more than 50 years of cooking primarily one thing (Harmon's does offer hot dogs in addition to hamburgers, though you'll never see anyone eating one), they've got the formula down, and your dumb requests for lettuce are not going to upset the careful balance of ingredients that Harmon's has settled on. The loaded version of their burger combines mustard, red relish, and sautéed onions on a buttered and heated soft roll.

The burgers at Harmon's are thin and cooked to a solid medium. They are topped with a thick layer of American cheese, which melts and oozes perfectly into the nooks and crannies on the surface of the burger. The "red relish" is a kind of pickle relish/tomato hybrid, and the onions are sublime—slow cooked for so long that they become incredibly sweet, with the consistency of marmalade. Skip the fries (which, though perfectly serviceable and admirably homemade, have a tendency to be a little on the limp side), and save the extra room for a second burger. It's a much better use of your stomach, and at only $2.45 each, a second burger will deservedly stay in your mind much longer than the French fries will. In fact, try the second burger plain. As delicious as the toppings on the loaded version of a Harmon's burger may be, as carefully balanced between sweet and savory as they are, a Harmon's burger eaten plain or with just cheese is a blissfully textural celebration. The bun is heated until just warmed through, and it combines with the grilled hamburger and the melted cheese into a whisper of a burger that you smell and feel as much as you eat.

Harmon's is exactly the kind of place we like to find on an autumn Friday afternoon. It feels like family, even on your first trip, and it feels like your neighborhood place even if you've driven in from Portland or Ellsworth. It's the kind of place where customers will pitch in and clean up some dropped napkins when they see them, or take a minute to mop spilled root beer off a table in a neighboring booth. Everyone works together, and the payoff is a round of delicate, ethereal little steamy burgers that you will find yourself eating one after another. Go.

DON'S LUNCH
517 Main Street, Westbrook, ME 04092

In the 1940s and 1950s, small diners and family restaurants popped up along major highway routes and in the suburbs of every major city, turning out inexpensive fast food for America's postwar expansion. It's easy to imagine how McDonald's got its start in this milieu, assembly-lining identical copies of small, simply topped, diminutive three-ounce hamburgers and cheeseburgers. For burger purists, a simply prepared and topped burger can hold its ground with any of the more exotic hamburger styles. Sixty-plus years later, this style of burger, with ketchup, onions, and a dab of pickle, manages to survive even as the rest of the world gets more and more weighed down by half-pound Wagyu patties and truffled aiolis.

Don's Lunch in Westbrook must have appeared wildly futuristic when it opened its doors in 1976, a small lunch truck with an angled, sloped front, neon signs, and bold orange and yellow racing stripes. The truck has moved from its original location across the street from Yudy's Tire and is now set back from the street, with plenty of signage to let you know you've arrived. There are a few picnic tables in the front, and as a line forms in front of the truck, you can see what it must have looked like when hungry tire workers lined up in front of the truck for a midday meal. The menu is dead simple, as it should be and as it has been for 35 years. There are chili dogs, grilled cheese sandwiches, French fries, onion rings, hamburgers, cheeseburgers, clam cakes, and a burger called The Big One. This $4 burger combines two thin, griddled hamburger patties with two slices of yellow, very melty American cheese on a soft, steaming-hot white bun.

It's the platonic ideal version of a McDonald's cheeseburger that can never possibly exist at the Golden Arches: The beef at Mickey D's is never this fresh and piping hot, the bun this soft and warm, or the cheese this melted and gooey. We paid exactly ten bucks for our entire order, and you'd be hard-pressed to get through a McDonald's for less. You can top the burger (or any of the lesser, single-patty versions) with anything you'd like for no extra charge. We went with mustard, raw onion, and sweet pepper relish. The onions provided a satisfying crunch, and the sweetness of the red pepper relish was a nice complement to the cheesy, beefy onslaught within.

After an initial tentative taste, I compulsively wolfed down the rest of the burger in seconds. I tried to make a show of nibbling at the frozen onion rings—crunchy little rehydrated, heavily battered hoops à la Burger King that tasted way more like onion than actual onions do—but they were not up to the burger standard. I congratulated myself on having ordered a second burger, which was steeping in a Styrofoam box, ready to be spirited home and eaten greedily as I stood in the kitchen. I didn't order French fries based on the disappointing, standard-issue onion rings. I suggest saving room for another burger.

I overheard one of the employees from deep inside the truck mention that Don's Lunch had been doing very well lately, due in part to its newly extended hours (until 2 a.m. on weekend nights) and in part to its newly instituted "Big One" burger special, which cuts the price of a burger in half from 9 p.m. to 11 p.m. I can imagine that this causes quite the late-night scene; according to the worker I spoke with, customers eat two or three burgers at a time while the special is on.

With every town in America looking more and more like the same slightly remixed combination of Best Buy, Starbucks, and Target, finding a dining option like Don's Lunch that gives you some sense of place is a relief. It harkens back to a time when real people made real food for hard-working customers, but this establishment isn't just coasting on reputation or nostalgia. It also happens to be serving some of the best burgers in the area.

WASSES HOT DOGS • *Malcolm*

2 North Main Street, Rockland, ME 04841; (207) 594-4347

No review of Wasses Hot Dogs can do justice to that smell. On warm days, the scent of grilling onions permeates the entire North End neighborhood between the ferry terminal and the Cumberland Farms convenience store around the corner to the north. It snakes in through your air-conditioning vents, into your hair, and under your skin. And it is heavenly.

The secret of Wasses' 30-year success is peanut oil. It's frying every living thing you can think of in peanut oil. They also use exceptionally high-quality links, with a satisfying snap to the casing, and nestle them in traditional New England split-side steamed buns. A sign clearly explains that asking for a hot dog with "everything" only gets you mustard and grilled onions, forcing you to somewhat painfully order your dogs with "everything and ketchup." They're almost as good served with no toppings; they are delicious enough, we think, to stand on their own. If bareback hot dogs aren't your thing, I am also a fairly recent convert to the Western Dog, which tops a hot dog with bacon, grilled onions, ketchup, and a heap of baked beans. It's like a bean hole supper on a bun, and it is remarkable.

The fries can be skipped; they are unremarkable frozen crinkle cuts, and besides, fries just take up space that could be otherwise occupied by another dog. A better pairing is with a tiny carton of Oakhurst Dairy chocolate milk or a homemade Rice Krispie treat.

At around two dollars per hot dog, Wasses represents a great value for anyone passing through the midcoast. Have a lobster, certainly, but make sure to stop and infuse the inside of your car with that Wasses smell the next time you are passing through. Try them once, and you'll have an obsession for life.

WEEKEND PROJECT:
Scratch-Made Lobster Roll •
Malcolm

Makes 9 lobster rolls

If you long for a last taste of summer when the leaves are falling, make yourself a lobster roll.

I once read that you can tell when a recipe for a Maine lobster roll has been written by someone from away, because it will have lots of things in it that aren't lobster. An authentic lobster roll shouldn't have dill, or celery, or scallions. It shouldn't have little bits of chopped-up chives sprinkled on top. Why? Because lobster doesn't need a thing to make it taste any better. It's nearly perfect as is, and when you eat a lobster roll, you should be tasting lobster. If anything, it should be tossed with just a dab of mayonnaise (no, not blobbed on top, and no, not spread on the inside of the bun) to bind everything together, and that mayonnaise should be Hellman's Blue Ribbon.

I regard a lobster roll as a celebration of texture and temperature as much as flavor. That's why it's so important to use New England–style hot dog rolls. Brushed with butter and then lightly grilled, the roll becomes warm and fluffy with a lightly crisped outside, and the combination of this with the cool, chunky lobster is simply heavenly. Because we recognize that New England split-top hot dog rolls are a regional item and might not be available everywhere, we are going to make our own. It's easy, but you'll need a special pan, which you can order online from King Arthur Flour. You'll need one 1¼-pound lobster per roll, steamed about five minutes in an inch or two of boiling water. You don't want to boil the lobsters; they'll become waterlogged and lose a lot of their flavor. If you're squeamish about cooking them, most fish markets and supermarkets will do it for you. (NOTE: We've heard the suggestion that it's more humane to put the lobsters into the kettle before heating the water. As the late Mike Brown wrote in his great book *The Great Lobster Chase*, that's the equivalent of killing a stockyard steer by pulling all its fur out strand by strand.) Once cooked, let them chill in the fridge until cool enough to handle. Then break the shells open and tear the meat apart with your hands; cutting the lobster with a knife can impart a metallic taste. You want big chunks, but not so big that you can't bite them in a single bite. Nobody likes pulling huge chunks of lobster out of a lobster roll with their teeth. Finally, a word about the Connecticut shoreline version of this sandwich, which is served warm and tossed in drawn butter instead of mayonnaise: Um, that's not a lobster roll. I'm not sure what you people are doing down there.

Method

For buns:

1. In a stand mixer, mix and knead all ingredients until dough is shiny and elastic, about 5 minutes or more. Place the dough in a lightly greased bowl and allow it to rise for 2 hours, until doubled in size.

2. Lightly grease a New England hot dog bun pan. Punch down dough and stretch out in pan, pushing the dough to the edges and corners as much as possible. Cover the pan with plastic wrap, and let the dough rest for 15 minutes.

3. Remove the plastic wrap and push dough all the way into the corners of the pan, leveling the top surface as best you can. Re-cover the pan and let buns rise for 45 to 60 minutes, until approximately ½ inch from top of pan. While the dough is rising, preheat your oven to 375°F.

4. Grease a baking sheet, and place it on top of the risen buns. Put the covered buns in the oven, weigh the baking sheet down with something oven safe (like a cast-iron skillet), and bake the buns for 18 minutes. Remove the baking sheet and bake a few minutes longer, if necessary, to brown the tops of the rolls.

5. Remove the buns from the oven and place the pan on a rack for 5 minutes. Turn the buns out of the pan onto a rack to finish cooling; make sure the top (rounded) side is up.

To assemble lobster rolls:

1. When buns are completely cool, slice each down the middle vertically, without cutting through the bottoms, then separate into individual buns.

2. Spread outsides of bun with butter, and toast in a skillet over medium heat until golden-brown.

3. Shred chilled lobster meat by hand into bite-sized chunks, and toss in a medium bowl with the mayonnaise.

4. Line a bun with lettuce (if desired), and top with the lobster salad. Serve with chips and a dill pickle.

INGREDIENTS

New England–style split-top hot dog buns:

3 cups all-purpose flour

2¼ teaspoons instant yeast

2 tablespoons sugar

¼ cup nonfat dry milk

⅔ cup instant mashed potato flakes

1½ teaspoons salt

2 tablespoons soft butter

1 large egg

1 cup lukewarm water

For each lobster roll:

One 1¼-pound lobster, steamed

¾ teaspoon Hellman's mayonnaise

Shredded lettuce (optional)

Tricks and Treats Continued

- Bacon and Egg Candies
- Pumpkin Butterscotch Cookies
- Salted Rolo Brownie Cookies

As everyone knows, Halloween is all about the candy—plastic pumpkins full, pillowcases full, caches and stashes of the stuff, parents stealing from kids, and kids counting their pieces, trading in the cafeteria, and making sure Mom and Dad are handing out something acceptable at their own front door. In the spirit of the season, we present one of our very few (maybe our one and only) candy recipes. The nights of October grow long, and although liquor may be quicker, candy is always dandy. And we say good–bye to October with two cookie recipes.

Bacon and Egg Candies • *Malcolm*
Makes about 24 candies

INGREDIENTS

4-ounce bar of good white chocolate

24 yellow M&M candies

24 pretzel sticks, each broken in half

I've never, ever been drawn to stuff like this. I don't craft, I don't make cute fondant cupcakes that look like the Muppets, and I don't get involved in all of that "bento" business, wherein what I imagine to be high-anxiety, Type-A parents spend hours meticulously decorating a cucumber roll to look like a surprised kitten, only for their children to trade their painstakingly crafted, Japanese-inspired lunch for a pizza-flavored Lunchable.

Maybe it's because I'm a new dad and I'm doing some kind of nesting thing. Maybe it's the first step toward irreversible lameness. I'm not sure. But these candies have a touch of homemade and combine sweet, salty, and crunchy in a way I love. Plus, they look like bacon and eggs. Innat cunnin'?

Method

1. In a small saucepan over medium heat, boil 1–2 cups of water. When the water boils, place a heat-safe bowl on top of the saucepan to serve as a double boiler. Break the white chocolate into small pieces and add to the bowl, stirring constantly until the chocolate melts.

2. On a parchment- or waxed paper–lined surface, dollop the white chocolate into pools about the size of a quarter. Place a single M&M on top of each chocolate pool, with the print facing down. Add two pieces of pretzel stick. Let cool completely at room temperature, and serve.

Pumpkin Butterscotch Cookies • *Jillian*

Makes about two dozen cookies

Mrs. Donahue was shaped like the calico cats we stitched together in sewing class, flat and lumpy in all the wrong places, and she wore the same calico fabric on the pocket of her long denim jumper. She taught us cooking and how to diaper a big bag of flour. We made tin scoops in metalshop, and I spray-painted mine pink and purple. And in woodshop, I made my sister a gumball machine that I kept for myself. I don't know how well these seventh-grade home economics lessons have served me as an adult. I never did become a seamstress, and I only rarely use my lathe to craft misshapen baseball bats. But I remember carefully placing six or seven butterscotch chips on rolled-out crescent roll dough and baking them into compact packages of melty goodness. I was so proud when I recreated this simple dessert at home for my mother, father, and sister. And I think that's what stuck, all these years later. Making food for your family is always an awesome achievement.

INGREDIENTS

2 cups all-purpose flour

1½ teaspoons baking powder

1 teaspoon baking soda

½ teaspoon salt

1 teaspoon cinnamon

2 eggs

1 cup brown sugar

1 cup pumpkin purée

1 teaspoon vanilla extract

½ cup canola oil

1 cup butterscotch chips

Method

1. Preheat the oven to 325°F. Line two baking sheets with parchment paper and butter the parchment.

2. In a mixing bowl, whisk together the flour, the baking powder, the baking soda, the salt, and the cinnamon.

3. In the bowl of a stand mixer, combine the eggs and the sugar. Add the pumpkin, the vanilla, and the oil. Slowly add the dry ingredients until just combined. Fold in the butterscotch chips.

4. Dollop the batter by the quarter cup onto the prepared cookie sheets, smooth, and bake for 16 minutes. Cool the cookies on the baking sheet for 5 minutes. Transfer to cooling racks to cool completely.

Salted Rolo Brownie Cookies • *Jillian*

Makes about 2 dozen cookies

File this recipe under "How to win friends and influence people." We once took these cookies with us on a family-filled weekend road trip through the wilds of Connecticut, snacking on them in the Jeep, proffering them as a hostess gift/dessert, and even using them to pay highway tolls in lieu of coins. I can't imagine a sane person who wouldn't like them—they are crisp on the outside and gooey and chewy on the inside.

Salted caramel has been a trendy flavor combination for a while, and I like how Rolos turn it just a tad trashy and ironic, like a mustache and PBR. (Is that still a thing? Probably not. The cool kids are probably growing mutton chops and drinking Crown Royal and Tab these days.) My only piece of advice is to buy more Rolos than you need. You think you are better than Rolos, but you're not. I'm not. Kate Middleton, Bishop Desmond Tutu, and Salman Rushdie may be, though we don't know for sure. The rest of us, I'm afraid, are stuck being plebeians and gobbling Rolos. It's not so bad.

INGREDIENTS

4 tablespoons (¼ stick) unsalted butter

16 ounces semisweet chocolate chips

4 eggs

1 cup brown sugar

⅓ cup granulated sugar

2 teaspoons vanilla extract

½ cup all-purpose flour

½ teaspoon baking powder

1½ cups Rolos, chopped

Flaked sea salt

Method

1. Preheat the oven to 350°F. Line baking sheets with parchment paper.

2. Over a double boiler, melt the butter and the chocolate.

3. In a large bowl, whisk together the eggs, the sugars, and the vanilla until well combined.

4. In a smaller mixing bowl, combine the flour and the baking powder.

5. Slowly stir the melted chocolate mixture into the eggs and sugar mixture in four batches. Stir vigorously to incorporate.

6. Mix in the dry ingredients. Fold in the chopped Rolos candies.

7. Drop heaping tablespoons of the batter onto prepared cookie sheets. Bake 10–12 minutes, until the centers are just set.

8. Remove from the oven and sprinkle with sea salt. Allow the cookies to cool on the baking sheet for 5 minutes. Transfer to cooling racks to finish cooling.

NOVEMBER

Thanksgiving Menu

- Blue Hubbard Squash Soup
- Achiote Butter-Basted Roast Turkey with Ancho Chile Gravy
- Cornbread Dressing with Fresh and Dried Fruit
- Bourbon Cranberry Compote
- Ancho Chile Pumpkin Pie

BONUS! Leftover Turkey and Chorizo Breakfast Hash

Our take on Thanksgiving is influenced both by growing up in New England and by our four-year adventure in Mexico. We love to mix traditional fare with exotic flavors. Ancho chile adds an unexpected flourish to a classic pumpkin pie and is exactly the warming spice that this sweet and mellow fall favorite needs.

Preparing for the big meal, planning a menu weeks in advance, shopping slowly to acquire all that we need—a bottle of wine here, a can of pumpkin there—waking up early to watch the parade and pop the bird in the oven, pulling from storage the placemats, table runners, salt and pepper shakers, and aprons we use every year is tradition, personal history, and comfort. We are grateful for all that we have, and we want nothing more than to share food, stories, and rituals with family and friends around a dinner table overflowing with bounty. And we are grateful, too, for those next-day leftover breakfasts.

Blue Hubbard Squash Soup • *Jillian*
Serves 6-8

The Blue Hubbard is a shabby-chic squash, a Gothic Cinderella gourd. It's gorgeous. Its exterior is mostly smooth with creamy custardy flesh. Last year I bought a few to display in our apartment and never for a moment considered eating one. The squash struck me as more aesthetic than edible, much like an artichoke or mussels in the shell, but I was mistaken, for it transforms into a most delectable soup—the perfect starter to Thanksgiving dinner, warming and filling and rich.

Method

1. Preheat the oven to 350°F. Quarter, seed, and roast the squash 1 hour. When cool, scoop out the flesh and purée in a food processor. Should yield roughly 4 cups. (As you only need half a squash for this recipe, freeze and save the rest for later.)

2. In a small pan, steep the bay and sage leaves in the heavy cream. Bring to a boil and then reduce the heat to low. Continue to steep on low while prepping the other ingredients.

3. In a soup pot, melt the butter and sauté the carrots, celery, and onion until softened. Add the nutmeg and cayenne, and salt and pepper to taste. Stir in the brandy, the squash, and the flour. Add the chicken stock. Cook for 30 minutes on simmer, stirring occasionally.

4. Discard the herbs and incorporate the heavy cream. Continue cooking until heated through, then serve with a dollop of crème fraîche.

INGREDIENTS

2 cups Blue Hubbard squash purée (½ of the squash)

½ pint heavy cream

1 dried bay leaf

2 fresh sage leaves

¼ cup (½ stick) unsalted butter

3 chopped carrots

2 chopped celery stalks

1 chopped onion

¼ teaspoon nutmeg

½ teaspoon cayenne

Salt and pepper, to taste

2 ounces brandy

¼ cup all-purpose flour

32 ounces chicken stock

Crème fraîche

Achiote Butter-Basted Roast Turkey with Ancho Chile Gravy • *Malcolm*

Serves 14

We had lived in Mexico for a little over a year when my dad arrived. He was determined, at 65, to have one last big solo adventure abroad, and had taken a caretaking position in a beach house about 45 minutes from the house Jillian and I had rented on the beach.

We were happy to see him arrive on that hot day in Merida. Though we'd figured out some basic survival strategies in our first year there, a familiar face from home (and one that spoke English) was a welcome addition to the family we were building south of the border. I had spent most of my childhood traveling from one exotic locale to another with my mom and dad; the closeness that is forged between family members depending on each other and surviving as a compact unit in a far-off land is something I feel very lucky to have shared with them. So here we were once again, only this time, I was an adult who was getting to spend more time than ever with my father. It's another privilege that I don't think a lot of people get to enjoy before their parents pass away.

A few months after his arrival, it was time to celebrate American Thanksgiving. The year before, Jillian and I had gathered with other expats at a mildly wretched buffet dinner at a local hotel. My memories of that event include a lot of cigarette smoke, gray skin, and grouchiness served with unlimited jalapeño peppers on the side.

This year, armed with just enough Spanish to navigate the supermarket and get ourselves hopelessly lost in complicated business transactions, we were ready to cook and prepare a traditional Thanksgiving meal. We'd found a ten-year-old can of Bruce's canned yams at the import store in the next city. It cost $8. There were ample fresh vegetables for sale in the local mercados. And just like in the States, the local chain supermarkets were filling with frozen, shrink-wrapped turkeys. Without hesitation, and more significantly, without examining labels, we picked out an 18-pound beauty, excited to celebrate a traditional American holiday together.

The meal preparation began smoothly. The side dishes were all done, the tequila was flowing freely, and we were waiting for the meat thermometer on the turkey to register 165°F. Nothing had gone wrong all day, which was unusual in a Mexican beach town that offered water, electricity, and propane for cooking, but almost never at the same time. The lights had stayed on and the oven had held out, and finally the turkey was done. It was beautiful—a big golden-brown beast with a caramel-colored crackly skin, oozing moisture from its joints. After letting it rest, I took carving knife and fork in hand (I was, after all, the man of the house now) and carved a few slices of that big brown beauty onto a platter.

We could tell as soon as I cut the first slice that something was wrong. Instead of the pale white turkey breast we had been looking forward to all day, this turkey's flesh was an alarming bright pink, the color of dried, day-old Big League Chew. We assumed at first that it simply wasn't cooked. We took its temperature again and again, in every portion of the poor bird's anatomy that we could think of, but every reading was the same. The turkey was definitely cooked. In fact, it was more than cooked; it almost looked cured, as if it had been cooked in a smoker for days on end.

I took a tentative bite. This gigantic turkey that we had slaved all day to prepare had the exact flavor and texture of an all-beef kosher hot dog.

We dug through the trash for the packaging, and on closer examination found the explanation: The Mexican turkey processing facility had thoughtfully added extra "flavoring" to the bird, along with, I assume, a fair amount of food dye. The exact flavoring wasn't mentioned, or perhaps we lacked the Spanish to pick out the words. I am certain, though, that "hot dog flavored" wasn't anywhere on the package.

The turkey was, sadly, inedible. As we tried to maintain our cheer, keeping our chins up and clapping each other on the back over the success of our side dishes, this enormous dark pink turkey carcass just sat there. Eventually, my dad and I decided that it would make a fine meal for one of the many homeless street dogs in the area, so we scooped it up and headed off. In retrospect, this was clearly a decision fueled by tequila. "You know what we need to do," someone must have said, "we need to take that thing outside," and the rest of us reacted as if Archimedes had just discovered the principle of displacement.

So that's what we did. Grabbing the turkey by one of its wretched, pink-hued wings, we headed out into the Progreso night, walking slowly up and down the street, looking for a stray dog. For once, impossibly, there were none around. So, laughing and joking in the balmy 95° November night, my dad and I shuffled up and down the street in the quiet darkness with a turkey no one wanted to eat. It's a Thanksgiving memory I will always cherish.

With this memory of my late dad in mind, I wanted to revisit the idea of introducing Yucatecan flavor to a Thanksgiving turkey, this time without making it taste like a hot dog. I settled on a liberal application of El Yucateco–brand achiote, a spice paste made of annatto, coriander, cumin, peppercorns, oregano, cloves, garlic, and sour orange, which imparts a shockingly bright-red hue to everything it touches. It's a flavor I became addicted to over the course of dozens of tortas de cochinita pibil eaten for breakfast on Sundays in the town square, and it's equally suitable for turkey. In fact, I think the high salt content acted as a sort of dry-brine for the bird,

INGREDIENTS

¾ cup (1½ sticks) unsalted butter, room temperature

3 tablespoons achiote paste

2 fresh poblano chiles

3 dried ancho chiles, stemmed, halved, seeded

A 22- to 24-pound turkey (neck and giblets discarded)

1 large white onion, quartered

2 oranges or tangerines, skins on, quartered

3½ cups (about) canned low-sodium chicken broth

¼ cup Masa Harina (Maseca brand or other instant corn tortilla mix)

which came out incomparably moist and juicy with a gorgeous dark-red hue to the skin. To finish it (and ourselves) off, we matched it with a gravy spiked with ancho and poblano chiles. It's a powerful version of a classic Thanksgiving dish that isn't particularly spicy but is still quite deep and complex. I urge you to try it.

Method

1. In a small bowl, mix the butter and achiote paste to blend, and set aside.

2. Under the broiler or over a gas flame, char the poblanos until blackened on all sides. Remove from the heat or oven, and seal in a plastic bag until the skins soften, about 10 minutes. Peel and seed the poblanos.

3. Place the anchos in a bowl and cover with hot water. Let stand until the anchos soften, about 15 minutes.

4. In a blender or food processor, purée four of the ancho chile halves with a half cup of the soaking liquid. Add the roasted poblano chiles and purée. Set aside the remaining two ancho chile halves.

5. Preheat the oven to 350°F. Rinse the turkey inside and out. Pat dry. Sprinkle the turkey with salt and pepper. Cut the remaining two ancho chile halves into strips. Place the chile strips, onion, and oranges in the turkey cavity.

6. Run your fingers between the turkey breast skin and the meat to loosen it. Rub half of the achiote butter between the turkey breast and the skin. Rub the butter over the outside of the turkey. Place the turkey in a large roasting pan. Tuck the wings under the turkey. Tie the legs together to hold its shape. Pour 1½ cups of the chicken broth into the pan.

7. Roast the turkey 45 minutes. Tent the turkey loosely with foil. Continue roasting until a meat thermometer inserted into the thickest part of the thigh registers 165°F, basting every 30 minutes with the pan juices, about 3½ hours. Transfer to a platter. Tent with foil.

8. Pour the turkey pan juices into a measuring cup. Spoon off the fat from the pan juices, reserving a quarter cup of the fat. Add enough of the remaining chicken broth to the pan juices to measure 3 cups. Return the quarter cup of fat to the roasting pan. Place the pan over two burners set at medium heat. Add the Masa Harina and whisk until the mixture resembles paste, scraping up any browned bits, about 2 minutes.

9. Gradually whisk in the pan juices. Add the chile purée and simmer 5 minutes to blend the flavors. Season the gravy with salt and pepper. Slice the turkey and serve with the gravy.

Cornbread Stuffing with Fresh and Dried Fruit
● *Jillian*
Serves 8

My ideal stuffing includes bread, butter, onion, and celery—you can hold the sausage and even the sage, thank you. One day I hope to be an extremely old and senile resident of an old folks' home, my every need attended to by robot-nurses, and my patient-care contract will include a rider that requires me to be fed mushy stuffing morning, noon, and night. Those robots better treat me right. I don't like texture or unexpected ingredients in my Thanksgiving stuffing. (I don't know why some people call it "dressing.") I don't care for oysters or anything slimy in my stuffing, nor anything that possibly grows underground, and I find chestnuts altogether creepy and suspect. But that's me, and Thanksgiving is for giving—it's right there in the name. It's for sharing and family, for watching parades and football games, and for getting grossly full on foods packed with butter and salt. It's for drinking before noon and laughing through tears when the dog steals the turkey from the counter. In that spirit, I made this stuffing because I knew my husband would like it. He is a WASP, after all, and wasps enjoy dried fruit. It's a very good stuffing; I recognize that. But I think I will make myself a secret stash of Stovetop to eat in the pantry while I drink my 10 a.m. wine.

Thanksgiving week is upon us! What are you cooking this week?

NOTE: The cornbread can be made ahead. It comes together quickly, and you can make it before or after work. No one will know if you taste just a little as you go.

Method

For the cornbread:

1. Preheat the oven to 375°F. Butter a 9-inch by 3-inch by 5-inch metal loaf pan. In a large mixing bowl, combine the cornmeal, flour, sugar, baking powder, and salt.

2. In another bowl, whisk together the butter, egg, and buttermilk. With a wooden spoon, stir the wet ingredients into the dry ingredients and let the mixture sit for 30 minutes. Pour into the prepared loaf pan and bake 40 minutes. Let the cornbread cool in the pan. Turn out onto a cutting board and cut into 1-inch pieces.

INGREDIENTS

For the cornbread:

1⅓ cups stone-ground yellow cornmeal

1 cup all-purpose flour

¼ cup granulated sugar

2 teaspoons baking powder

¾ teaspoon salt

9 tablespoons (1 stick plus 1 tablespoon) unsalted butter, melted

1 large egg, plus one yolk

1 cup plus 2 tablespoons buttermilk

For the stuffing:

1 loaf day-old or dried cornbread, cut into pieces and toasted

½ cup (1 stick) unsalted butter

2 large white onions, diced

4 stalks of celery, ribs and leaves, diced

4 pears, unpeeled and diced

4 fresh sage leaves, chopped

6 ounces dried apricots, roughly chopped

3 ounces dried cherries

3 ounces raisins or pitted prunes

Kosher salt and ground black pepper

1½ cups chicken broth

3. Turn the oven down to 200°F. Bake the cornbread pieces on a baking sheet for 30 to 40 minutes or until beginning to crisp. You can also make the cornbread one day ahead and leave covered overnight.

For the stuffing:

1. Preheat the oven to 375°F. Butter a large baking dish. In a large skillet over medium-high heat, melt the butter. Sauté the onions until translucent, about 10 minutes. Add the celery, pear, and sage and sauté another 10 minutes.

2. In a very large mixing bowl, combine the sautéed mixture, the dried fruits, and the cornbread pieces. Season with salt and pepper and slowly add the chicken broth. The mixture should be wet but not saturated. Transfer to the prepared baking dish and bake 40 minutes.

Bourbon Cranberry Compote • *Malcolm*
Serves 8

INGREDIENTS

A 12-ounce bag of fresh cranberries

¼ cup granulated sugar

½ cup apple juice

¼ cup bourbon

¼ teaspoon cinnamon

Cranberry sauce is one of those great "make-ahead" Thanksgiving or Christmas dishes, and now that we see how easy it is to make at home, we'll never suffer through a slice of the canned stuff (with can lines intact) ever again. This cranberry sauce is cooked just until the cranberries begin to split, which helps them retain their character and keeps them from turning into a gluey mess. Don't leave your simmering cranberries unattended. If they boil, they will foam up and out of the saucepan. If this starts to happen, reduce the heat and give a quick stir.

And, of course, adding bourbon to a dish never hurts. It simmers long enough to cook off all the alcohol but not all the taste; this cranberry sauce ends up just the right amount of boozy.

Method

1. Combine all the ingredients in a medium saucepan.

2. Simmer over medium heat, stirring occasionally, until the cranberries burst and the sauce thickens, about 20 minutes. Let cool completely (or chill) before serving.

Ancho Chile Pumpkin Pie • *Malcolm*

Adapted from a recipe by Lisarae Lattin

Serves 8

My sister, a transplant to New Mexico and master pie baker, uses ancho chile by the handful. Having transplanted ourselves from New England to Mexico and back again, we also tend to use it a lot in cooking, particularly in Mexican dishes and in chili. Anchos are just dried poblanos, and they're not particularly hot—they just add a mysterious, pleasant background glow to your dish.

Unfortunately, there's a real dearth of ancho chiles here in Maine. We tracked some down at Whole Foods to the tune of around three bucks for two whole, dried chiles. This recipe calls for ground ancho chiles, which you can make yourself using the pepper pods or order online if they aren't available in your area. We went a different route and added the ancho the same way we do when we make chili; we soaked the seeded pepper for a few minutes and squeezed it dry before finely chopping it into mush and adding the whole thing. This method leaves pleasing little chunks of chile in your pie, but it also makes the heat level more difficult to control. Whichever method you choose, you'll love the way the gentle heat of the chiles complements the pumpkin. And remember, if it gets too spicy, you can always cool it down with more vanilla ice cream.

Method

For the crust:

1. Preheat the oven to 375°F. In a mixing bowl, combine the flour and salt. Add the butter and break apart using two knives until the mixture resembles tiny, irregular chunks the size of coarse breadcrumbs. Add water a teaspoon at a time until a rough dough forms.

2. Flour your work surface and roll out the dough into a circle, about 12 inches in diameter. Lay the pie crust into a 9-inch pie pan, gently pressing it into the bottom and sides of the pan. Fix any cracks or tears in the crust by pressing them together. Prick the pie crust all over with the tines of a fork and flute the edges of the crust.

3. Bake the pie crust until it just begins to turn golden-brown, about 15 minutes. Remove from the oven. Lower the oven to 350°F.

For the filling:

1. In a mixing bowl, combine all the ingredients. With a hand mixer, whisk or mix until smooth. Pour into the hot pie crust and return to the oven. Bake about 60 minutes or until the center of the pie filling is just set and barely wiggles. Remove from the oven and let cool completely, at least 2 hours, before serving.

INGREDIENTS

For the crust:

1½ cups all-purpose flour

½ teaspoon salt

¼ cup (½ stick) unsalted butter

4 teaspoons cold water

For the filling:

A 15-ounce can puréed pumpkin

1⅔ cups whipping cream

3 large eggs

½ cup firmly packed brown sugar

½ cup granulated sugar

1 tablespoon ground dried ancho chile (or use dried whole chiles; see note above)

1 teaspoon cinnamon

½ teaspoon nutmeg

½ teaspoon salt

INGREDIENTS

2 tablespoons vegetable oil or turkey fat

6 ounces fresh Mexican chorizo

1 medium onion, diced

2 cloves garlic, minced

2 cups Brussels sprouts, raw or cooked, thinly sliced

1 large russet potato, cooked, diced into ¼-inch pieces

2 cups roasted turkey meat, white and dark meat, diced into ¼-inch pieces

½ cup heavy cream

1 tablespoon chile sauce

Kosher salt and freshly ground black pepper

3 or 4 eggs

Sriracha hot sauce (optional)

BONUS! Leftover Turkey and Chorizo
Breakfast Hash • *Malcolm*

Serves 3-4

The morning after a big family meal like Thanksgiving is the perfect opportunity to whip up a breakfast hash. Most of the ingredients are already cooked, and hash makes use of a lot of the leftovers, adding new flavors completely unlike what you experienced the day before. The secret to a good breakfast hash, as I learned from last year's version using prime rib, is to use a spot of heavy cream and to keep mashing and scraping the hash out of the bottom of the pan. This gives you a breakfast hash with a phenomenal crust. It's also important to cut all the ingredients as close to the same size as possible, to ensure that everything cooks evenly.

Don't worry much about the measurements; there is a lot of flexibility in this dish, which is one of its beauties. Making little wells in the nearly finished hash cradles the eggs, allowing you to cook them to runny-yolked perfection in the same pan. It's an amazing way to work through your fridge full of leftovers, and even Jillian made an exception to her ordinarily negative position regarding the juxtaposition of poultry and eggs on the same plate. And you wouldn't want to take a break from being breathtakingly full, would you?

Method

1. In a large cast-iron skillet over medium-high heat, heat the vegetable oil. Add the chorizo and break up with a spoon. Add the onion, garlic, Brussels sprouts, and potato, and cook, stirring occasionally, until the onions become translucent and the potatoes begin to brown, about 5 minutes. Add the turkey meat, the heavy cream, the chile sauce, and a dash of salt and pepper, and stir until combined.

2. Using a spatula, press the mixture into the bottom of the pan. Let cook without stirring until a crust forms on the bottom, about 2 minutes. Scrape up the hash, mix, and press the mixture back into the bottom of the pan. Repeat every 2 minutes until brown crusty bits appear throughout the hash, about 10 minutes total.

3. Make three or four wells (depending on the size of your pan) in the hash, and crack three or four eggs into the wells. Cover the pan and cook until the eggs reach the desired doneness, about 5 to 7 more minutes. Add a swirl of Sriracha if desired, and serve with leftover cranberry sauce.

A 1 DINER • *Malcolm*
3 Bridge Street, Gardiner, ME 04345; (207) 582-4804; a1diner.com

It's hard to miss the A1 Diner. Perhaps that's because the restaurant is a bright spot of activity in a downtown that must have been adorable once and may become so again, but is at present struggling through a twilight interregnum of empty storefronts and half-empty streets. The yesteryear downtown of family-owned stores selling hardware, groceries, medicine, books, shoes, and clothing to loyal customers is gone and almost forgotten. Walmart, Lowe's, Rite-Aid, and their ilk won that war; we don't have to like it, but we have to acknowledge it. Downtowns all over Maine and America huddle forlorn in the November dusk, too many storefronts unlighted, waiting for something to happen. There are rebirths—Portland's Old Port, Bath, Rockland, Belfast, and others—where local heroes and visionaries make the most of luck and circumstance to coax a town back to life. Like a long idle engine, a reawakening needs help at first. You need a center of gravity—you need a "there" there—before more life comes. And when the creative economy finds Gardiner and brings it roaring back to life, one good reason for the discovery will be the A1 Diner.

Maybe the A1 Diner stands out because you just don't see many 1940s-era Worcester Lunch Cars in pristine condition, deco chrome glinting in the sunlight, floating in midair atop a set of steel pilings at traffic level next to a bridge above a rushing stream.

When the restaurant opened in 1946, it served fast, hot, home-cooked meals to hungry factory workers. The diner has reinvented itself several times since then, changing owners and names while working hard to keep up with current trends. This innovative ability has given the A1 Diner its longevity and has led to the unusual menu served today.

> *Jillian:* I didn't know why Malcolm was driving me to a diner in Gardiner. It seemed a long way to go for eggs and bacon. But as we turned onto the town's main street, I became more hopeful. This was a cute town, and perhaps something cool was happening here after all. Then I saw the antique car, the classic, long, narrow interior all wood-paneled and stocked with original stools and red-lettered menu signage. As we settled into a booth and took a look around, I saw a creativity at work that I hadn't anticipated.

In spite of its conventional diner-car appearance, the A1 Diner harbors its share of surprises. The first thing that indicated we might be on to something a little out of the ordinary was the outstanding beer and wine list that was laminated next to a menu at every table. When you can sit down in a leather booth and crack a Maudite or a Delirium Tremens with your blue-plate pot roast special, it's clear that the owners are paying attention. A quick run through the menu revealed the classic diner fare we expected, including fried chicken, meatloaf and gravy, and an assortment of burgers made with locally sourced Oaklands Farms beef. Allow your eye to wander to the black plastic board with the slide-on letters above the counter that runs the length of the restaurant, however, and all hell breaks loose.

The A1 Diner has at least a dozen daily specials, and these routinely escalate standard lunchcar fare to the level of modern American cuisine, featuring dishes that you never expect to see in a diner. We have dined there several times now, and we've seen plates of chicken mole tacos, flank steak, ginger-carrot soup, and curried beef meatloaf passed from the kitchen through a tiny window accompanied by the "ding" of a bell to indicate each new order. It's a diner, sure, but one that happens to make a mean pan-seared duck breast and a flavorful cardamom-spiked North African lamb stew.

On our most recent visit, we were after more traditional diner fare, which the A1 Diner also (mostly) delivers well. Because I am watching my figure, I opted for the hot meatloaf sandwich ($8.99) covered in brown gravy. I was served a massive tower of thick-cut, pillowy-soft country white bread, served closed-face around an enormous stack of three thick slices of meatloaf, each piece seared on the flattop grill for extra crust. A drizzle of satisfyingly salty brown gravy was deemed insufficient by the waitress, who immediately brought me a sidecar of the finest brown sauce ever to come out of a bottle of Gravy Master, which I happily emptied onto my sandwich. The meatloaf was a tiny bit crumbly, but this is a knife-and-fork sandwich, and once everything gets covered in gravy, it hardly matters.

Plenty of mid-century diners remain in New England, most having been handed down among family members or purchased by aging hipster dot-com burnouts. Most such diners seem content to focus on nostalgia, turning out mediocre $3 bacon-and-egg plates and weak cups of coffee and expecting that you will be dazzled by the neon, the jukebox, and the pedigree. Rarely do they try to reinvent themselves, and it is here that the A1 Diner excels, turning out inexpensive, surprisingly modern dishes in an environment you would expect to be covered in a thick fog of Elvis records and poodle skirts. It's refreshing to see a diner make an effort with their menu, and for the most part, it works.

WEEKEND PROJECT: Porchetta • *Malcolm*

Serves 12–15 people

INGREDIENTS

A 5- to 6-pound fresh pork belly, skin on

A 3-pound boneless, center-cut pork loin

3 tablespoons fennel seeds

2 tablespoons crushed red pepper flakes

2 tablespoons minced fresh sage

1 tablespoon minced fresh rosemary

4 garlic cloves, minced

Kosher salt

Half an orange, seeded, rind on, thinly sliced

Porchetta is an Italian street food, particularly in Rome, where it is served in market stalls or from trucks, often in sandwich form. Frequently made from an entire gutted, spit-roasted pig and stuffed with citrus, rosemary, fennel, and other aromatics, the key characteristic is that each portion is a miniature celebration of the best parts of the entire pig: the fat, the lean, and the crackly skin.

I wish I could claim that my first experience with this Italian specialty was on a crisp January day in Rome, wandering aimlessly around the Trevi fountain, a steaming porchetta sandwich wrapped in waxed paper in my hands. It wasn't. Instead, my introduction to the wonders of the porchetta sandwich, a life-changing day that addicts refer to as their "moment of clarity," came from the lower level of the Brooklyn flea market, where tiny, one- and two-man operations set up tables and carts in an impromptu food court. There, the flea market outpost of the East Village's PorchettaNYC sells a small, fist-sized version of their porchetta sandwich, a $7 calorie bomb carved from a giant pork shoulder, each slender piece of meat hand selected to form the perfect combination of pure pork fat, lean meat, and skin that has crackled and burst sufficiently that the entire pork shoulder seems to be wrapped in a giant pork rind. It's a sandwich that represents one of my favorite things about that city, where the population density is sufficient that you can start a business, gain a following, and make a living selling just one thing that you cook exceptionally well. And if you are going to cook one thing, this porchetta is a great place to start.

Rather than cook a whole pig or mess with a finicky shoulder, our version of porchetta has been adapted for the home cook. We use a huge piece of skin-on pork belly wrapped around a boneless pork loin, seasoned with spices, and tied into a roast. Explain to your butcher what your intentions are; they will trim the pork belly and the loin for you as needed. Once you've got it assembled, it's nearly foolproof: Stick it in the oven, turn it a few times, adjust the temperature as needed, and you're done. The result is astonishingly delicious, all crunchy skin and moist, flavorful meat, a celebratory meal that is equally appropriate for a holiday dinner or eaten in sandwich form standing over the sink.

Method

1. First, let's prepare by doing a test-fit of the two pieces of pork. Place the belly skin-side down and arrange the loin in the center. Roll the belly around the loin so the ends of the belly meet. If any of the belly or the loin overlaps, trim the meat with a sharp knife. Unroll and set aside.

2. In a small pan over medium heat, toast the fennel seeds and red pepper flakes until fragrant, about 1 minute. Let the spices cool, then grind in a spice mill or clean coffee grinder until very fine. Transfer to a small bowl and toss with the sage, rosemary, and garlic. Set aside.

3. Arrange the belly skin-side down on a counter or large cutting board. Using a knife, score the belly flesh in a checkerboard pattern about a third of an inch deep to help the roast cook evenly.

4. Flip the belly over, and with a paring knife, poke dozens of eighth-inch-deep holes through the skin, all over the belly.

5. Using a spiked meat mallet, pound the skin side of belly all over for at least 3 minutes. This will tenderize the skin and help it puff up and get crispy when roasted.

6. Turn the belly and salt both the loin and the belly generously with kosher salt. Rub the flesh side of the belly and the entire loin with the fennel mixture. Arrange the loin down the middle of the belly, and top with the orange slices.

7. Wrap the belly around the loin, and tie crosswise tightly at ½- to 1-inch intervals with kitchen twine.

8. Trim the twine and transfer the roast to a wire rack set on a baking dish. Refrigerate uncovered for at least 24 hours to allow the skin to air-dry.

9. When ready to cook, let the porchetta sit at room temperature for two hours. Preheat the oven to 500°F, and season the porchetta with salt. Roast on a rack on a baking sheet for 40 minutes, turning once. Reduce the heat to 300°F and continue roasting, rotating the pan and turning the roast about every 20 minutes, until a thermometer inserted into the center of the roast reads 140°F, about 1½ to 2 hours more. If the skin is not yet a deep brown mahogany, crank the heat back up to 500°F and roast for 10 minutes more. Let rest for 30 minutes before slicing into ½-inch round slices with a serrated knife. Serve in slices or in sandwich form.

NOTE: I feel compelled to mention that, at approximately 850 calories per ½-inch slice, this dish is one of the worst things for you that you could ever eat. All it means is that you should probably make this dish now, before you begin the post-Thanksgiving run-up to New Year's resolutions.

CLAYTON'S CAFÉ • *Malcolm*

447 Route 1, Yarmouth, ME 04096; (207) 846-1117; claytonscafe.com

Like any self-respecting white Anglo-Saxon Protestant, I expect a certain amount of fruit in my mayonnaise-based salads. My mom's coleslaw always had raisins in it, and often pineapple. I have eaten Ambrosia salad at a picnic. And yes, I have known the cooling touch of a summer Waldorf salad. Under normal circumstances, I'll favor savory, stinky sandwiches piled high with peppered salami and smeared with taleggio. But when my fancy turns to chicken salad, I want it jammed with things other than chicken. I want candied pecans. I want curry and apples. And, as the chicken salad is served at Clayton's Café, I want halved red seedless grapes and chunks of blue cheese.

Clayton's Café is exactly what a fine sandwich shop should be—a large space with plenty of tables for dining alone with a newspaper or with a group. It features a gorgeous case of bakery items, including homemade pop tarts, oversized cupcakes, giant chocolate-dipped macaroons, and bins of old-timey penny candy. One entire wall is devoted to prepared salads, entrées, a daily selection of soups, and freshly made sandwiches. Local art and photography line the walls, and the staff is friendly, outgoing, and

hospitable without a trace of the smugness sometimes found in places that know how special their beautiful, handcrafted food is.

When you unwrap a sandwich from Clayton's, it's hard to believe just how much lunch you've gotten for so little money. In Portland's West End, this would be a $12 sandwich. Clayton's seems to understand that an excellent sandwich is only partly about what's inside it, starting with insanely thick-cut, pleasantly sharp sourdough bread. The chicken salad itself is made with 100% white meat chicken breasts cut into ¾-inch cubes and tossed with just the right amount of mayonnaise. A few studs of earthy blue cheese are a surprise in every other bite but never manage to overpower the sandwich. The halved grapes burst and pop in your mouth, mellowing the otherwise strong flavors of the sandwich and changing the consistency of the sandwich filling as you eat it.

Can you base where you live on proximity to a sandwich you really love? If so, I expect Yarmouth's population to swell as Clayton's becomes ever more popular. If I lived closer, I would be at Clayton's Café every day. This sandwich was perfect; quite simply, one of the best I have had since moving back to Maine.

Cake for Jillian's Birthday

It may not be a nationally recognized holiday, but Jillian's birthday happens to fall in November, and she takes it seriously and celebrates as much as possible. So our last thought for November has to be birthday cake.

Jillian has a personal tradition of tossing birthday cake out the window to make room for the year ahead. What else could the last bite be than a ridiculously simple but balanced cake with a crunchy crust and gooey crumb?

- Ferrero Rocher Stuffed Chocolate Cupcakes with Nutella Buttercream
- Coconut Drippy Cake
- Black Magic Grasshopper Cake
- Gooey Butter Cake

Ferrero Rocher Stuffed Chocolate Cupcakes with Nutella Buttercream • *Malcolm*
Makes 12 cupcakes

Nutella, the chocolate hazelnut spread that Italians seem to love putting on everything, is a food item that our family has deemed strictly off-limits. It's not that we don't love slathering a chunk of leftover crusty baguette with a spoonful of the stuff to go with our morning coffee; rather, we love it too much and are simply not responsible enough to have it in the house. Like Cheez-It crackers, marinated mozzarella, and peanut butter granola bars, we just can't have a jar around without devouring it in one sitting, so we choose to skip it altogether.

But when it's your birthday, you get to throw good sense out the window and eat your favorite things. And that's what today is: It's Jillian's birthday. I wanted to bake her something special, something that combined all her favorite sweets into one over-the-top cupcake that would make her senses explode and her body start racing furiously to produce extra insulin. The Nutella buttercream was a no-brainer for Jillian's ideal cupcake, but the real surprise here is inside, where an entire Ferrero Rocher hazelnut chocolate candy is baked right in. They're weapon-grade bombs of sugar, fat, and butter, perfect for special occasions or to tell someone you love them. Happy birthday, Jillian.

P.S. Do not keep tasting the buttercream as you work, or by the time the cupcakes are ready, the sugar overload will have made your heart explode.

Method

For the cupcakes:

1. Preheat the oven to 350°F. Line a muffin tin with 12 paper muffin cups. Place on a baking sheet and set aside.

2. Whisk together the flour, the cocoa powder, the baking soda, the baking powder, and the salt. Set aside.

3. In the bowl of a stand mixer, beat the butter at medium speed until soft and creamy. Add the sugar and beat until incorporated, about 2 minutes

INGREDIENTS

For the cupcakes:

1 cup all-purpose flour

¼ cup cocoa powder

¼ teaspoon baking soda

¼ teaspoon baking powder

¼ teaspoon salt

8 tablespoons (1 stick) unsalted butter, at room temperature

¾ cup granulated sugar

1 egg

½ teaspoon vanilla extract

½ cup buttermilk

2 ounces bittersweet chocolate, melted and cooled

12 Ferrero Rocher candies, unwrapped

For the Nutella buttercream:

1 cup (2 sticks) unsalted butter, softened and cut into cubes

4 cups confectioner's sugar

1 tablespoon heavy cream

2 teaspoons vanilla extract

½ cup Nutella or other chocolate-hazelnut spread

Pinch of salt

more. Add the egg and the vanilla, and reduce the mixer speed to low. Add half the dry ingredients, mixing until combined. Scrape down the bowl and add the buttermilk, mixing until incorporated. Mix in the remaining dry ingredients. Scrape down the bowl, add the melted chocolate, and mix it in by hand with a rubber spatula.

4. Divide the batter evenly into the paper cups. Press one Ferrero Rocher into the center of each cupcake. Try to cover the chocolates with batter by nestling it, but don't worry if it's not completely covered. Bake for 22–25 minutes or until a tester inserted in the centers comes out clean. Don't worry if you can see the candies after baking; we'll be covering the tops with frosting.

5. Transfer the muffin pan to a cooling rack and allow the cakes to cool for 5 minutes before taking them out of the pan. Cool to room temperature before frosting.

For the Nutella buttercream:
1. In the bowl of a stand mixer, whip the butter for 5 minutes on medium speed until the butter is pale and creamy. Add the remaining ingredients and mix on low speed for 1 minute, then on medium speed for 5 minutes. The frosting will be light, creamy, and fluffy.

2. Frost the cupcakes generously and serve.

Coconut Drippy Cake • *Jillian*
Serves 8–10

Take my mother-in-law, please. I kid! I am lucky to have a terrific, fun, lovely mother-in-law; she has been back visiting from a stint in the Deep Dirty South. She recently recounted some of her adventures in the heart of Dixie over many cups of strong coffee and coconut drippy cake.

What is coconut drippy cake, you ask? Well, it's not nearly as gross as it sounds. In fact, it's wonderful stuff. It's neither drippy nor syrupy. It's light and sweet and lovely. I tried to come up with a new name for it, but as it turns out "completely saturated cake," "mushy cake," and "sweet mellow goop" are all far worse than the original. Coconut drippy cake, it is.

It's a thing, a standard dessert, in the backwoods of Georgia, along with frequent black bear sightings, aquamarine pedicures, and big Aqua Net hair. I had to tweak the traditional recipe a bit because I wanted to make my cake from scratch and replace the traditional Cool Whip topping with my own whipped cream. We have also replaced the too-sweet coconut cream with unsweetened Thai coconut milk, because there are so many other sweetened parts in this cake.

INGREDIENTS

For the yellow cake:

4 cups plus 2 tablespoons cake flour

2 teaspoons baking powder

1½ teaspoons baking soda

1 teaspoon table salt

1 cup (2 sticks) unsalted butter, softened

2 cups granulated sugar

2 teaspoons vanilla extract

4 large eggs, room temperature

2 cups buttermilk

For the topping:

1 can condensed milk

1 can unsweetened coconut milk

2 cups whipping cream

2 tablespoons powdered sugar

1 teaspoon vanilla extract

Generous handful shredded coconut

Don't want to scratch-bake a cake? Feel free to buy a boxed mix and jazz it up from there. (I'm a big fan of jazzing stuff up.) But this is how we do a Southern classic up north in Maine. Thanks for the great recipe, Pen!

Method

1. Preheat the oven to 350°F. Butter a deep rectangular cake pan.

2. Sift together the flour, the baking powder, the baking soda, and the salt in a medium bowl.

3. In the bowl of a stand mixer, beat the butter and the sugar at medium speed until pale and fluffy. Beat in the vanilla. Add the eggs one at a time, beating well and scraping down the bowl after each addition. At low speed, beat in the buttermilk until just combined.

4. Add the flour mixture in three batches, mixing until each addition is just incorporated.

5. Spread the batter evenly in the prepared cake pan. Tap the pan on the counter several times to eliminate air bubbles. Bake until golden and a wooden pick inserted in the center of the cake comes out clean, 35–40 minutes. Cool in the pan on a rack for 10 minutes.

6. Use a fork to puncture the surface of the cake several times. Combine the condensed milk and coconut milk and pour over the cake. Let the cake cool in the refrigerator for at least 2 hours. Using the whisk attachment on a stand mixer, gently whip the cream, the sugar, and the vanilla.

7. Spread over the cake in a wonderful heap and cover this frosting with a generous sprinkling of shredded coconut. Store in the refrigerator.

INGREDIENTS

For the cake:

1¾ cups all-purpose flour

2 cups granulated sugar

¾ cup cocoa powder

2 teaspoons baking soda

1 teaspoon baking powder

1 teaspoon salt

2 eggs

1 cup buttermilk

1 cup strong black coffee, cooled

½ cup vegetable oil

1 teaspoon vanilla extract

For the peppermint icing:

½ cup (1 stick) unsalted, softened butter

2 cups powdered sugar

1 tablespoon water

½ teaspoon peppermint extract

3 drops green food coloring (optional)

For the chocolate glaze:

6 tablespoons unsalted butter

1 cup milk chocolate chips

½ cup semisweet chocolate chips

¼ teaspoon peppermint extract

Black Magic Grasshopper Cake • *Malcolm*

Serves 8–10

This chocolate cake is so good it will melt your face. If you've only ever had cakes made from a mix, as I did growing up, this will change your entire opinion of cake and, possibly, life. It's more than moist; it's this side of gooey and rich as a robber baron. Nothing complicated or fancy, just damn fine cake that keeps the kids off the street. And I support that.

Method

For the cake:

1. Preheat the oven to 350°F. Oil and flour a 13-inch by 9-inch cake pan. Whisk to combine the dry ingredients. Add the eggs, the buttermilk, the coffee, the oil, and the vanilla. Pour into the prepared pan. Bake for 35 minutes. Let cool for 15 minutes, then invert onto a wire rack to finish cooling. Let cool completely before frosting.

For the peppermint icing:

1. Use a spatula to blend all the ingredients thoroughly.

For the chocolate glaze:

1. Melt all the ingredients in the microwave, about 3 minutes.

To assemble, frost the cooled cake first with peppermint frosting, then spread with chocolate glaze.

Gooey Butter Cake • *Jillian*

Serves 8–10

Want to make a house feel like a home? Bake this cozy butter cake on the afternoon of your second day after moving, when you're surrounded by boxes stuffed with newspaper and odd objects stacking up precariously close to your ears while a determined toddler marches past carrying framed photos, clothespins, the dog's bowl, a Cleopatra head, tongs, a flyswatter, the checkbook, dominoes, a bag of flour, and finally, her pants. It is chaos in here—the complicated, happy chaos of life in motion. We're settling into a little house on a hill with space to cook and write and work in the warm sunlight. This family life is good in our little town in Maine. Okay, so this cake is crazy sweet. And rich. So. Much. Butter. Simple and decadent, with three lovely, distinct layers of texture: crackling, gooey, and buttery.

Method

For the cake:

1. In a small bowl, combine the milk and the 2 tablespoons of warm water. Whisk in the yeast; the mixture will foam slightly.

2. In the bowl of a stand mixer, using the paddle attachment, cream the butter and the sugar. Beat in the egg. Add the flour and the salt, alternating with the yeast mixture, scraping down the sides with a rubber spatula. Continue to beat on medium speed, 7–10 minutes, until the dough pulls away from the sides of the bowl. Press the dough into an ungreased, 9-inch by 13-inch ceramic baking dish. Cover with a clean dishcloth and let the dough rise in a warm spot for 3 hours.

For the filling:

1. Preheat the oven to 350°F. In a small bowl, whisk together the corn syrup, the 2 tablespoons of warm water, and the vanilla extract.

2. In the bowl of a stand mixer, using the paddle attachment, cream the butter and the sugar for 5 minutes. Beat in the egg. Add the flour and the salt, alternating with the corn syrup mixture, scraping down the sides with a rubber spatula.

3. Spread the filling evenly over the dough. Bake 40–45 minutes, until golden-brown. Allow the cake to cool in the pan before cutting into large squares and dusting with confectioner's sugar to serve.

INGREDIENTS

For the cake:

3 tablespoons whole milk, room temperature

2 tablespoons warm water

1¾ teaspoons active dry yeast

6 tablespoons unsalted, softened butter

3 tablespoons granulated sugar

1 egg

1¾ cups all-purpose flour

1 teaspoon kosher salt

For the filling:

3 tablespoons plus 1 teaspoon light corn syrup

2 tablespoons warm water

2½ teaspoons vanilla extract

¾ cup (1½ sticks) unsalted, softened butter

1½ cups sugar

1 egg

1 cup plus 3 tablespoons all-purpose flour

½ teaspoon kosher salt

Confectioner's sugar

DECEMBER

A Christmas Spirit Menu

- Chipotle and Rosemary Roasted Nuts
- Our Family's Creamy Lobster Bisque
- Roasted Bone Marrow with Parsley Salad
- Cauliflower Gratin
- Beef Wellington
- Eggnog Cake

Knowing we might get snowed in on Christmas Day, we make a contingency plan to spend the morning sleeping in, opening gifts, and later taking a long walk through the deep drifts, visiting neighboring horses, and sledding down the slight hill in our own backyard. It is a day to watch movies and snuggle on the couch.

Our tradition is for family and friends to gather the night before in a big, festive, splashy Christmas Eve celebration, complete with Malcolm's family's lobster bisque, a recipe his mother has made hundreds of times for her children and grandchildren. The year is ending, and it is a good time for rich food and making memories, savoring favorite bites done the same way for generations.

It's also a time for creating new traditions that are just ours, for our little nuclear family.

Chipotle and Rosemary Roasted Nuts • *Malcolm*

Makes one pound of nuts

This was my first batch of homemade roasted nuts, and I am officially a believer. You will be, too. Regular ol' bulk mixed nuts (I found unsalted, unroasted mixed nuts at Trader Joe's) are transformed by a few herbs and spices into a completely new dish, served warm, and are perfect for holiday get-togethers. This version uses chipotle and fresh rosemary, a flavor combination that never would have occurred to me in a thousand years. The chipotle and maple syrup provide an interesting if somewhat predictable contrast, but the charred bits of rosemary and chunks of kosher salt introduce a brand-new flavor that you never quite see coming and that ends up tasting like a hot bowl of Christmas. The only thing that's a tiny bit tricky is that you must work quickly and confidently to keep the nuts from melting into a giant, sticky mass. It's pretty easy once you get the hang of it; cook the nuts in a single layer on a well-oiled baking sheet, and then, when the nuts are cooling, remember to give them a quick toss with a spatula every 2 to 3 minutes until their coating firms up and turns into a spicy shellack.

Method

1. Preheat the oven to 350°F.

2. Coat a baking sheet with a generous amount of vegetable oil. In a bowl, toss the mixed nuts with 1 tablespoon vegetable oil, the maple syrup, light brown sugar, orange juice, and chipotle powder, until coated evenly. Add 1 tablespoon rosemary, 1 teaspoon salt, and toss again.

3. Transfer the nuts to the prepared baking sheet and spread out into a single layer. Roast for 25 minutes until the nuts are glazed and golden-brown, pausing twice in the cooking time to stir the nuts with a metal spatula before arranging back into a single layer. Remove from the oven and sprinkle with another teaspoon of salt and the remaining minced rosemary.

4. Toss well and set aside, stirring every few minutes to prevent the nuts from sticking together as they cool. Taste for seasoning. Serve warm, or let cool completely.

INGREDIENTS

Vegetable oil

1 pound mixed nuts (almonds, walnuts, pecans, cashews, hazelnuts, brazil nuts, or any combination), unsalted and unroasted

3 tablespoons pure maple syrup

2 tablespoons light brown sugar

4½ teaspoons freshly squeezed orange juice

1 teaspoon ground chipotle powder

2 tablespoons fresh rosemary leaves, minced, divided

2 teaspoons Kosher salt, divided

INGREDIENTS

Three 1½-pound Maine lobsters

½ cup (1 stick) salted butter

½ cup all-purpose flour

6 cups whole milk

¾ cup half-and-half

8 to 10 dashes Tabasco sauce

2 tablespoons Worcestershire sauce

6 teaspoons Dijon mustard

1½ cups shredded Parmesan cheese

½ cup white wine

Salt and pepper, to taste

Our Family's Creamy Lobster Bisque • *Malcolm*
Serves 6

Every Christmas Eve for as long as I can remember, my family has served lobster bisque. Okay, some years, depending on where we were in the world, or for that matter, where we were economically, the lobster was swapped for shrimp. But this dead-simple creamy, cheesy, boozy burgoo is a perfect light meal to begin the festival of eating that is Christmas Day. It always makes my insides feel snuggly and warm, as if my grandmother is giving my stomach a big hug.

There's just one problem. There's no recipe. I tried to recreate this soup for my father-in-law about five years ago based on my mother's over-the-phone directions of "you just kind of keep adjusting as you go." I ended up with a thin, lumpy, watery bowl of yuck, utterly devoid of flavor. The ingredients were all present and accounted for, but my proportions were woefully off.

During my mother's most recent visit, we made it our mission to finally get this old family recipe down on paper in a form that would be reliably reproducible. "But I don't measure anything, I just keep tasting," she protested, but finally she agreed to use measuring cups and call out the measurements of everything that went in as she slurped, sipped, and adjusted. We watched what she did, not what she said. "Okay, one cup of milk," she would say, pouring a half cup of milk into the pot. "Can we just say 'a healthy glug of wine?'" she would ask, while sipping white wine directly from the metal measuring cup as she stirred, tweaked, hummed, and adjusted some more. When all was said and done, we ended up with not just a stunning example of this dish, but for the first time in the family's history, precise instructions on how to replicate it. Here are those instructions.

Method

1. Fill a large stock or lobster pot with 2 to 3 inches of water and bring to a boil. Add the lobster and cover. Steam for 10 minutes. Drain in the sink, allow the lobster to cool, and remove the meat from the claws, knuckles, and tail. Coarsely chop the lobster meat.

2. In a medium saucepan, melt the butter over low heat. Stir in the flour and cook until the flour is absorbed, whisking constantly, about 1 to 2 minutes. Slowly add the milk and the half-and-half, whisking constantly, and cook until the mixture thickens, about 8 to 10 minutes. Whisk in the remaining ingredients, including the chopped lobster. Continue cooking over very low heat, stirring, for 8 to 10 minutes or until desired thickness is reached. (Be careful not to let the soup simmer after you add the wine. It can break and separate.) Remove from the heat, cover, and let rest for 20 minutes before serving.

Roasted Bone Marrow with Parsley Salad

● *Malcolm*

Serves 8

I've realized recently that there are no foods I actively dislike; instead, there are only degrees of desire. "Favorite" foods and "hated" foods are concepts for kids, I'm now thinking. We adults should be slower and more open-ended in our judgments, more catholic in our tastes. Certainly I "like" frozen custard more than boiled cabbage, but I am trying to appreciate both for the different sensations they provide, and to stop thinking of one as "better" than the other. I am trying to taste everything, and the foods I find challenging have become opportunities to stretch and exercise this new sensibility. I want to find out if I'm discovering a new, more expansive me or if I'm just full of it.

Given this new approach to food, I deemed it time to challenge one of my few remaining "problem" categories. You see, I have an immature aversion to the parts of an animal that seem too (spiritually? ethically?) fundamental to its being. This means, for whatever reason, that tongue and heart are fine, liver is perfectly acceptable, and stomach is passable, but brain and bone marrow give me base-level heebie-jeebies. You can argue that these distinctions are completely arbitrary, and that a steer needs its heart and stomach every bit as much as its brain and marrow. I'm with you intellectually, but emotionally I'm just not there yet. I'm not particularly spiritual or even ethical; I don't dwell on whether the meat I'm eating had a face, even a particularly adorable one. So what gives? This is what's been eating me. As a meat eater worth my salt, I should eat the entire animal, not just the usual, familiar parts.

With this in mind, I set out to conquer my irrational fear of bone marrow, because nothing asserts your dominance over a cow more than splitting its bones open and scooping its marrow onto toast points. Let's get started, shall we?

Ask your butcher to saw the bones lengthwise; this provides for more even cooking and easier scraping. Marrow bones are dirt cheap. We got eight split bones for about five bucks. Be careful not to overcook your bones. You should stop cooking before the marrow starts oozing out of the bone, as it has a tendency to become chewy. The finished product is much, much different than I expected; the marrow smells strongly of beef (I found myself referring to it as "super beef") with a loose consistency not unlike that of half-rendered fat. Spread onto toast and topped with the

INGREDIENTS

Four center-cut beef or veal marrow bones, 3 inches long, cut lengthwise

1 cup roughly chopped fresh parsley

Two shallots, thinly sliced

2 teaspoons capers

1½ tablespoons extra-virgin olive oil

2 teaspoons fresh lemon juice

Coarse sea salt to taste

At least four ½-inch-thick slices of crusty bread, toasted

parsley salad, each bite was satisfying, with the sharpness of the salad preventing the heavy beef notes from becoming overwhelming or the heavy fat from coating my lips. After my first bone, I was hooked, and I didn't stop until they were all clean.

Method

1. Preheat the oven to 450°F. Place the bones in a cast-iron skillet and roast, cut side up, until the marrow is soft and begins to pull away from the bone, about 15 minutes. While the bones cook, combine the parsley, shallots, and capers in a small bowl. Add the olive oil and lemon juice and toss to combine. Scoop the marrow out of the bones, spread on the toast slices, and top with sea salt and the dressing. Serve immediately.

Cauliflower Gratin • *Jillian*

Serves 8

It's the most decadent meal of the entire year. For some, the most anticipated. The coziest. The richest. Though Thanksgiving may have more breadth and volume, our Christmas dinner is rich beyond belief. We take the cream, the fat, the marrow, and marry it all on a table shining with ornaments, pinecones, and candles. This holiday sparkles in Maine, with our majestic pine trees making it feel special and holy every way you look. When it is so cold and dark outside, we turn inward with fireplaces and family members, giving gifts and making our own light in the darkest time of year. I think this cauliflower gratin is the only vegetable side dish that could possibly stand up to and balance everything else we have on our menu. It's a lovely winter vegetable and lots of nutty, warm cheese nestled together.

Method

1. Preheat the oven to 375°F. Cook the cauliflower florets 5–6 minutes in a large pot of boiling water. Drain. and set aside.

2. In a medium-sized saucepan over low heat, melt half the butter. Add the flour, stirring constantly for 1 minute. Slowly pour in the milk and stir until the mixture comes to a boil. Whisk until thickened. Remove from the heat and season with the salt, pepper, and nutmeg. Add ½ cup of the Gruyère, all of the Parmesan, and all but a half clove of garlic.

3. Combine the remaining ¼ cup Gruyère with the bread crumbs. Slice the remaining butter into very small pats. Rub the baking dish with the remaining half clove of garlic. Ladle a third of the cheese sauce into the baking dish. Add the cooked cauliflower and the rest of the cheese sauce. Top with the bread crumb mixture and butter pats. Bake 30 minutes until golden-brown and bubbly.

INGREDIENTS

1 large head cauliflower, cut into florets

4 tablespoons (½ stick) unsalted butter, divided

3 tablespoons all-purpose flour

2 cups hot milk

Kosher salt and freshly ground black pepper

¼ teaspoon ground nutmeg

¾ cup grated Gruyère, divided

½ cup grated Parmesan cheese

3 garlic cloves, peeled and halved

½ cup bread crumbs

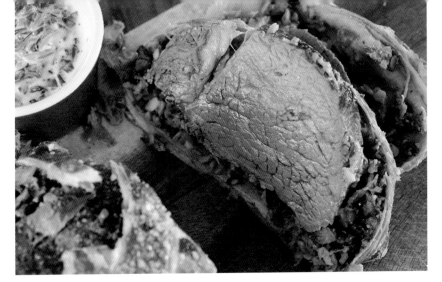

Beef Wellington • *Jillian*
Serves 6

This recipe is a classic, savory and rich. You need time but no special skill or equipment to achieve an impressive and delicious dinner for a holiday or special occasion, or even for an unremarkable Thursday in May.

The butcher cut a beautiful piece of fillet. I chopped wild mushrooms, fragrant of the middle woods, and used my favorite long rolling pin to form the puff pastry into the right shape (Mississippi-ish) and size. I added a good glug of wine to the cooking-down of the earthy vegetables, with marjoram instead of the more traditional thyme. I brushed lovingly with egg.

It came out of the oven golden-brown, and when we sliced it, the medium-rare meat was pink in the center. There are textures and layers and such a sweet reward for the effort. I cannot recommend this one highly enough. Please enjoy!

Method

To prepare the beef:

1. In a large skillet over medium-high heat, add a tablespoon of vegetable oil, and allow to get very hot. Season the beef with salt and pepper. Sear the meat on all four sides until deep brown. Remove to a plate and allow to rest for 10 minutes, then rub with Dijon mustard.

For the mushroom duxelles:

1. In the same skillet used to sear the beef, melt the butter over medium-low heat. Sauté the shallots, mushrooms, garlic, and marjoram. Add the vermouth and cook down until almost a paste. Season with salt and pepper.

INGREDIENTS

Vegetable oil

2 pounds beef tenderloin fillet

Kosher salt and freshly ground pepper

2 tablespoons Dijon mustard

2 tablespoons (¼ stick) unsalted butter

1 large shallot, minced

12 ounces mixed mushrooms (shiitakes and creminis), very finely diced

2 garlic cloves, minced

4 sprigs marjoram, leaves removed from stems

¼ cup vermouth or dry white wine

6 to 8 pieces of prosciutto

Flour, for dusting work surface

1 sheet puff pastry

2 egg yolks, beaten

For the Wellington:

2. Preheat the oven to 400°F.

3. Lay 12 inches of plastic wrap on your work surface. Layer the prosciutto in a shingled fashion in two columns, overlapping.

4. Spread the mushroom duxelles evenly over the prosciutto.

5. Center the beef fillet on the mushroom mixture. Fold up the sides of plastic wrap and secure tightly around the fillet. Refrigerate while you prepare the pastry.

6. On a lightly floured work surface, roll out one sheet of (thawed) puff pastry into a rectangle.

7. Paint the edges with beaten egg yolks. Unwrap the beef and center on the puff pastry. Fold up the sides of the pastry and seal. Seal the ends, making sure to remove any excess pastry. More than two layers of pastry will not cook completely.

8. Place on a baking pan, seam side down. Brush with the egg yolks and score with the back of a knife, taking care not to go all the way through the pastry. Cook 30 minutes or until a meat thermometer inserted into the center of the roast reads 125° to 130°F. Allow the Wellington to rest for 10 minutes before slicing into 1-inch-thick slices.

Eggnog Cake • *Jillian*
Serves 8

Food is an integral part of holiday gatherings. We feast, break bread, come to the table together to experience constancy and continuity in this ever-changing life. We bake and share sweet cookies, make a much-too-big roast, mull wine, and even leave a carrot for Santa's favorite reindeer.

There is one tasty Christmas treat that is humble yet more sacrosanct than all the rest. It can be handcrafted, but I will always argue that the very best of its kind comes from the refrigerated section of your local supermarket. Yes, friends, I speak of eggnog, that sweet, delicious, and faux-boozy boxed dairy drink that is only available during the holidays. Have you tasted homemade eggnog? It's mostly pretty gross. And there are so many kinds of delicious nonalcoholic nog for sale right now. I used a carton of plain Oakhurst Dairy eggnog to make this rich, dense cake.

Method

For the cake:

1. Preheat the oven to 350°F. Prepare two 9-inch round cake pans with baking spray. In the bowl of a stand mixer, cream the butter and sugar. Add the eggs, one at a time, beating after each one. Add the vanilla. In a separate bowl, whisk together the dry ingredients, then pour into the mixer, alternating with the eggnog. Transfer to the prepared cake pans and bake 25 to 30 minutes, until a toothpick comes out clean. Let cool completely in pans before inverting onto wire rack.

For the frosting:

1. In a small saucepan over medium heat, combine the flour and salt. Whisk in the eggnog and keep whisking. Bring to a boil and let the mixture thicken, stirring constantly. Cool to room temperature.

2. In the bowl of a stand mixer, cream the butter and sugar. Add the vanilla, rum, and nutmeg. Pour in the cooled flour/eggnog mixture. Beat until well blended and smooth. Once the cakes are completely cool, frost and keep refrigerated.

INGREDIENTS

For the cake:

½ cup (1 stick) unsalted butter, softened

1¼ cups granulated sugar

3 eggs

1 teaspoon vanilla extract

2 cups all-purpose flour

2 teaspoons baking powder

1 teaspoon salt

1 cup eggnog

For the frosting:

¼ cup all-purpose flour

¼ teaspoon salt

1½ cups eggnog

1 cup (2 sticks) unsalted butter, softened

1½ cups confectioner's sugar

1 teaspoon vanilla extract

1 teaspoon rum

½ teaspoon nutmeg

WEEKEND PROJECT: The Ultimate Maine-Style Italian Sandwich • *Malcolm*

Makes one sandwich

In 1902, in his tiny bakery on Portland's working waterfront, Giovanni Amato allowed local dockworkers to talk him into splitting his bread loaves lengthwise, then piling them with meat, cheese, and vegetables. The resulting sandwich, which today typically includes a thin layer of boiled ham, sliced American cheese, sliced tomatoes, green pepper, onion, olives (black or kalamata), and a finish of oil, salt, and pepper, is one of the last truly regional food specialties. Travel south of Kittery, and you'll continue to see lots of sandwiches for sale at gas stations. You'll find hoagies, grinders, subs, and heroes. But you'll be hard pressed to find a real Italian. (For more on Italians à la Amato's or Anania's, see the "February" chapter.)

After eating hundreds of versions of this sandwich, I decided it was time to work up my own variation. Such a project is fraught with peril, of course. Mainers are protective of their Italians; too much mucking around with the ingredients might produce a perfectly good sandwich, but it would not be a tried-and-true Maine Italian. I knew I had to find a way to tweak the original without changing what the sandwich fundamentally is.

What better month than December to tackle a project like this? You're indoors anyway. Mild weather is a distant memory. Snow for skiing is a mere promise. Nothing out there now but frozen ground, your breath in the air, and early dark. Heat up the kitchen. Here's what I've come up with, broken down by ingredients.

The Bread The bread on a traditional Italian is light, white, and fluffy. It's the kind of loaf that is so tied to the sandwich's identity that to change it would mean changing the sandwich itself. It's also the kind of loaf that I suspect is out of reach for most home bakers; these things need to be mass produced, made of hyper-bleached enriched white flour, and slurped dry of any nutritional value.

For our sandwich, I went with something off the shelf: a bag of four 12-inch giants from the supermarket bakery that were helpfully labeled "Italian Sandwich Loaves." If you live in a part of the country where these aren't available—which I suspect is anywhere outside Maine—try making "mini Italians" using hot dog buns. While less than ideal, this option is preferable to changing the texture of the bread in any way. To repeat, an Italian in anything other than light, white, fluffy bread is simply not a true Italian. Ask any native Mainer.

The Cheese I considered swapping out the traditional American cheese for something with a little more flavor, such as provolone, but the weird properties of American cheese are such a major part of the Italian sandwich experience that I couldn't bear to do it. In a Maine Italian, the American cheese liquefies, presumably in response to the moisture from the vegetables and oil, forming a thin protective layer that guards the bottom slice of bread from too much oil seepage, especially when wrapped in butcher paper and stored overnight. I left the cheese alone.

The Meat For our signature version of this sandwich, I had to part ways with tradition just a little. The meat is a great place to get creative; the boiled ham on a Maine Italian is such a minor component of the finished product that you can make some substitutions here without raising too many eyebrows. For our sandwich, I went with fatty mortadella and a few slices of Genoa salami for texture and a hint of spice.

The Vegetables Again, there's not a lot of room to substitute here. When you're making a Maine Italian, tomatoes, onions, and green peppers are mandatory. But I like to add tart sour pickles, sliced into thin spears so that you get a little pickle in every bite. And rather than choose between black and kalamata olives, I prefer to buy a mix of assorted pitted varieties and chop them in a food processor with a few banana peppers, creating a kind of poor-man's tapenade, which I spread on one side of the bread.

A final word about vegetables: Stack them vertically in the sandwich, so that it can be closed and eaten normally. The Amato's chain doesn't do this, which can make eating an Amato's Italian seem more like eating a soft tray of oily vegetables.

The Oil Opinions vary here; Amato's uses a blend of vegetable and olive oils. I prefer the stronger flavor of a good olive oil, particularly a garlic- or chile-infused one.

The resulting sandwich breaks from tradition here and there but honors the original. And like the original, our version of the Maine Italian is a pure junk food addiction that pings all your pleasure receptors: salty, sour, spicy, crunchy, oily, and messy. It's food meant to be eaten either at the beach, where you can clean off afterward with a dip in the frigid ocean, or more likely in the middle of the night, standing over the sink, with half a bottle of Moxie for a chaser.

Method

1. Slice the bread two-thirds of the way through. Line the bottom half with the cheese, then the sliced meat. Top with the tomato, green pepper, onion, and pickles, arranged vertically for easy eating.

2. In a food processor, pulse the olives and banana peppers into a coarse paste, and spread on the top half of the bread. Drizzle liberally with olive oil, and finish with salt and pepper. Serve immediately, or allow everything to melt together in the fridge overnight.

INGREDIENTS

A 12-inch soft white sub sandwich roll

2 or 3 slices American cheese, cut in half

4 to 6 slices mortadella

4 to 6 slices Genoa salami

Sliced tomato, green pepper, onion, and sour pickles

1 cup assorted pitted olives (green, black, and Kalamata)

¼ cup banana peppers

Olive oil

Salt and pepper, to taste

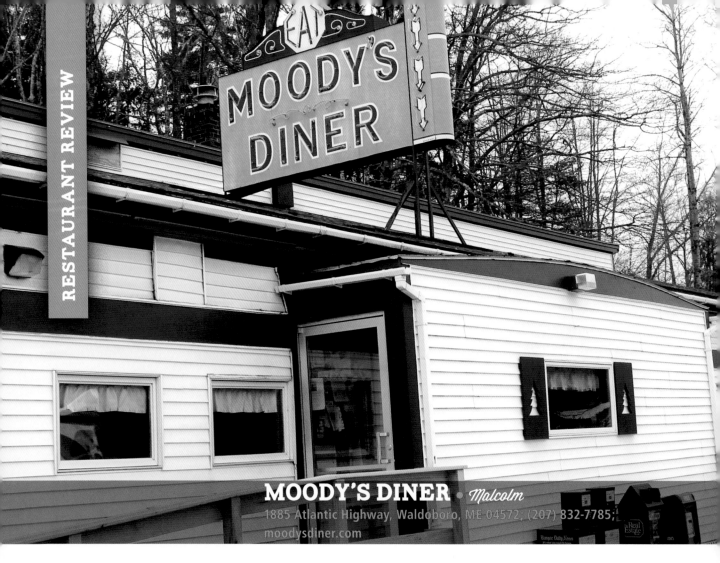

MOODY'S DINER • *Malcolm*

1885 Atlantic Highway, Waldoboro, ME 04572; (207) 832-7785; moodysdiner.com

Ask anyone from away about iconic Maine road food and the conversation will turn, inevitably, to Moody's Diner in Waldoboro. One key to the legendary diner's fame is its location; a plum U.S. Route 1 location means that nearly every tourist en route up the coast to attend the Maine Lobster Festival in Rockland or spend a few nights in a tent in Camden Hills State Park will pass the restaurant and take notice of the unassuming white trailer with the big art-deco orange neon sign that commands us to "EAT."

Jillian: It's been many years since Malcolm first absconded with me from Connecticut to visit his childhood home on the craggy, peninsular coast of Maine. After that first visit we made the epic journey once a year, escaping the humidity of New Haven summers and Yucatan winters to stay at the Samoset, where we would swim and brunch and walk the breakwater. Now I'm a license-holding Maine resident, yet there are still mysteries to be uncovered. Malcolm's been threatening me with Moody's for I don't know how long. I quietly resist and we sail on by, stopping somewhere else for hot dogs or lobster rolls, depending on the season. Is now a good time to share my theory that force-feeding a lobster one of Wasses' awesome hot dogs, then eating that lobster, would be the ultimate Maine eating experience?

The Moody's empire began in 1927 as a motel with three cabins featuring screened porches but no running water that rented for $1.00 per person per night. Built to capitalize on the expected influx of summer visitors over yet-to-be-built Route 1, the motel grew over the years into a full-blown compound that includes 18 cabins, a 104-seat diner, and a gift shop.

My first experience at Moody's was as a kid in the early 1980s, watching my dad somehow manage to eat plates full of liver and onions while simultaneously drinking coffee and chain-smoking Marlboro Reds. By the time I got to high school, Moody's had done away with their smoking section, but their (then) 24-hour schedule made it something of a late-night destination for bored teenagers from the surrounding hinterlands. After a night spent driving between the parking lots of Wal-Mart, Ames, and Shop 'n' Save, where we would sit for hours in one of our cars, a slice of pie at Moody's was often a final stop, a focused destination during a decidedly unfocused time in our lives. The 20 minutes that separated Moody's from our hometown was enough to ensure that we didn't visit often, but I was always happy when we did.

My best friend from childhood now has a teenaged stepson of his own, who was briefly a dishwasher at Moody's. His mother-in-law worked there for 30 years. That's the kind of multigenerational impact a family business like Moody's has on everyone who grows up here. Though we returned to Maine several years ago, and despite countless trips up the coast to visit friends and family, it didn't occur to me until recently to stop at Moody's and write a review. When a place has been around for 80 years and has become such a central institution in the collective mind—and has in fact become a legendary piece of scenery—it almost doesn't dawn on you to stop and eat there. It doesn't occur to you that you could possibly add anything to its story.

When you first step into Moody's, you have a choice to make. On the left, the diner's original Formica counter and leather-and-chrome stools run the length of the building, some of which are occupied by locals who eat at Moody's every day. Hang a right, and Moody's opens into a slightly more spacious dining room with a few freestanding tables and another row of booths. On most weekdays during the winter, you can sit wherever

you like. The pale green linoleum on the floor is mirrored by the low foam dropped ceiling that runs throughout.

Jillian: It felt strangely temporary for a place as enduring as this. Where I'm from, diners resemble Tomorrowland, chrome-shiny and neon-new. I like how barely indoors Moody's feels, like an extension of the coniferous forest just beyond its walls. It's a diner in many ways that are familiar: waitresses who carry the weight of the world on a plate with two fried eggs but can be coaxed by a cute newborn into smiling, bottomless cups of coffee, substantial plates of fries and onion rings greasy enough to get you through those bleary-eyed mornings that once were caused by whiskey and now are the result of the 3 a.m. feeding.

After settling into a booth, ordering a cup of coffee, and reviewing the daily specials, I cursed my bad luck for not stopping at Moody's on American Chop Suey Wednesday. I settled instead on the Salisbury Steak with Mushroom Gravy ($7.99). Jillian usually opts for breakfast when visiting a diner and was pleased to find that Moody's offers the morning meal all day. There are, she learned, a few peculiar exceptions to this. You can order breakfast all day at Moody's unless you want a poached egg. Those are only served until 11 a.m. and after 9 p.m. The same holds true for omelets. If you want breakfast, that's fine. But if you want an omelet, well, those aren't served after 11 a.m. Throwing up her hands in a last-minute panic, she settled on a grilled cheese on rye with a side of onion rings ($5.38). We also sampled the pan-fried haddock cakes with pickled beets and potato salad ($7.99).

Jillian: Rye bread is a diner essential.

Expecting standard diner fare, I was pleasantly surprised by my Salisbury Steak. The two hamburger patties were nondescript—a little dry, a little underseasoned, a little puckish—but with a fantastic sear and crust around the outside. The star of the dish was the mushroom gravy. Moody's makes their own gravy, and it is studded with tons of fresh sautéed mushrooms, adding a salty, beefy layer of flavor to the meat and mashed potatoes it covers. I kept making (and breaking) mental bargains with myself about how much of the dish I would eat, ultimately nearly finishing it.

Jillian's grilled cheese sandwich was unremarkable, but certainly good, with golden-toasted rye bread and lots of melted Swiss cheese. The onion rings were nothing short of remarkable; tender ribbons of perfectly cooked onion wrapped in a crunchy batter that positively begged for additional salt and ketchup. Jillian ordered coleslaw for me, but the dish of slaw that accompanied my dinner was plenty.

I was most surprised by the haddock cakes, a dish I would never ordinarily order. I expected them to be bready and mushy, with lots of filler and little fish. Instead, these perfectly crisped rounds of haddock were packed full of my favorite fish, and the sear from the pan added a delicious crunch that proved the perfect vehicle for tartar sauce.

While all our entrées were good, it is the pie at Moody's that has become iconic over the years. With eleven varieties of homemade pie available at any given time of the day or night, the shortening-laden flaky crust at the bottom of a Moody's pie ($3.69/slice) is enough to warrant a visit. We tried two huge slices of chocolate cream and coconut cream pie, both double the size of a regular slice of pie and covered in a thick mound of whipped cream. Both slices were perfect—not too sweet, impossibly creamy, thick and velvety, with tons of chocolate and coconut flavor in each slice. I can imagine skipping lunch altogether, ordering a slice of four-berry pie à la mode, and foregoing other meals for the rest of the day.

Jillian: Moody's is a roadside icon, as much a part of the fabric of that Route 1 drive as Bath Ironworks and the Wiscasset Bridge. I like being a small part of this place, though I may just be passing through.

What started as a summer rental-cabin business founded by a serial entrepreneur who also had his hand in cattle and Christmas tree businesses has evolved with the times into a family enterprise that has kept the Moody family employed for generations. What is most surprising is that in spite of its prime location and attention to summer business, Moody's has never felt like a tourist trap. Visit in the winter, and you'll find customers that have been eating there for years, enjoying the same low-priced, hearty diner fare. While the locals may be mostly absent during the summer, and there

may be a bit of a wait, tourists will receive the same treatment and be served the same good meals. There are no $40 shore dinners made with six bucks' worth of seafood at Moody's. Instead, locals and tourists alike have been delighted by Moody's versions of classic diner cuisine executed faithfully, quickly, and inexpensively for over 85 years. It's a Maine institution.

HOT SUPPA • *Malcolm*
703 Congress Street, Portland, ME 04102; (207) 871-5005; hotsuppa.com

If I had to sum up my father's life in one epic, sweeping goal, it would be this: to find the ultimate hand-cut, perfectly flattop-crusted corned beef hash. How happy he would be, then, to see that Hot Suppa delivers 100% in this regard. Word is traveling fast, too; *Bon Appetit* called the corned beef hash at Hot Suppa "Portland's best breakfast dish." They take the element of corned beef hash that everyone loves, that crusty outer layer, and manage to extend it throughout the dish, a combination of hand-cut potatoes, carrots, and onions, and piles of house-made shredded corned beef. Add a side of hash browns and you'll find that crusty exterior extended over the whole plate into one giant, beautifully crunchy layer of hot, meaty mashed deliciousness; add a couple of poached eggs and a hit of Sriracha, and you've got a hangover cure and a guaranteed afternoon nap on one perfect plate.

Hot Suppa has also recently started offering alcoholic beverages at breakfast; the Cajun Bloody Marys are terrifically spicy and potent. Because their new liquor license still has its sheen, be sure to bring some identification . . . You will be flatly denied service should you look less than forty and not be able to produce proof of age.

The specials board contains some treasures, from specialty bacons of the day to diabolical breakfast concoctions that will instantly put a smile on your face, not to mention give you the gout. Beef brisket eggs Benedict? Shrimp and grits? This is "one meal per day" eating. Finish the plate, and the only place you'll be going is back to bed.

If you can rally for lunch, Hot Suppa has some tasty options there as well. The "Hot Suppa Double Double" burger consistently makes the "Best Burger Roundup" lists in Portland, and the consideration is deserved: This burger is a fast food–style burger done right, with two thinnish burger patties, pleasingly shellacked with dual layers of melted American cheese, caramelized onions, and a few slices of pickle. Dipped directly into ketchup, the Double Double is burger heaven.

Hot Suppa's list of side dishes is impressive as well, including Fried Green Tomatoes, Macaroni and Cheese, and Baked Beans. Hot Suppa is proud enough of their sides, in fact, that a lunchtime option is to build an entire meal out of sides for a flat price.

You may hit a bit of a wait on the weekends. The tables turn quickly, though, and seeing the smiling, satisfied faces on their way out will inspire you to wait just a little longer. Hot Suppa has emerged as one of our favorite places to take guests for a cozy, bleary-eyed breakfast.

More December Dishes: Everything in Moderation, Including Moderation

- Yukon Gold Potatoes with Crème Fraîche and Lobster Roe
- Chicken Liver Pâté
- Super Crispy Slow-Roasted Pork Shoulder

In December, you can't have too much anything—too much Christmas or Hannukah, too much decadent, rich food, too many lights and parties, too many glasses of champagne and mugs of hot chocolate. We take advantage of every treat we can think of to get us through this dark, cold month. For us, it is all about celebrating, indulging, gathering, and sharing wonderful food with family and friends. And of course, in Maine, it's always time for lobster!

Yukon Gold Potatoes with Crème Fraîche and Lobster Roe • *Jillian*

Serves 8–10

Lobster roe lends just the right light essence of lobster to this sumptuous canapé. We use Yukon Gold potatoes because they are creamy and roast nicely, but use your favorite. This dish is a perfect party hors d'oeuvre—easy, decadent, and satisfying in taste and texture. Enjoy Maine's land-and-sea appetizer the next time you want a simple, indulgent supper.

INGREDIENTS

2 pounds Yukon Gold potatoes, cut in 1-inch slices

1 tablespoon olive oil

Kosher salt and freshly ground black pepper

1 tablespoon fresh rosemary, minced

1 cup crème fraîche

1 ounce lobster roe

Method

1. Preheat the oven to 400°F. Toss the potato slices with the olive oil, the salt, pepper, and the rosemary. Roast on a cookie sheet until browned and crisp, approximately 40 minutes. Allow the potatoes to cool before topping them with dollops of the crème fraîche and the lobster roe.

Chicken Liver Pâté • *Malcolm*

Adapted from a recipe by David Lebovitz

Makes about two cups

Rendered duck fat gets a lot of play here in Maine, and for good reason. There are few better fats to use for frying impossibly rich, golden-brown potatoes (just ask the good folks at Portland's Duckfat), and it's also fantastic in pie crusts or rubbed on the outside of a chicken prior to roasting. It's marginally better for you than most hydrogenated oils, and it keeps practically forever in the refrigerator or freezer. If you suddenly find yourself with an abundance of duck fat around, you lucky dog, you can also use it to lend structure to a light chicken liver mousse pâté.

To be fair, chicken liver pâté may not be for everyone, but I think it represents a painless introduction to the wonderful world of organ meat spreads and terrines. Unlike its chunkier, bacon-wrapped, country-style cousin, the smooth, silken texture of this pâté is a little easier for the uninitiated to approach. It was certainly the first pâté I tried as a kid, thanks to a mother who has what can only be considered an addiction to the stuff; she'd spread it on crackers with plenty of capers and lemon juice. It's the anchor component of any self-respecting charcuterie board, and it's remarkably easy to make yourself at home using inexpensive ingredients (though the duck fat may require a trip to a specialty grocery store).

If you have any lingering squeamishness about working with cooked and puréed chicken livers, it will be gone by the time you finish making this recipe for the first time, since the process for some reason seems to require the mixture getting on dozens more dishes and spoons than you planned on using, as well as many paper towels, your hands, and maybe even the baby. After chilling for a few hours in the fridge, we top ours with a port wine gelatin (though, as David Lebovitz points out with regard to gelatins and aspics, "People get weird about things that are jellied, so it's optional") to give the pâté a finished look and a touch of sweetness to offset its richness. Once set, the pâté will keep for a few days in the fridge, developing even more flavor the second day. Serve it spread on a crusty slice of baguette or cracker, with a squeeze of lemon, capers, and a few cornichons on the side.

Method

For the pâté:

1. In a large skillet over low heat, cook the onions with ¼ cup of the duck fat, stirring often, until the onions begin to brown and caramelize, about 20 minutes. Use a slotted spoon to transfer the onions to paper towels to drain.

INGREDIENTS

For the pâté:

¾ cup melted duck fat

1 onion, peeled and diced

1 pound chicken livers

1 teaspoon salt

1 teaspoon freshly ground pepper

Pinch cayenne powder

3 large hard-boiled eggs

2 teaspoons red wine vinegar

1 teaspoon bourbon

For the port wine gelatin:

2 tablespoons water

½ cup plus 2 tablespoons port wine

1 teaspoon unflavored gelatin

2 teaspoons granulated sugar

Pinch of ground allspice

2. Increase the heat to medium-high and add the chicken livers, the salt, the pepper, and the cayenne to the pan. Cook, stirring often, until the chicken livers are just cooked through but still pink in the middle, about 4–5 minutes.

3. Transfer the chicken liver mixture and the pan drippings to the bowl of a food processor. Add the hard-boiled eggs, the vinegar, the bourbon, the caramelized onions, and the remaining duck fat. Purée until completely smooth. Transfer the mixture to a small mold (mini loaf pans work well) or bowl. Cover with plastic wrap and chill in the refrigerator for a few hours until set.

For the port wine gelatin:

1. In a small bowl, combine the water and the two tablespoons of the port. Sprinkle with the powdered gelatin and let rest for 5 minutes.

2. In a small saucepan over medium heat, warm the remaining ½ cup port, the sugar, and the allspice. When the mixture begins to simmer, pour over the softened gelatin, stirring until the gelatin is dissolved. Let the mixture cool to room temperature, then pour in a thin layer over the chilled pâté. Return to the refrigerator until the gelatin is set.

Super Crispy Slow-Roasted Pork Shoulder • *Malcolm*

Serves 8

Each year we try to make something extra special to serve for Christmas Day dinner. It's usually a pretty informal affair; I try to make something that can sit all day, served alongside a simple salad and the other amazing DIY food presents we receive from friends and family, so that anyone who drops by to help us with our holly jollies can have a bite to eat. But nothing we have made for Christmas dinner (and I stress, NOTHING!) compares to this recipe for slow-cooked pork shoulder, the inexpensive cut of meat rendered spoon tender while the skin puffs and inflates to make the finished product more like a blissfully tender and moist pork roast topped with a thick layer of deep-fried chicharrón.

For such impressive, foolproof results, the technique couldn't be simpler. Find an 8- to 10-pound skin-on pork shoulder (often referred to as a "picnic roast" here in Maine), and rub it all over with salt and pepper. Cooking it in a 250°F oven for eight hours allows all the connective collagen in the hard-working pig's shoulder to break down into gelatin, resulting in an almost otherworldly tenderness, while retaining as much moisture as possible.

INGREDIENTS

1 bone-in, skin-on pork shoulder, 8–10 pounds (sometimes called a "picnic cut" in the Northeast)

Kosher salt and freshly ground black pepper

Crusty rolls

Chimichurri, or barbecue sauce (optional)

EASY CHIMICHURRI

INGREDIENTS

¼ cup oregano

1 cup packed parsley

3 cloves garlic, peeled

½ cup olive oil

2 tablespoons white wine vinegar

1 teaspoon red pepper flakes, or to taste

Pinch of salt

Combine all ingredients in food processor, and pulse until combined and mixture is nearly smooth. Allow to marinate in the fridge for a few hours before serving.

This slow-and-low treatment doesn't do the skin any favors, however, leaving it tough and almost inedibly chewy. Fixing that requires nothing but some extra heat. After letting the roast finish cooking, we take it out of the oven to rest while we bring the oven up to 500°F. A blast at this high heat causes all of the tiny pockets in the skin to fill with steam from the meat underneath so that it turns light, crunchy, and a beautiful golden-brown, with a layer of succulent fat underneath.

The resulting roast can be picked apart with your bare hands, dipped into sauce and eaten as is, or pulled and chopped to make into sandwiches. Encourage your guests to put a little lean meat, a little fat, and a few bits of crunchy skin on a Portuguese roll. The combination of textures and temperatures is stunningly delicious. For good measure, top your sandwich with a bit of homemade chimichurri.

Method

1. Move the oven rack to the middle position, and preheat the oven to 250°F.

2. Line a rimmed baking sheet with foil, and set a wire rack inside it. Season the pork on all sides with salt and pepper (or whatever you'd like), and place on the wire rack. Transfer to the oven and roast until the pork shows little resistance to a fork, about 8 hours.

3. Remove the pork from the oven and tent with foil. Allow the pork to rest at least 15 minutes, although the pork can be held at this stage until just before you are ready to serve, up to several hours. Increase the oven temperature to 500°F, and allow to preheat. Remove the foil and return the pork to the oven. Roast until the skin is blistered and puffy, rotating every 5 minutes, about 20 minutes total. Remove from the oven, tent with foil, and allow the pork to rest an additional 15 minutes.

4. To serve, either bring the roast to the table as is and let your guests pick at it themselves to dip in accompanying sauces, or cut up the pork in the kitchen and serve bits of meat, fat, and crispy skin on Portuguese rolls.

Achiote paste
  Achiote Butter-Basted Roast Turkey, 240
  Cochinita Pibil, 116–117
American Chop Suey, 47–48
ancho chiles
  Ancho Chile Gravy, 240
  Ancho Chile Pumpkin Pie, 243
  Smoky Lamb and Chorizo Chili, 206–207
The Angelique's Gingerbread Cake, 195
apples
  Apple Fritters, 218–219
  Baked Apple, 209–210
  Maine Lobster Fondue, 34–35
  Sweet Potato Soup, 17
Apricot-Shellacked Ghost Chile Chicken Wings, 212–215
artichokes
  Kale and Artichoke Soup, 76
  Steamed Artichokes with Roasted Garlic Aioli, 33
asparagus
  Asparagus Soup, 94–95
  Boiled Egg, Sautéed Asparagus, and Pickled Red Onion Sandwich, 90–91
Atlantic Baja-Style Fish Tacos, 162

bacon
  Bacon & Egg Potato Salad, 97
  Big Homemade Barbecue Burgers, 167–168
  Brown Ale and Cheddar Soup, 55–56
  Brown Butter and Bacon Chocolate Chip Cookies, 91–92
  Chicken and Corn Summer Chowder, 161
  Haddock Chowder, 111–112
  Haddock Ragout with Mussels, Bacon, and Peas, 135
  Homemade Bacon Jam, 110–111
  Orecchiette with Yellow Squash, Corn, and Bacon, 140–141
  Sweet Corn and Poblano Chowder, 115
  Welsh Rarebit Bites, 52–53

Yankee Pot Roast, 46–47
Bacon and Egg Candies, 232–233
Baileys Buttercream, 59–61
Baked Apple with Ginger Cookie and Whiskey Whipped Cream, 209–210
Banana Pancakes, Gluten-Free Two-Ingredient, 187
Barbecue Burgers, Big Homemade, 167–168
Barbecue Sauce, North Carolina, 172–173
beef
  American Chop Suey, 47–48
  Beef Wellington, 263–264
  Big Homemade Barbecue Burgers, 167–168
  Corned Beef Hash, 62
  Eggs Florentine Burgers, 71–72
  Grilled Flank Steak Tacos with Chipotle Rhubarb Salsa, 100–102
  Prime Rib Breakfast Hash, 18
  Roasted Bone Marrow with Parsley Salad, 261–262
  Scratch-Made Corned Beef and Cabbage, 57–58
  Scratch-Made Grownup Sloppy Joes, 65–66
  Scratch-Made Ultimate Cheeseburger, 199–201
  Short Ribs with Tagliatelle, 29
  Yankee Pot Roast, 46–47
beer
  Atlantic Baja-Style Fish Tacos, 162
  Beer & Bison Burgers with Garlic Pub Cheese, 96–97
  Brown Ale and Cheddar Soup, 55–56
  Chocolate Guinness Cupcakes, 59–61
  Scratch-Made Corned Beef and Cabbage, 57–58
  Welsh Rarebit Bites, 52–53
Beets, Spicy Lamb Meatballs with Roasted Golden, 44
Bhut Jolokia chile, Apricot-Shellacked Ghost Chile Chicken Wings, 212–215
Big Homemade Barbecue Burgers, 167–

168
Bison Burgers, Beer &, 96–97
Black Magic Grasshopper Cake, 256
Blue Hubbard Squash Soup, 237
blueberries
  Blueberry Velvet Cake, 168
  Fourth of July Ice Cream Pie, 143
Boiled Egg, Sautéed Asparagus, and Pickled Red Onion Sandwich, 90–91
Bourbon Cranberry Compote, 242
Braised Leg of Lamb, 78
breads
  Cranberry Cardamom Monkey Bread with Clementine Glaze, 49–50
  English muffins, 84–86
  Gluten-Free Corn Spoonbread with Tomatoes, 116
  "Japanese Big Mac" Pork Belly Buns, 26–27
  New England-style hot dog buns, 231
  Sloppy Joe Buns, 66–67
Broccoli Rabe, Spicy Sausage, and Ricotta on Garlic-Rubbed Bread, 136
Brown Ale and Cheddar Soup, 55–56
Brown Butter and Bacon Chocolate Chip Cookies, 91–92
Brussels sprouts, Leftover Turkey and Chorizo Breakfast Hash, 244
Butterscotch Cookies, Pumpkin, 233

cakes
  The Angelique's Gingerbread Cake, 195
  Black Magic Grasshopper Cake, 256
  Blueberry Velvet Cake, 168
  Chocolate Guinness Cupcakes, 59–61
  Coconut Drippy Cake, 254–255
  Eggnog Cake, 265
  Ferrero Rocher Stuffed Chocolate Cupcakes, 252–254
  Gooey Butter Cake, 257
  Mexican Chocolate Cake, 117–118
  Rosemary Olive Oil Cake, 37
  Snickerdoodle Cake, 30–31
  Sour Cream Coffee Cake, 20

Cauliflower Gratin, 262

Cheddar Soup, Brown Ale and, 55–56

chicken

    Apricot-Shellacked Ghost Chile Chicken
        Wings, 212–215

    Chicken and Corn Summer Chowder,
        161

    Chicken Fricassée, 208

    Chicken Liver Pâté, 275–276

chile oil, Lobster Noodles with Hot and
    Spicy Scallion Butter, 216–218

chile sauce

    Leftover Turkey and Chorizo Breakfast
        Hash, 244

    Scratch-Made Grownup Sloppy Joes,
        65–66

chiles japoneses, Spicy Lamb Meatballs
    with Roasted Golden Beets and Moroccan
    Couscous, 44

Chilled Sriracha Lobster Salad Lettuce
    Cups, 184

Chimichurri, Easy, 278

Chinese Spare Ribs, 215–216

chipotle

    Atlantic Baja-Style Fish Tacos, 162

    Chipotle and Rosemary Roasted Nuts,
        259

    Chipotle Rhubarb Salsa, 100–102

    Mexican Chocolate Cake, 117–118

    Sweet Potato Soup, 17

chocolate

    Bacon and Egg Candies, 232–233

    Black Magic Grasshopper Cake, 256

    Brown Butter and Bacon Chocolate
        Chip Cookies, 91–92

    Chocolate Ganache, 37

    Chocolate Guinness Cupcakes, 59–61

    Chocolate Moxie Whoopie Pies,
        189–190

    Coffee S'mores Pie, 112–113

    Ferrero Rocher Stuffed Chocolate
        Cupcakes, 252–254

    Hazelnut and Chocolate Chip Biscotti,
        208–209

    Mexican Chocolate Cake, 117–118

    Salted Rolo Brownie Cookies, 234

    Short Ribs with Tagliatelle, 29

chorizo

    Chorizo y Papas Grilled Cheese

        Sandwich, 70–71

    Leftover Turkey and Chorizo Breakfast
        Hash, 244

    Scratch-Made Grownup Sloppy Joes,
        65–66

    Smoky Lamb and Chorizo Chili,
        206–207

Clementine Glaze, Cranberry Cardamom
    Monkey Bread with, 49–50

Cochinita Pibil, 116–117

coconut

    Coconut Drippy Cake, 254–255

    Macaroon Whoopie Pies, 97

coconut milk, Lobster Tom Kha, 144

Coffee Alexander Belle Orange, 16

Coffee Brandy Buttercream, Allen's,
    189–190

Coffee S'mores Pie, 112–113

cookies

    Brown Butter and Bacon Chocolate
        Chip Cookies, 91–92

    Ginger Cookies, 210

    Pumpkin Butterscotch Cookies, 233

    Salted Rolo Brownie Cookies, 234

corn

    Chicken and Corn Summer Chowder,
        161

    Cornbread Stuffing with Fresh and
        Dried Fruit, 241–242

    Gluten-Free Corn Spoonbread with
        Tomatoes, 116

    Lobster with Sweet Corn Linguine, 185

    Orecchiette with Yellow Squash, Corn,
        and Bacon, 140–141

    Sweet Corn and Poblano Chowder, 115

Cornbread Stuffing with Fresh and Dried
    Fruit, 241–242

Corned Beef Hash, 62

Couscous, Moroccan, 44

cranberries

    Bourbon Cranberry Compote, 242

    Cranberry Cardamom Monkey Bread,
        49–50

Crème Fraîche and Lobster Roe, Yukon
    Gold Potatoes with, 274

Deviled Ham, 75

Easy Chimichurri, 278

Eggnog Cake, 265

eggs

    Bacon & Egg Potato Salad, 97

    Boiled Egg, Sautéed Asparagus, and
        Pickled Red Onion Sandwich, 90–91

    Eggs Benedict, 84–86

    Eggs Florentine Burgers, 71–72

    Gluten-Free Two-Ingredient Banana
        Pancakes, 187

    Leftover Turkey and Chorizo Breakfast
        Hash, 244

    Spinach and Gruyère Strata, 19

English muffins, 84–86

Ferrero Rocher Stuffed Chocolate Cupcakes
    with Nutella Buttercream, 252–254

fish

    Atlantic Baja-Style Fish Tacos, 162

    Haddock Chowder, 111–112

    Haddock Ragout with Mussels, Bacon,
        and Peas, 135

    Swordfish Puttanesca, 36

five-spice powder, 215–216

Fondue, Maine Lobster, 34–35

Fourth of July Ice Cream Pie, 143

Fried Oyster Po' Boy Sandwiches with
    Spicy Remoulade, 133–134

frostings

    Allen's Coffee Brandy Buttercream,
        189–190

    Baileys Buttercream, 59–61

    Brown Sugar Buttercream, 30–31

    Chocolate Ganache, 37

    Nutella Buttercream, 252–254

    peppermint icing, 256

garlic

    Garlic Pub Cheese, 96–97

    Roasted Garlic Aioli, 33

Ghost Chile Chicken Wings, Apricot-
    Shellacked, 212–215

Ginger Cookies, 209–210

Gingerbread Cake, The Angelique's, 195

Gluten-Free Corn Spoonbread with
    Tomatoes, 116

Gluten-Free Two-Ingredient Banana
    Pancakes, 187

Goat Cheese Pie, Leek and, 77

Gooey Butter Cake, 257

Grilled Cheese Sandwich, Chorizo y Papas, 70–71

Grilled Flank Steak Tacos with Chipotle Rhubarb Salsa, 100–102

Gruyère Strata, Spinach and, 19

habanero peppers
Chipotle Rhubarb Salsa, 100–102
Mellowed Habanero Peppers, 117

Haddock Chowder, 111–112

Haddock Ragout with Mussels, Bacon, and Peas, 135

ham
Deviled Ham, 75
Eggs Benedict, 84–86

Hazelnut and Chocolate Chip Biscotti, 208–209

hollandaise sauce
Eggs Benedict, 84–86
Eggs Florentine Burgers, 71–72

Homemade Bacon Jam, 110–111

Homemade Marshmallow Fluff, 188

Hungarian Mushroom Soup, 28

Ice Cream Pie, Fourth of July, 143

Insta-Cure #1, 57–58, 59

jalapeños
Atlantic Baja-Style Fish Tacos, 162
Brown Ale and Cheddar Soup, 55–56
Chicken and Corn Summer Chowder, 161
Chorizo y Papas Grilled Cheese Sandwich, 70–71
Pickled Red Onions, 117
Smoky Lamb and Chorizo Chili, 206–207
Zucchini Fritters, 164

"Japanese Big Mac" Pork Belly Buns, 26–27

Jello Shots, Lemon Meringue Pie, 138

Kale and Artichoke Soup, 76

lamb
Braised Leg of Lamb, 78
Manchego Lamb Burgers with Fried Potato Chive Cakes, 142–143

Smoky Lamb and Chorizo Chili, 206–207

Spicy Lamb Meatballs with Roasted Golden Beets and Moroccan Couscous, 44

leeks
Asparagus Soup, 94–95
Haddock Chowder, 111–112
Leek and Goat Cheese Pie, 77
Spinach and Gruyère Strata, 19

Leftover Turkey and Chorizo Breakfast Hash, 244

Lemon Meringue Jello Shots, 138

lobster
Chilled Sriracha Lobster Salad Lettuce Cups, 184
Lobster Fra Diavolo, 147–148
Lobster Macaroni and Cheese, 149–150
Lobster Noodles with Hot and Spicy Scallion Butter, 216–218
Lobster Tom Kha, 144
Lobster with Sweet Corn Linguine, 185
Maine Lobster Fondue, 34–35
Our Family's Creamy Lobster Bisque, 260
Scratch-Made Lobster Roll, 230–231
Warm Maine Lobster Dip, 145–146
Yukon Gold Potatoes with Crème Fraîche and Lobster Roe, 274

Macaroon Whoopie Pies, 97

Maine Lobster Fondue with Oyster River Riesling and Bartlett Estate Wild Blueberry Wine, 34–35

Manchego Lamb Burgers with Fried Potato Chive Cakes, 142–143

Marshmallow Fluff, Homemade, 188

Mayan-Style Slow-Cooked Pork with Pickled Red Onions and Mellowed Habanero Peppers, 116–117

Mellowed Habanero Peppers, 117

Mexican Chocolate Cake, 117–118

Moxie soda
Chocolate Moxie Whoopie Pies, 189–190
Moxie Cocktail, 160

mushrooms
Beef Wellington, 263–264

Chicken Fricassée, 208
Hungarian Mushroom Soup, 28
Lobster Tom Kha, 144

Mussels, Bacon, and Peas, Haddock Ragout with, 135

New England Boiled Dinner, 57–58

New England-style hot dog buns, 231

North Carolina Barbecue Sauce, 172–173

Nutella
Coffee S'mores Pie, 112–113
Hazelnut and Chocolate Chip Biscotti, 208–209
Nutella Buttercream, 252–254

Nuts, Chipotle and Rosemary Roasted, 259

Olive Oil Cake, Rosemary, 37

Orecchiette with Yellow Squash, Corn, and Bacon, 140–141

Our Family's Creamy Lobster Bisque, 260

Oyster Po' Boy Sandwiches, Fried, 133–134

Pancakes, Gluten-Free Two-Ingredient Banana, 187

pancetta, Short Ribs with Tagliatelle, 29

Parsley Salad, Roasted Bone Marrow with, 261–262

pasta
American Chop Suey, 47–48
Lobster Fra Diavolo, 147–148
Lobster Macaroni and Cheese, 149–150
Lobster with Sweet Corn Linguine, 185
Orecchiette with Yellow Squash, Corn, and Bacon, 140–141
Short Ribs with Tagliatelle, 29
Sun-Cooked Heirloom Tomato Pasta Sauce, 166–167

Peas, Haddock Ragout with Mussels, Bacon, and, 135

Pickled Red Onions, 117

Pimiento Cheese, 165

poblano chile peppers
Achiote Butter-Basted Roast Turkey with Ancho Chile Gravy, 240
Corned Beef Hash, 62
Sweet Corn and Poblano Chowder, 115

Porchetta, 248–250

pork
  Cochinita Pibil, 116–117
  "Japanese Big Mac" Pork Belly Buns, 26–27
  Manchego Lamb Burgers, 142–143
  Porchetta, 248–250
  Slow-Smoked Pulled Pork, 171–173
  Super Crispy Slow-Roasted Pork Shoulder, 277–278
potatoes
  Bacon & Egg Potato Salad, 97
  Chicken and Corn Summer Chowder, 161
  Corned Beef Hash, 62
  Haddock Chowder, 111–112
  Leftover Turkey and Chorizo Breakfast Hash, 244
  Manchego Lamb Burgers with Fried Potato Chive Cakes, 142–143
  Prime Rib Breakfast Hash, 18
  Scratch-Made Corned Beef and Cabbage, 57–58
  Sweet Corn and Poblano Chowder, 115
  Yankee Pot Roast, 46–47
  Yukon Gold Potatoes with Crème Fraîche and Lobster Roe, 274
Prime Rib Breakfast Hash, 18
prosciutto, Beef Wellington, 263–264
pumpkin
  Ancho Chile Pumpkin Pie, 243
  Pumpkin Butterscotch Cookies, 233

red chiles, Lobster Noodles with Hot and Spicy Scallion Butter, 216–218
Red Onions, Pickled, 90–91, 117
Remoulade, Spicy, 133–134
rhubarb
  about, 101
  Chipotle Rhubarb Salsa, 100–102
  Sparkling Rhubarb Water, 102
  Strawberry Rhubarb Sangria, 94
  Vanilla-Roasted Rhubarb and Strawberries, 103
Ricotta on Garlic-Rubbed Bread, Broccoli Rabe, Spicy Sausage, and, 136
Roasted Bone Marrow with Parsley Salad, 261–262
Roasted Garlic Aioli, 33
Rolo Brownie Cookies, Salted, 234

rosemary
  Braised Leg of Lamb, 78
  Chipotle and Rosemary Roasted Nuts, 259
  Rosemary Olive Oil Cake with Chocolate Ganache, 37
  Yankee Pot Roast, 46–47
rum
  Eggnog Cake, 265
  Moxie Cocktail, 160
  The Scurvy and Spice, 212
  Strawberry Rhubarb Sangria, 94

Salted Rolo Brownie Cookies, 234
sausage
  American Chop Suey, 47–48
  Broccoli Rabe, Spicy Sausage, and Ricotta on Garlic-Rubbed Bread, 136
  See also chorizo
Scallion Butter, Lobster Noodles with Hot and Spicy, 216–218
Scratch-Made Corned Beef and Cabbage, 57–58
Scratch-Made Grownup Sloppy Joes, 65–66
Scratch-Made Lobster Roll, 230–231
Scratch-Made Ultimate Cheeseburger, 199–201
The Scurvy and Spice, 212
serrano chile, Watermelon Salad Bites, 95
Short Ribs with Tagliatelle, 29
Sloppy Joe Buns, 66–67
Slow-Smoked Pulled Pork, 171–173
Smoky Lamb and Chorizo Chili, 206–207
Snickerdoodle Cake with Brown Sugar Buttercream, 30–31
soups
  Asparagus Soup, 94–95
  Blue Hubbard Squash Soup, 237
  Brown Ale and Cheddar Soup, 55–56
  Chicken and Corn Summer Chowder, 161
  Hungarian Mushroom Soup, 28
  Kale and Artichoke Soup, 76
  Our Family's Creamy Lobster Bisque, 260
  Sweet Corn and Poblano Chowder, 115
  Sweet Potato Soup, 17
Sour Cream Coffee Cake, 20

Spare Ribs, Chinese, 215–216
Sparkling Rhubarb Water, 102
Spicy Lamb Meatballs with Roasted Golden Beets and Moroccan Couscous, 44
Spicy Remoulade, 133–134
spinach
  Eggs Florentine Burgers, 71–72
  Spinach and Gruyère Strata, 19
squash
  Blue Hubbard Squash Soup, 237
  Orecchiette with Yellow Squash, Corn, and Bacon, 140–141
  Zucchini Fritters, 164
Sriracha
  Chilled Sriracha Lobster Salad Lettuce Cups, 184
  Corned Beef Hash, 62
  Deviled Ham, 75
  "Japanese Big Mac" Pork Belly Buns, 26–27
  Leftover Turkey and Chorizo Breakfast Hash, 244
  Lobster Noodles with Hot and Spicy Scallion Butter, 216–218
  Warm Maine Lobster Dip, 145–146
  Zucchini Fritters, 164
Steamed Artichokes with Roasted Garlic Aioli, 33
strawberries
  Fourth of July Ice Cream Pie, 143
  Strawberry Rhubarb Sangria, 94
  Vanilla-Roasted Rhubarb and Strawberries, 103
Sun-Cooked Heirloom Tomato Pasta Sauce, 166–167
Super Crispy Slow-Roasted Pork Shoulder, 277–278
Sweet Corn and Poblano Chowder, 115
Sweet Potato Soup, 17
Swordfish Puttanesca, 36

Thai red curry paste, Lobster Tom Kha, 144
Toasted Almond Blondies, 73
tomatoes
  American Chop Suey, 47–48
  Gluten-Free Corn Spoonbread with Tomatoes, 116
  Lobster Fra Diavolo, 147–148
  Scratch-Made Grownup Sloppy Joes,

65–66
Sun-Cooked Heirloom Tomato Pasta
Sauce, 166–167
Swordfish Puttanesca, 36
Tomato Pie, 139–140
Welsh Rarebit Bites, 52–53
turkey
Achiote Butter-Basted Roast Turkey, 240
Leftover Turkey and Chorizo Breakfast
Hash, 244

Ultimate Maine-Style Italian Sandwich,
266–267

Vanilla-Roasted Rhubarb and Strawberries,
103

Warm Maine Lobster Dip, 145–146
Watermelon Salad Bites, 95
Welsh Rarebit Bites, 52–53
whiskey
Jameson Ganache, 59–61
Whiskey Whipped Cream, 209–210
whoopie pies
Chocolate Moxie Whoopie Pies,
189–190
Macaroon Whoopie Pies, 97

Yankee Pot Roast, 46–47
Yukon Gold Potatoes with Crème Fraîche
and Lobster Roe, 274

Zucchini Fritters, 164

EATING ON THE TOWN AND ON THE ROAD
Index of Restaurants

A1 Diner (Gardiner), 245–247
Amato's (locations vary), 38–39, 43, 267
Anania's (Portland), 40

Big G's Deli (Winslow), 220–222
Bite Into Maine (Cape Elizabeth), 155

Caiola's (Portland), 63–64, 107
Clayton's Café (Yarmouth), 28, 251–252
Cod End Seafood (Tenants Harbor),
196–198
Coffee By Design (Portland), 108
Cook's Lobster House (Bailey Island),
169–170

DiMillo's (Portland), 109
Don's Lunch (Westbrook), 227–228
Duckfat (Portland), 158–159
Dysart's Restaurant and Truck Stop
(Bangor), 202–204

El Camino (Brunswick), 174–177
El Frijoles (Sargentville), 128–132

Fat Boy Drive-In (Brunswick), 224–225
Five Fifty-Five (Portland), 182–183

Fore Street (Portland), 21–22, 107
Front Room, The (Portland), 24

Gilbert's Chowder House (Portland), 108
Grammy's Country Inn (Linneus), 204–
206

Hacienda Pancho Villa (Brunswick),
125–128
Harmon's Lunch (Falmouth), 226–227
Holy Donut, The (Portland), 24
Hoss and Mary's (Old Orchard Beach),
151–154
Hot Suppa (Portland), 25, 106, 272–273

J's Oyster (Portland), 41–42, 109

Lobster Shack at Two Lights (Cape
Elizabeth), 106, 156
Local 188 (Portland), 98–99
Long Grain (Camden), 87–89

Mellen Street Market (Portland), 24
Micucci's (Portland), 83, 108–109
Moody's Diner (Waldoboro), 268–271

Novare Res (Portland), 109

158 Pickett Street (South Portland), 23
Otto Pizza (Portland), 107

Pai Men Miyake (Portland), 26
Patty's Seafood Takeout (Edgecomb),
156–157
Po' Boys and Pickles (Portland), 104–105
Portland Lobster Company (Portland),
107–108
Punky's (Portland), 23

Red's Eats (Wiscasset), 156

Samuel's Bar and Grill (Portland), 108
Scratch Baking Co. (South Portland), 25
The Slipway (Thomaston), 178–181
Standard Baking Company (Portland), 108
Suzuki's Sushi Bar (Rockland), 79–82

Trattoria Athena (Brunswick), 68–69
Tu Casa (Portland), 120–121

Wasses Hot Dogs (Rockland), 229

Zapoteca (Portland), 108, 122–124

Bailey Island
Cook's Lobster House, 169–170

Bangor
Dysart's Restaurant and Truck Stop, 202–204

Brunswick
El Camino, 174–177
Fat Boy Drive-In, 224–225
Hacienda Pancho Villa, 125–128
Trattoria Athena, 68–69

Camden
Long Grain, 87–89

Cape Elizabeth
Bite Into Maine, 155
Lobster Shack at Two Lights, 106, 156

Edgecomb
Patty's Seafood Takeout, 156–157

Falmouth
Harmon's Lunch, 226–227

Gardiner
A1 Diner, 245–247

Linneus
Grammy's Country Inn, 204–206

Old Orchard Beach
Hoss and Mary's, 151–154

Portland
Anania's, 40
Caiola's, 63–64, 107
Coffee By Design, 108
DiMillo's, 109
Duckfat, 158–159
Five Fifty-Five, 182–183
Fore Street, 21–22, 107
Front Room, The, 24
Gilbert's Chowder House, 108
Holy Donut, The, 24
Hot Suppa, 25, 106, 272–273
J's Oyster, 41–42, 109
Local 188, 98–99
Mellen Street Market, 24
Micucci's, 83, 108–109
Novare Res, 109
Otto Pizza, 107
Pai Men Miyake, 26
Po' Boys and Pickles, 104–105
Portland Lobster Company, 107–108
Punky's, 23
Samuel's Bar and Grill, 108
Standard Baking Company, 108
Tu Casa, 120–121
Zapoteca, 108, 122–124

Rockland
Suzuki's Sushi Bar, 79–82
Wasses Hot Dogs, 229

Sargentville
El Frijoles, 128–132

South Portland
158 Pickett Street, 23
Scratch Baking Co., 25

Tenants Harbor
Cod End Seafood, 196–198

Thomaston
The Slipway, 178–181

various
Amato's, 38–39, 43, 267

Waldoboro
Moody's Diner, 268–271

Westbrook
Don's Lunch, 227–228

Winslow
Big G's Deli, 220–222

Wiscasset
Red's Eats, 156

Yarmouth
Clayton's Café, 28, 251–252

ACKNOWLEDGMENTS

We owe an enormous debt of gratitude to Dr. Susan L. Cole, a lifelong friend whose commitment to educating us has extended far beyond her college humanities classroom and into our adult lives.

We'd also like to thank everyone in Maine who welcomed us, made us feel at home, and encouraged us to write about this place. This includes Anestes Fotiades at Portland Food Map, Kendall Kurtz, the Maine Beauru of Tourism, the team at BVK, and the staffs of *Down East* and *Dispatch* magazines as well as the thousands of readers who visit our website each day.

Jillian: I would also like to thank my family for always supporting my writing, and Malcolm for checking my work, making me more diligent, and consistently coming up with big ideas I fall in love with.

Malcolm: I'd also like to thank Jillian for her seemingly endless reservoirs of patience, faith, and love; my mother, for encouraging my cooking and letting me use the stove at an inappropriately young age; and my father, for being the last true pirate in the western hemisphere. Yar.

Finally, a huge thank you is due to everyone who believed in this book even when it was just a blog, and whose work and assistance helped create a result we are insanely proud of. This includes everyone at Tilbury House Publishing, but especially Jon Eaton, Kendra Millis, and Elizabeth Ilgenfritz.

ABOUT THE AUTHORS

Jillian and Malcolm Bedell are grateful that their lives led them first to each other and then to Maine (by way of Brooklyn and a tiny fishing village in Mexico). Upon their return to Malcolm's home state, guided as always by the siren call of food, they said hello to the clam shacks, drive-ins, and diners of Malcolm's youth, ate up Maine's newly cosmopolitan food scene, and were inspired to start From Away, which has become one of Maine's leading food blogs. They have also become the doting parents of a beautiful daughter, Violet. This is their first book.